YOGA
Its Scientific Basis

KOVOOR T. BEHANAN

DOVER PUBLICATIONS, INC.
Mineola, New York

Bibliographical Note

This Dover edition, first published in 2002, is an unabridged republication of the work published by Dover in 1959 under the title *Yoga: A Scientific Evaluation*, which was originally published in 1937 by The Macmillan Company, New York. The Preface to the Dover Edition was added for the 1959 edition.

Library of Congress Cataloging-in-Publication Data

Behanan, K. T.
     Yoga : its scientific basis / Kovoor T. Behanan.
         p. cm.
     Originally published: New York : Macmillan, 1937. With new pref.
     Includes index.
     ISBN 0-486-41792-1 (pbk.)
       1. Yoga. I. Title.

B132.Y6 B4 2001
181'.45—dc21

2001047466

Manufactured in the United States of America
Dover Publications, Inc., 31 East 2nd Street, Mineola, N.Y. 11501

TO ALL THOSE WHO, LIKE WILLIAM JAMES,
ARE INTERESTED IN THE
DEEPER AND BROADER ASPECTS
OF
HUMAN MOTIVATION

ACKNOWLEDGMENTS

Thanks are due to Charles Scribner's Sons for permission to quote passages from Santayana's *The Realm of Essence*, and McDougall's *Outline of Abnormal Psychology*; to Yale University Press for the passage from Hocking's *The Meaning of God in Human Experience*; to Dodd, Mead and Co. for the passage from Jung's *Collected Papers on Analytical Psychology*; to Harvard University Press for the passage from Moore's *Metempsychosis*; to Princeton University Press for the passage from Whitehead's *The Function of Reason*; to Harcourt, Brace and Co. for two passages from Leuba's *The Psychology of Religious Mysticism*; to W. W. Norton and Co. for the passage from Russell's *Mysticism and Logic*; to D. Appleton-Century Co. for the passage from Jastrow's *Wish and Wisdom*; to Longmans, Green and Co. for the passages from James' *A Pluralistic Universe*, and Seal's *The Positive Sciences of the Ancient Hindus*; to Henry Holt and Co. for the passages from James' *On Vital Reserves*; to the Open Court Publishing Co. for two passages from Garbe's *Philosophy of Ancient India*; to The Macmillan Co. for the passage from Nietzsche's *Beyond Good and Evil*; to the Oxford University Press for the passage from Smith's *The Oxford History of India*; to Edward Arnold and Co. for three passages from McTaggart's *Some Dogmas of Religion*; to the Liveright

Publishing Corp. for the passage from Freud's *A General Introduction to Psychoanalysis;* to Methuen and Co. for the passage from Underhill's *The Life of the Spirit and the Life of To-day;* to John M. Watkins for the passage from Underhill's *The Cloud of Unknowing;* to Swami Kuvalayananda for the passage from his *Pranayama;* to Dr. Ernest Jones for two passages from Freud's *Collected Papers* and *The Ego and the Id;* to Dr. A. A. Brill for the passage from his translation of Freud's *Selected Papers on Hysteria and Other Psychoneuroses.*

FOREWORD

To MANY inhabitants of the Western world Yoga means something ancient and curious, Hindu mystery, the magic of the supernatural. Among the followers of certain Western cults Yoga is believed to contravene the laws of physiology, to abolish basic principles in psychology, as well as to reveal the ultimate in religious philosophy. The historians of philosophy have included the fundamental Hindu systems in their world surveys, and a few Western philosophers have sought to penetrate deeply and understandingly into Hindu teachings. That this endeavor has not been more often or more completely accomplished is patently due to the difficulties involved first in the language as the medium of understanding and more fundamentally in the unfamiliarly esoteric quality of the Eastern concepts.

In the history of thought the Hindu contributions have been characteristically philosophic and mystical. It appears natural that the forces of biology and culture, of mental growth and expression in a land where earth and sky are ruled by the tropical monsoons, have inevitably conspired to produce a philosophical tradition congenial to the world-remote psychological soil from which it has sprung and in which it has continued to flourish from generation to generation. The Western mind, even in its idealistic or transcendental phases, has not sought characteristically to carry on its most profound speculations in an isolated world of pure mental experience. Western mystics have generally closed their eyes in order to view more clearly that which would guide them later in the real world. They have looked for the infinite in the self and in the world. In Oriental thinking the soul seeks typically for escape from the real or present world; here the ultimate problem is the search for the self in the universe. The language attests this contrast: for the treasury of Sanskrit speech available for religious and philosophical exchange is said to be more than the corresponding vocabularies of Greek, Latin and German combined.

Yoga is one of the several Hindu systems of thought that developed from the ancient philosophical concepts contained in the Vedic writings of the first millennium B.C. In common with the other systems Yoga has sought for an ultimate union of the individual personality with the infinite. To yoke the individual soul to the world-soul is, like the attainment of any idealistic goal, an end much more easily thought than won. Not comfortably content, as were some other Hindu philosophies, in the intellectual assurance that an abstract knowing about the nature of things was adequate to extricate the believer from the meshes of mortal existence and the "woes of rebirth", Yoga added to an essential profession of faith the arduous training and discipline of a difficult routine of physical and mental self-development. Beginning at the physiological level with the systematic control of reflexes, postures and respiratory functions the Yogic training regime progresses to the higher mental processes, especially seeking the development of minute control in states of mental concentration. Rather than submit to the "effortless custodian of automatism" or than passively allow social conditioning to find its way by some kind of instinct the Yogic disciple takes himself in hand, seeking by his regimen consciously tó organize and master his entire self. This combination of a practical physical development and discipline with a mystical objective which it is its purpose to facilitate has served to attract world-wide attention to Yoga. The coördination of a system of thought with a program of daily-life exercises proves of interest in physiological psychology as well as in religious philosophy.

The reader who approaches the study of Hindu mysticism in a negative and doubting mood will be surprised and intrigued by the temper and type of treatment that the author of this volume has given to his subject. On the other hand, ardent readers may at first be disappointed in the lack of supernatural content, but I believe that ultimately they will be grateful for the enlarged view presented here. For those who read without preliminary prejudice or bias either for or against Yoga and its teachings a fascinating educational experience is in store.

In this volume a sympathetic presentation and appraisal of Yoga is given without a championing of it as a final or finished system of philosophy. Objective or subjective creations built up by long and earnest human endeavor, on whatsoever plan or by whomsoever wrought, constitute material worthy of study by other human beings; and, when these are examined critically, they must serve to broaden our views in their several fields. As we should expect of any system of thinking intended to be a comprehensive theoretical psychology or philosophy, Yoga is formulated about such basic concepts as existence and self-existence, energy and inertia, cause and effect, body and mind, blind drive and intelligence, death and rebirth. We have never had the opportunity of discovering what men from Mars think about these things, but perhaps in the chapters of this book some readers will find ideas or slants as novel to them as a Martian's view of our philosophical foundation stones.

The reader will, I believe, appreciate Dr. Behanan's intimate use and definition of a considerable number of Yogic terms. Those for whom these terms are new may derive from them a sense of more direct touch with the concepts represented, while others to whom they are already somewhat familiar will appreciate the author's fresh English translations further defined by many apt phrases and illustrations in our American idiom. The use of a Yogic vocabulary of at least moderate size seems essential in a work of this kind, as the translated terms provide the points of reference for the orientation of novices and for the identification of the terrain by scholars already familiar with this region of thought. Differences of opinion on certain points of fact in the history and thought of Yoga will doubtless appear. However, I believe that we may have confidence in the author's portrayal of this intricate subject matter and in his interpretations based as they are upon thorough and conscientious study and upon a soundly critical point of view.

A Hindu by birth, early experience and education, Dr. Behanan is also a well qualified student of Western philosophy and culture, not only in terms of years of academic experience but also in terms of respect and confidence among a wide circle of scholars. He has carried on distinguished work in the study of religion, of philosophy and of psychology. This unusual breadth of competence will become evident to the reader as he notes the different aspects of Yoga in the detailed presentation of this book.

Dr. Behanan was born in Travancore, India, of a family conspicuous for leadership in the legislative assembly of the Travancore State. He received the B.A. degree in 1923 from Calcutta University, graduating *with distinction,* and then spent two years in government service in the Madras Presidency. After a year devoted to the study of philosophy in the University of Toronto, he came to Yale, where he continued his philosophical and religious investigations. In 1929 and 1930 Dr. Behanan carried on his studies at Yale in the Graduate Department of Psychology; and a year later the University awarded him a Sterling Fellowship for two years of study at first hand of the Yoga discipline in India. Some of the studies carried on in the following year at Yale (part of which is reported in the concluding chapter of this book) served to complete the dissertation for the degree of doctor of philosophy awarded in 1934. I shall not attempt to detail the success with which our author acquainted himself at first hand with the personalities and activities of Yogic groups in India and with the Yogic literature and traditions. He was fortunate in coming under the tuition of Swami Kuvalayananda, a modern Yogin sympathetic to scientific interest. So great a man attracts aspiring followers and from these some are accepted as "ripe for discipleship". In the older tradition he who went into Yoga did so for life; after a suitable period of instruction by the master he in turn became a teacher of other disciples. Dr. Behanan's interest and purpose was in this respect different from that of the usual disciple; but the master was willing to accept him as a pupil, recognizing his sympathetic and genuine desire to study the system of Yoga objectively and critically. By entering the discipleship himself he has undergone the specified discipline and learned the techniques as a willing student, so that he might be competent to understand the phenomena and be able as a trained specialist to observe other Yogins and their practices. I do not know of any other student who has similarly prepared himself through a combined course of philosophic, scientific and systematic prescribed Yogic training for scholarly research and writing in this field.

Dr. Behanan has set as his goal the preparation of a relatively complete description of the major physical and mental exercises and the theoretical formulations composing the Yogic system. Because of the comprehensiveness of his plan both scientists and religious philosophers will, I believe, find material of specific interest in the volume. The chapters on the "Process of Knowing", "Ethical Preparation", and "Exercises in Concentration" are of direct psychological interest. That on "Evolution and Its Stages" presents a cosmological view in terms of the physicist. The discussions of "Postures" and "Varieties of Breathing" have import for the physiologist. Psychiatrists may discover in "Yoga and Psychoanalysis" some interesting theoretical parallels. The chapters on "Rebirth" and "Yoga and Psychic Research" will surely interest students in the psychology of religion, while the first four chapters of the volume are more especially in the field of religious philosophy. The many-sided approach gives the work as a whole the value of completeness appreciated by the general reader.

Philosophers and systematizers generally view their systems as adequately complete; their critics oft-times insist on as complete a repudiation. The author of the present volume does not press the reader to accept or to reject the Yogic system; he is neither over-protective and over-zealous on the one hand, nor is he coldly destructive in his analysis. The reader is free to take or to leave; but whatever his temper or the angle of his observation he will, I feel confident, find material here for deep thought and a basis for increased respect for the subtleties of the Hindu mind.

WALTER R. MILES
Institute of Human Relations
Yale University

JANUARY 15, 1937

PREFACE TO THE DOVER EDITION

IN THE relatively long period of more than two decades since the first publication of this volume in 1937, I have been preoccupied with other things; consequently no new experimental work has been carried out by me. Nevertheless, during all these years, I have continued to practise yoga for my own benefit, and occasionally kept in touch with new publications.

The rash of steadily increasing numbers of books would testify to the public interest in this subject. But one cannot escape noticing the unduly large proportion of popular literature that is still weighted with wild and unverified claims. That such claims could still appeal to the public is an index of the high degree of emotional maladjustment and sense of insecurity that characterizes our time.

For my part, I see no reason to revise either my approach to yoga or the conclusions reached in this volume. As a system of practices for inducing a high level of relaxation, yoga is unsurpassed. The longer the practice, the more easily one is able gradually to gain control over the nervous system, central and autonomic. This will explain the emotional mastery of the yoga practitioners.

I know of no verified yogic phenomena that would justify any hypothesis other than the generally accepted scientific one that mind is the special mode of existence of matter evolutionarily organised in a particular way. What is called for is more experimental work, and less mystery—mongering and grandiose metaphysical speculation.

I express my thanks to Dover Publications for bringing out a new edition. It is gratifying to any author to learn that there is still demand for a volume exactly as it was first published even after more than two decades.

K. T. BEHANAN

Gandhinagar,
Bangalore — 9
India.

JANUARY, 1959

PREFACE

THIS book is a study of the philosophical basis, motivations, and methods of a group which, through continuous psychological and physiological practices, achieves and maintains a state of emotional stability. I have tried to appraise yoga from the standpoint of science and Western culture. It was my scientific interest which led me to undertake this study and to undergo some of the yogic practices myself. I have made every effort to remain critical and objective throughout the book. The reader may form his own judgment as to how far this effort has been successful.

I am deeply indebted to my countryman and teacher, yogin Swami Kuvalayananda of Lonavla, who for over a period of one year patiently instructed me in the technique of the yogic practices. I am further obligated to him for his kind permission to make use of the illustrations in Chapter X. A brief description of his work is given in the Appendix.

Thanks are due to Professor Walter R. Miles, under whose direction the experimental research was performed, and who so generously wrote the Foreword for this book; and to Professors Roswell P. Angier and Raymond Dodge for their keen interest and valuable guidance throughout my work.

I am indebted to Miss Ann Abelson for her invaluable

assistance throughout the entire period of writing. Miss Ethel Davis is to be remembered for her painstaking technical assistance.

Chapters I and VIII were gone over carefully by Mr. Wallace H. Wulfeck, and Chapter XIII by Mr. Glen L. Heathers. I am most thankful for their suggestions.

The entire manuscript was read by Dr. Leonard W. Doob and many suggestions for its improvement were made by him.

My deepest gratitude is due Mr. Tom J. Gorham for his trenchant criticism of the entire manuscript and his patient coöperation in reading and revising the text.

This study was made possible by Yale University and the Department of Psychology through the means of a Sterling Fellowship.

K. T. BEHANAN

Institute of Human Relations
New Haven, Conn.
January, 1937

CONTENTS

ILLUSTRATIONS

POSTURES
(Pages 186-187)

BREATHING
(Page 238)

Chapter I

THE APPARENT COMPLEXITY OF INDIAN CULTURE

No word can bring to Western minds a greater number of esoteric associations than the name India. The entice-ment of romance, the lure of gold and diamonds, wander-lust, a desire to face the tiger in the jungles of Bengal, the reputed unerring precision of the mongoose in sub-duing the cobra, or even a sneaking suspicion that there is a catch somewhere in that tall "rope-trick story"; these and many others are mingled together as elements in a hazy picture of India. While there is a basic residuum of truth in such a conception, a correct understanding of the complexity of modern India is impossible without some historical knowledge of the cultural evolution of the country.

The cultural history of India begins with the Aryan invasion. Leaving aside for the moment the vague origins of what is now one of the oldest cultures of the world, we may profitably summarize the high points of India's later history. Although thousands of miles away from Europe, India has figured recurrently in historic times as the goal of a succession of military conquests from the Western world. Blazing new trails and overcoming great obstacles, Alexander the Great of Macedon subjugated the northwestern regions of India in 326 B.C. He came not to establish a kingdom, but merely to conquer. Like a bird of passage he disappeared soon after his arrival. The cultural influence of this invasion survives today in some of the architectural monuments of North India. During the next great wave of conquest, which began in the eleventh century and finally culminated in the establishment of the Mohammedan Empire, Europe lost contact with India. But with the breakup of feudal Europe and the beginning of the modern era of Western expansion, a sea route to India was discovered by the Portuguese. After a period of struggle for power between the various nations of Europe, the English established their rule and built an Indian Empire on the ruins of that of the Mohammedans, which had been slowly disintegrating since the beginning of the eighteenth century. The coming of the English to India was in many respects different from the previous conquests, in that two distinct cultures came into intimate contact with one another. After the consolidation of their political power, English scholars were not slow in initiating research in various directions to reconstruct India's past.

What strikes any keen student of present-day India is its incomprehensible diversity. It is a veritable museum of beliefs, a finely interwoven tapestry of multifarious sects and secret rites. Side by side with the most abstruse and sublime metaphysical speculations about the nature of reality, one may see primitive animistic beliefs and worship of natural forces. The introduction of Western education has made these anachronisms all the more incongruous. Until recently, for example, there existed in a section of the country a hospital for rats endowed by public subscription! What can be more paradoxical to the Westerner than the sight of painted, sacred bulls mingling nonchalantly with the pedestrians on the streets of Calcutta, the second largest city in the British Empire?

Social life is even more incomprehensible—a rigid caste system, with the Untouchables at the bottom and the Brahmins at the top, is the very bedrock of Indian civilization. The rigidity of such social stratification is to be seen in two communities of fishermen in a certain section where the members of one weave their nets from right to left and the other from left to right; there is no intermarriage between the two groups.

Religion, like salt in the ocean, pervades all aspects of life. Because of the religious sanction which underlies all social institutions, caste has continued to flourish for centuries in spite of the moral and material degradation to which a vast number of India's population has been consigned. Even highway robbery was once considered as having religious sanction. A "thug" in American newspapers is an armed robber. But the name is derived from a North Indian community of the last century, whose members not only gained a livelihood through armed robbery but considered it a religious duty.

The contradiction between theory and practice and the wide prevalence of the most barbaric social customs and religious practices alongside sublime philosophic thought and ideals of self-abnegation have led many modern observers to contradictory evaluations of India's culture. But this contradiction would fade away on deeper analysis. The sociologist and the social psychologist aim to understand culture. They are not averse to introducing changes in society, though they do not consider it their province. On the other hand, reformers all over the world have one thing in common, namely a desire to change existing institutions when they have outlived their usefulness. Their praise and blame are influenced by relative standards of what is, or what is not, desirable. A modern example may help us here. The reformers of the extreme left today attribute all the ills of society to the private ownership of the means of production, hence, they clamor for a collectivist society. But such an attitude does not help us to understand how and why private ownership became an economic institution all over the world. To comprehend this, it is necessary to study the various factors which influence the evolution of changing relationships in the means of production. Without an understanding of the past the present becomes inexplicable.

Gradual evolution from lower to higher forms is the pivotal truth of biology; forms of thought and attitudes toward life, religion, and philosophy are also better understood in terms of evolution. Ancient Greece and Rome are dead, but who would deny that the legacy of these two civilizations may be traced in modern Europe and America? The exaggerated dictum that nothing moves in the world that is not Greek in origin may be true of the West, but it is equally true that India moves on foundations that are thoroughly Hindu in origin.

With the exception of the Chinese, Indian civilization is the only one that has come down to us from antiquity with an unbroken tradition. Conquerors may have come and gone and at Delhi may be seen the ruins of half a dozen empires, but the culture of India has remained untouched through the ages. In spite of repeated political convulsions, religious reforms, and foreign invasions, the spirit of Hindu culture today is not very different from what it was centuries ago. Today, after nearly two centuries of British rule, the ways of the man in the street remain unchanged. Politically and economically, in India, as everywhere else, threatening clouds are gathering on the horizon. Whether this will lead to a disintegration of the age-old Hindu culture remains to be seen. The words of the English historian, V. A. Smith, are very significant in this connection:

European writers, as a rule, have been more conscious of the diversity than of the unity of India. . . . India beyond all doubt possesses a deep underlying fundamental unity, far more profound than that produced either by geographical isolation or by political suzerainty. That unity transcends the innumerable diversities of blood, colour, language, dress, manners, and sect.[1]

It is generally believed that the important factor which makes for this unity has been the Hindu religion and its philosophical tenets. And so, if we are to understand yoga, which is an important part of the philosophical tradition, in its natural setting in Hindu thought and with a correct perspective, it is necessary to trace briefly the history of this culture with reference to religion and philosophy.

Evidence gathered from the earliest Indian literature leads us to believe that a group of warlike tribes invaded India from the northwest and spread to the east and to

[1] Smith, V. A.—*The Oxford History of India*, Introduction, x; Oxford University Press, 1919.

the south, subjugating the natives and imposing their speech and civilization upon them. The exact date of this invasion remains conjectural, but was probably the first half of the second millennium B.C.

The language spoken by these tribes was the earliest form of Sanskrit, the classical language of India. In the beginning of the last century, the first generation of scholars that studied India's past discovered that Sanskrit was closely related to several European languages. This group of languages, known as Indo-European, may be traced all the way from Western Europe to the banks of the Ganges. The following list of words gives an indication of this interrelationship: [2]

Sanskrit	Latin	Old Irish	Old High German	Old English
bhrātar	frāter	bráthir	bruoder	brōthor
dvāu	duo	dáu	zwei	twā
akshi	oculus	—	ouga	ēage
nāman	nōmen	ainm	namo	nama
yuvan	juvenis	óac	jung	geong
deva	deus	día	Zio	Tīg

Lithua-nian	Czech	German	French	English
broterelis	bratr	Bruder	frère	brother
du	dva	zwei	deux	two
akis	oko	Auge	oeil	eye
—	jmeno	Name	nom	name
jaunas	—	jung	jeune	young
dievas	—	—	dieu	Tues-day

The philologists soon concluded that a race of people known as Aryans must have lived, in pre-historic times, in their original home somewhere in Central Asia or Eastern Europe. In the third or second millennium B.C.

[2] The author is indebted to Professor Edward Sapir and Dr. Stanley Newman for this list.

they migrated in various directions, the tribes that spoke Sanskrit and that invaded India being the most easterly branch of this race. For a long time it was the pastime of the philologists to attribute superiority of mental development and the great achievements of the ancient world to the Aryans who were regarded as a distinct race. The latest excavations in Mesopotamia and Egypt have taught us to think differently. The concept race in its original sense has no meaning, and the present tendency is to discard the word and substitute "ethnic group" (a group sharing the same culture, irrespective of the ancestry of its members) in its place. But the human mind is so prone to accept what is pleasing that the word "Aryan" has been resurrected for political purposes in Germany.

When the invaders poured into India from the northwest they were confronted with dark-skinned, long-nosed aborigines. What little culture these indigenous peoples possessed was either destroyed or absorbed by the conquerors. Since we have had only glimmerings of the period preceding the Aryan conquest, it has been taken for granted that the second millennium was the dawn of civilization in India. But a new chapter of India's pre-historic past has been suddenly opened by the accidental discovery, about a decade ago, of the site of Mohenjo Daro in the Indus valley. No less than ten superimposed pre-historic cities have been identified, although only the latest three have been explored. According to Sir John Marshall, the leader of the excavations, ". . . the civilization of which we have now obtained this first glimpse was developed in the Indus valley and was probably as distinctive of that region, as the civilization of the pharaohs was distinctive of the Nile." [3]

It is too early to decide the racial origin of the people who evolved this civilization, since it came to an end about 3000 B.C., but it has been suggested that it was probably destroyed by the conquering Aryans. Or, on the contrary, it may have died out leaving no observable influence on the later development of civilization in India.

After this brief historical digression we may now come back to the culture as revealed in the earliest literature which originated with the Aryans. The word "Veda" (from *vid*, "to know") means "sacred knowledge or Scripture" and the first compositions, four in number, are known as the Vedas. For the most part these books contain collections of sacrificial hymns sung on religious occasions. The recovery of the Vedas and the extensive work of scholars like Max Müller in interpreting this literature have revealed a fascinating side of Indian history. It has been clearly established that writing was unknown in India before the fourth century and the oldest known inscriptions do not go back further than the third century B.C., whereas the oldest extant manuscripts of the Vedas belong to the sixteenth century A.D. Yet it has been established beyond doubt that the major part of the Vedas was composed before 1000 B.C. Evidently these hymns were handed down from generation to generation by a select group of people who learned the passages by heart. Take, for example, the Rig-Veda. It is the oldest product not only of the Indian, but of the Indo-

[3] Marshall, Sir John—*Annual Report of the Archaeological Survey of India*, 1923–24, 49; Government Press, Calcutta.

European literature, consisting of 1017 poems, 10,550 verses, and about 153,826 words. When Max Müller, toward the end of the last century, decided to translate and publish the Rig-Veda, instead of collecting manuscripts, as scholars do in Greek and Latin, various Vedic students were asked to recite the whole book from memory. Strikingly enough, if every manuscript of the Rig-Veda were lost today, we should be able to recover the whole of it from the memory of professional Vedic students known as *Srotrayas*. Inasmuch as oral transmission is a religious function, the candidates are selected at a very early age and made to undergo vigorous physical and spiritual discipline in preparation for their task. Eight years spent with a teacher *(guru)* is the minimum.

The Rig-Veda and the culture it reveals remind one of the *Iliad* of the Greeks. In both literatures we have a picture of a society molded by invasions, showing the full vitality of the conquerors. Nobles and kings ruled the various tribes. The indigenous peoples were enslaved. The unit of society was the patriarchal household of freemen; farming and sheep-grazing the means of livelihood.

To the student of the evolution of thought, the religious ideas embodied in the Vedas are of paramount importance, for here we see the development of mythology, magic, and religion from a very primitive to an advanced form. Every phenomenon of nature which showed power and beauty was personified. The Sun, Dawn, Rain, Thunder, Rivers and Mountains, all became gods and rulers of the world. Their food is the same as that of men. They could be placated by sacrifices and made to bestow gifts on men. The world was

pictured as a cosmic Punch and Judy show, controlled
and administered by the will of the divine officers.

One stage of great importance in the evolution of religion, in general, is the attribution of moral majesty or
goodness to the deities. This is nowhere to be found in
Vedic religion. Shepherd tribes migrating constantly
could not be expected to devote any serious and consistent thought to ethical problems. Material comfort, not
soul-searching philosophy, dominated the minds of the
Vedic people.

The Vedas were followed by a group of theological
treatises *(Brahmanas)*, written in prose, detailing mi-
nutely the various steps in sacrificial ceremonials. The
priest became the guardian of the secrets of sacrifice and
thus gained a dominant position in social life. The theological intricacies and hair-splitting arguments of this
literature present a close parallel to the Hebrew Talmud.
The four castes and their duties are mentioned for the
first time in these books, which consequently shed considerable light on the social origins of caste and the vul-
garized nature of the organized religious forms of a later
period.

The whole of India was not caught in the meshes of
this popular theological religion and ritualism. We find
the emergence of a number of treatises known as *Upanishads* containing a highly idealistic exposition of the
problems of philosophy and metaphysics. These became the basis of all the subsequent schools of philosophy in India. The subject matter of all these volumes
is essentially the same: i.e., speculations on the nature of
the supreme soul. They constitute the latest phase of the
Vedic literature. Before proceeding any further we

would do well to recapitulate the main trends of our discourse thus far.

We have said that the Vedic period began with the conquest of the Aryan tribes sometime in the early part of the second millennium. The simple civilization of the pastoral people embodied in the Vedas was followed by one in which the priests, by becoming the custodians of sacrifice, began to exercise economic and social power and influence. It was primarily against the money-making priests that Buddha directed his reform movement in the sixth century B.C. But the hold that the sacrificial mysteries had gained over the masses was a strong one, and with characteristic human intolerance the priesthood spared no pains in rooting out of India the teachings of Buddha.

The precepts of the Upanishads (c. 1000-sixth century B.C.) constitute a new turn in the development of Indian thought, having nothing to do with the old theological magic of the priests. Inasmuch as the teachings contained in the Upanishads were aimed at the salvation of the soul, and not concerned with the reformation of society, like those of Buddha, they did not fall under the ban of the official priesthood. This period of daring speculative philosophy came to a close around 300 B.C. Modern India becomes less of a paradox when we realize that these two traditions, the sacrificial religion of the masses which is dominated and controlled by the priests and the philosophic idealism of the Upanishads (which is free from the shackles of caste and creed), have continued to flow along side by side ever since they came into existence in the later Vedic period.

We turn now to the Upanishads. The word literally

means "secret teachings". Since the distinctive character
of the Upanishadic doctrines constituted an uncompromising departure from the prevailing sacrificial religions,
it is very probable that certain formulae embodying philosophical principles—as for example, *tat tvam asi*, meaning the identity of the cosmic (Brahman) and individual
souls (Atman)—were communicated by the teacher to
the disciple as hidden truths to be guarded as priceless
treasure. In the course of time, when the various literatures were brought together, the Upanishads were ap-
pended to the end of the Vedas; hence the name Vedanta,[4] which literally means "end of the Vedas". It was
in the same way that Aristotle's Metaphysics received its
designation; because it was placed after his writings on
Physics.

More than two hundred Upanishads are known to be
in existence, some of them having been composed as late
as the eighteenth century A.D. It has been established,
however, that the most important of them, about twelve
in number, were actually composed after the completion of the Vedic hymns and before the Buddhist period
(c. 1000-sixth century B.C.). The style of presentation is
mostly in philosophic-poetic dialogues and is reminiscent
of the Dialogues of Plato. We learn of the authors only
indirectly, for their modesty made them attribute their
works to mythical heroes and deities, a practice current
in modern India among philosophers in the old tradition.

The main problems of the Upanishads are the central
themes of philosophy. They are the questions that persistently rise in thoughtful minds of all ages: whence do

[4] Vedanta today is the name of the most uncompromising idealistic
school of philosophy in India.

we come? whither do we go? what is the unchanging reality behind the flux and change in the phenomenal world? It was not a sheer accident of history that these questions came to be asked in India. In Greece, the spiritual home of Western civilization, we find a parallel development. The religion of the *Iliad* with its Olympic gods was soon eclipsed, at least among the thinkers, by the fundamental philosophical questions raised by a succession of philosophers culminating in Aristotle. The Upanishadic sages do not all teach the same doctrine; the diversity of their teachings reminds us of the "schools" in Greek thought. For the various subsidiary problems dealt with are subject to an infinite variety of interpretations. Yet nowhere do these men lose sight of the cardinal teaching, that the reality behind the flux of phenomena is identical with the individual principle, the true Self within. This is a far cry from the popular religion of gods and sacrifices, for which the Upanishadic teachers had only veiled contempt. The priests were satirically represented as a procession of dogs, each holding the tail of the one in front and saying: "Om! [5] Let us eat! Om! Let us drink. . . ." [6] The pleasures of the senses are all ephemeral and only the realization of the timeless Self within can bring true bliss and joy.

Two terms, Brahman [7] and Atman, on which the whole edifice of Indian philosophy rests, may well be explained here. The original meanings of the terms are obscure. Brahman in the Vedic vocabulary meant prayer, and later came to signify the power inherent in the

[5] A syllable believed to have symbolic spiritual significance and uttered by worshippers.

[6] *Chandogya Upanishad,* I.12.5.

[7] Brahman or Brahmin is also the name of the priestly class.

prayer of the devotee. In the magic-ridden religion of the priests the sacrificial formulae were believed to contain the spell which would make the gods reward the worshippers with gifts. Finally, in the Upanishadic times, it came to connote the cosmic reality underlying the phenomenal world. The etymology of the word "Atman" is more clear. The root term meant breath at a time when breath was considered the vital essence of man or of any living organism. With the development of critical thinking it acquired the meaning of self or soul as a spiritual principle. Thus Atman came to mean the imperishable Self within, the ultimate principle in man which ever remains the unifying ground of all experience sometimes referred to as the psychical principle or self-consciousness.

In an interesting Upanishadic dialogue between Prajapati and Indra,[8] the conception of the self as the ultimate substratum underlying all experience is brought out. It is said that the gods and demons had jointly decided to learn about the nature of existence and deputed Indra to ascertain from Prajapati the real truth of the matter. Prajapati had held that "that entity, which is free from sin, free from old age, free from death and grief, free from hunger and thirst, which desires nothing, must be regarded as the ultimate self." This pronouncement was much easier made than understood, and the gods and demons decided to get further light on the matter.

After a long interval during which Indra has served as a disciple, Prajapati deludes him further by the remark that the self is the image of the person as seen in water or in a mirror—nail and hair all included. Prajapati

[8] *Chandogya Upanishad*, VIII.7-12.

wants Indra to learn from experience the truth of any proposition, but the latter, taking what the former had said for gospel truth, goes back to the gods in perfect complacency. After a time doubts arise in his mind: when the body is well adorned, the self is well adorned; when the body is clean, the self is clean; but what would happen when the body is lame, blind, or crippled? "I see no good in this," says Indra, and goes again to the teacher for further instruction.

After another long interval of learning, Indra is told that the true self is he "who moves about happy in dreams". Thus dream-consciousness is made identical with the self. This time, before he reaches the gods, Indra realizes that what had seemed to him to be precious truth is in reality full of contradictions. It is true that in dreams our thoughts seem relatively independent of the body. They are free from bodily deformities. Dreams do not differ from individual to individual because a few are crippled and others are not. "But," says Indra, "do we not feel as if we are struck or chased in our dreams? Do we not experience pain, and do we not shed tears in dreams? I see no good in such a self." Dissatisfied, and eager for more light, Indra again approaches Prajapati.

This time Indra is told that the true self is to be identified with the consciousness in deep sleep. While there are fluctuations in dream states, deep sleep is a state of continuous repose and perfect rest. There is a changeless unity of the self in deep sleep which is entirely different from the succession of states characteristic of waking and dream conditions. A self to be the true self must itself be permanent and yet be the ground of the stream of consciousness. Prajapati realizes that Indra would perceive the desirability of such a conception of the self. Immanuel Kant recognized that such a unity was necessary to explain knowledge and called it "transcendental unity of apperception". This self, according to Prajapati, must exist if knowledge of the external world is to be registered on a common ground. It may only be a shadow, but a necessary shadow. Although there are no objects to be perceived Devadatta (John Doe) after sleep is the same Devadatta as before sleep. Sleep is not a break as far as the real self is concerned; otherwise it is difficult to explain the continuity of experience. A necklace of pearls could not exist without the string, but the string could remain without the pearls. The subject is supreme over the object, maintains Prajapati; and Indra is satisfied for a time and goes back to the gods.

Constant meditation, the creator of doubts, begins to spread dark clouds over Indra's mental horizon. He reflects: if the self knows no objects, does not react, knows not that it exists, what is it but a barren fiction, a euphemistic term for unconsciousness, non-existence, and mere nothingness? Who could take this for final wisdom? A box without the sides, bottom, or top, is not a box, but empty space. The concept of a self deprived of positive qualities has been deemed inadmissible again and again in the history of thought.

Like the empirical psychologist of the modern day, the indomitable Indra could find no useful purpose served by such a shadowy self. But, while the psychologist is prepared to rest content without any self at all, Indra continues his quest. Seeking light, he again puts his difficulty to Prajapati thus: ". . . in truth that dreamless sleeping subject does not know himself that he is, nor does he know anything that exists. He is gone to utter annihilation. I see no good in this."

Whereupon Prajapati gives his final answer: Atman is nothing but Self-consciousness, existing in itself and for itself. Through all the phenomena and processes of the universe, in the subject and in the object, in the finite and in the infinite, Atman constitutes the basic reality. Being the universal self, it is both the subject and the object. It is not in experience because it is the permanent possibility and basis of experience; it is not consciousness, for it illuminates consciousness. The eye which sees cannot itself be seen. It is the Kantian "I am I", the supreme Self-spectator.

Throughout the dialogue, Prajapati is trying to point out that the Atman is not an empty abstraction. In its true state, it knows only itself. But the problem was, and remains: is it possible to realize this self? According to the Upanishadic teachers, the way of the intellect with its reason and logic all molded after the demands of the objective world is not the path to the realization of the Atman. Mystical intuition, or whatever else it may be called, is the condition of this knowledge. Ultimate reality from the subjective side, Atman, is attainable only through a super-intellectual, mystical process.

When confronted with a new phenomenon, the scientist will try by analysis to trace the particular causal relationships that produced the event. The test of correctness is verifiability. On the other hand, throughout history we find philosophers seeking an ultimate cause that would explain the whole universe. They are not interested in piecemeal relationships in terms of immediate causes, but in an ultimate basis of existence itself. In the early days of philosophy, at one time or another, fire, water, earth, sun, moon, etc., were each considered the substratum of the phenomenal world. With the advance in thought such crude formulations were one after another abandoned; and quite naturally the ultimate reality, of which the world is a manifestation, progressively became a concept endowed with spirituality.

Such was the evolution of the concept "Brahman" in Upanishadic philosophy. It is one thing to lay down the dictum that all things flow from the Brahman and quite another thing to picture it in understandable language. The various attempts in the Upanishads to describe the Brahman aim to illuminate two aspects, viz., that the Brahman is definable and yet unknowable. To define it is to do injustice to its supreme transcendence, but not to define it at all would be tantamount to making the ultimate a fiction, a negative abstraction, a zero. Much ingenuity has been brought to bear on the problem by the "ultimate-intoxicated" authors of the Upanishads in their attempts to straddle the horns of the dilemma.

On the positive side Brahman is said to be pure existence, consciousness, bliss. Bliss appears not as an attribute or state of Brahman, but as its essence. Without existence, attribute has no meaning; therefore Brahman is continuous existence. It is a unity of existence and essence, the latter being conceived in terms of bliss.

The unknowability of Brahman is most dramatically revealed in the celebrated refrain of the sage Yajnavalkya, who, when questioned, invariably answered in the negative, saying: "Brahman is not this, Brahman is not that, . . ." More than all other modern Western philosophers, Immanuel Kant has pointed out that our empirical order of things is subject to the laws of space, time, and causality, and that the self-existent, in contrast with the empirical system of the universe, is not in space but spaceless, not in time but timeless, not subject to, but independent of the law of causality. Upanishadic philosophy has brought out this point very clearly by ascribing contradictory and irreconcilable qualities to Brahman:

> *"He stays, yet wanders far from hence,*
> *He reposes, yet strays everywhere around,*
> *The movement hither and thither of the god,*
> *Who could understand besides me?"* [9]

> *"One,—motionless and yet swift as thought,—*
> *Departing; not even by gods to be overtaken;*
> *Standing still he yet overtakes all runners,—*
> *In him the god of the wind interwove the*
> *primeval waters.*

> *"Resting is he and yet restless,*
> *Afar is he and yet so near!*
> *He is within all,*
> *And yet yonder outside of all."* [10]

Perhaps the following story is more expressive than the above stanzas: Vashkali, the disciple, questioned Bahva, the teacher, about the nature of Brahman. "Teach me, most revered sir, the nature of Brahman," said Vashkali.

[9] *Katha Upanishad*, II.21 (Paul Deussen's translation, *The Philosophy of the Upanishads*, 149).

[10] *Isa Upanishad*, 4-5 (Paul Deussen's translation, *The Philosophy of the Upanishads*, 149).

The other, however, remained silent. The knowledge-loving disciple pursued the matter and repeated the question several times, whereupon the teacher answered, "I teach you indeed, but you do not understand; this Brahman is silence." [11]

The reader may ask, what is the difference, if any, between the two concepts, Brahman and Atman? Well, the answer is "none". The most important step in the development of Indian philosophy was taken when the Brahman, the cosmic principle, and Atman, the psychic principle in man were looked upon as identical. Thenceforth the two have been used synonymously. Long before Plato recognized the identity of subject and object, the notion was accepted as a cardinal doctrine of metaphysics in India. The identity is briefly expressed by the saying, "that art thou" (*tat tvam asi*); and "I am Brahman" (*aham brahma asmi*).

Is this identity an empty formula or something that really expresses the truth of ultimate existence? As our general knowledge goes, it is an unverifiable dogma, but several great thinkers of history have, independently in some cases, arrived at the same conclusion. It is a tacit assumption of mystics all over the world, irrespective of credal affiliations. Paul Deussen, a student of both Eastern and Western philosophy, has the following to say on the subject:

This idea [the equation Brahman=Atman] alone secures to the Upanishads an importance reaching far beyond their land and clime; for whatever means of unveiling the secrets of Nature a future time may discover, this idea will be true for ever, from this mankind will never depart,—if the mys-

[11] Deussen, P.—*The Philosophy of the Upanishads*, 156.

tery of Nature is to be solved, the key of it can be found only there where alone Nature allows us an interior view of the world, that is in ourselves.[12]

What the Upanishadic philosophers sought, a unity behind the changing phenomena of the world and life, was discovered with the Brahman=Atman equation, and it has remained ever since, most often explicitly and at times implicitly, the pivotal point of nearly all the schools of Indian philosophy. Alongside this conception of the ultimate nature of reality, there were developed certain minor doctrines which also were destined to influence the course of Indian culture and philosophy. Foremost among them was the question of the relation of Brahman to the universe.

If Brahman is the only source of all that is manifest, it is fair to ask what is the status of all that we experience. The evolution of the organic and the inorganic world from the less to the more complex, the reality of an objective world which only madmen could deny, a sense of plurality which no theoretical belief in ultimate unity can explain away; these and many other problems need to be elucidated. The Upanishads, like all philosophies, are sometimes vague and often self-contradictory in their attempts to answer these problems. Humility born of a realization of the limitations of human intellect made them admit the impossibility of obtaining a satisfactory explanation of many things that we would like to know. Heroic attempts, however, were made with the help of symbols, metaphors and parables to bring about some kind of understanding.

[12] Deussen, P.—Outlines of Indian Philosophy, 23; Berlin, 1907.

According to the prevailing conception, the material world and the multiplicity that it nurtures are a transformation of the essential nature of Brahman. Through the plethora of this changing world of experience, which we call the universe, runs a single thread of unity, the Brahman. Here are some fine images showing this relationship:

"*As a spider ejects and retracts (the threads),*
As the plants shoot forth on the earth,
As the hairs on the head and body of the living man,
So from the imperishable, all that is here." [13]

"*As the sparks from the well-kindled fire,*
In nature akin to it, spring forth in their thousands;
Living beings of many kinds go forth
And again return into him." [14]

What is implied here is the relationship of cause and effect. The world is not to be considered either as external to or apart from Brahman. The cause and effect are never identical, yet the effect is a transformation of the cause; similarly, Brahman is not identical with the world, yet the world is in an essential sense the transformation and expression of Brahman. There is nothing in the Upanishads to suggest that the phenomenal world is unreal, a fiction of the imagination, a foggy illusion like the "stuff of which dreams are made". Earlier interpreters of the Upanishads, Western scholars in particular, conveyed the impression that the Upanishadic teachers considered

[13] *Mundaka Upanishad,* I.i.7.
[14] *Mundaka Upanishad,* II.i.i.

the world an illusion. But the overwhelming majority of subsequent investigators have discredited this interpretation.

It has sometimes been maintained that the Upanishadic conception is pantheistic. This is equally erroneous. Pantheism is generally understood to be the view that identifies ultimate reality and the world, as against the deistic view that reality stands apart and outside the world—that is, it is transcendental. According to the pantheistic view reality is so completely exhausted by the world that there is nothing beyond it; in the deistic view reality is so detached that the world bears no trace of it. Neither of these views is entirely applicable to the Upanishads. Brahman is both in the world and above it. The world of experience derives its reality because it is in Brahman like a net in the ocean; but in a very real sense it is also transcendental. By manifesting itself in the world process, Brahman has not exhausted its nature. The logic of the intellect, which is the logic of the finite, may not be able to grasp fully this relationship; just the same, one of the Hindu sages expresses this relationship between the eternal Brahman and the finite world in the following paradoxical image: "That is full and this is full. From that full rises this full. Take away this full from that, what remains is yet full." [15] From all these images that run counter to the practical logic of everyday life, the reader may very well see that the order of truth embodied in the Brahman=Atman equation is not intellectually demonstrable. The Upanishadic teachers were themselves willing to leave it here.

[15] Radhakrishnan, S.—*The Philosophy of the Upanishads*, 78; The Macmillan Company, 1924.

The next doctrine for our consideration, and one which has become a nuclear feature of Hindu culture, concerns the problem of death. The answer to the important question of what becomes of the individual after death has led to a firm assertion of immortality in the various religions of the world, but in Hinduism it resulted in the development of a unique Upanishadic doctrine which has been accepted as an axiomatic truth of life by that extensive mass of people owing spiritual allegiance to the different persuasions of the Hindu religion. The doctrine has two closely related notions: namely, *karma* and rebirth, each supplementing the other.

Karma, stripped of the metaphors and allegorical language in which the doctrine is expressed, is an expression of the belief in the inviolability of the natural sequence of cause and effect. We are all familiar with the law of the uniformity of nature in the physical world where every event must have its antecedent cause or causes. In the moral world, so the Upanishadic teachers argued, what we do is determined by past habits. Chance and the timely help of a beneficent god are entirely ruled out of the moral world and individual responsibility is brought to the foreground. Every act, good or bad, leaves a trace in the organism which becomes a potential determiner of future action and progress. Karma follows us like the shadow follows the figure. By right conduct we can slowly, but surely, undo the effects of the past bad habits; evil conduct will only lead to a further strengthening of the knots in the net that has entangled us, the net of mundane existence with its attendant suffering.

But, the critics might say, that is not true of the world in which we live. Instead of moral retribution, we see the wicked flourishing like the "Oaks of Lebanon", and the good go through suffering like a Job. It was this real paradox of life that led to the doctrine of rebirth or cycles of existence, the counterpart of karma. Only in a long series of successive lives are the effects of our deeds and our actions undone. We live now because of our past karma and for the same reason we shall live again. Life is thus an expiation of the deeds of the previous existence and as long as it is accompanied by action and deeds the necessity for further expiation makes rebirth inevitable.

It is startling how a doctrine of rebirth like this, which can never be verified, has been accepted and believed as a solution for the riddle of existence. Cultured and illiterate alike find in it a just answer to the inequalities and sufferings of life. It inspires in its adherents a hope for the future coupled with submissive resignation in the face of present suffering. To say the least, the theory is, so far as the moral order is concerned, as logical as any other, which perhaps accounts for its acceptance. In its cardinal features the doctrine is found in the teachings of the ancient Greek philosopher, Pythagoras. Plato, too, believed in it.

When appraised against the background of the priestly religion, then current, the doctrine of karma and rebirth was an improvement on the more primitive sacrificial religion. But it did not remain so very long. Instead of undermining the influence of the custodians of the traditional religion, it had the opposite effect. The evil-doer, according to the priests, would be reborn as serpent, tortoise, or worm, and his soul would migrate even into inanimate objects! The caste system and the misery it heaped upon countless human beings were complacently explained on the basis of karma. Thus a theory developed to free men from primitive bonds served only to enslave them all the more. It is easier to preach a democratic religion than to establish it. Doctrines evolved to explain human suffering have sometimes been utilized to make it greater. The way to heaven becomes the way to hell. At any rate it was so in India.

The equation, Brahman=Atman, and the doctrine of karma and rebirth constitute the essential teachings of the Upanishads. The field was now ready for systematization. It is not necessary for our purpose to trace the development of the various schools of Indian philosophy, all of which claimed to represent the essential teachings of the Upanishads.

Following the formulation of the doctrines of the Upanishads, there was no further attempt to interpret the universe or speculate on the nature of the ultimate. To be sure, great strides were made in logic, ethics, and allied disciplines. But these were only minor advances. Six classical systems of philosophy evolved from the Upanishadic teachings. All of them accepted the Upanishadic teachings and claimed to point the way to emancipation from mundane existence, which to them was an obstacle to be overcome. "Realize the Atman in you", became the watchword of every system.

Among these systems, yoga was one. Some of the elements of yoga may be seen in the Upanishadic writings, but not as a system. With the emergence of the various schools, each pointing the way to salvation, yoga achieved popularity as an independent system. More than all others it offered a practical way to realize the Atman through a graduated series of physical and mental exercises. We may now turn our attention to the subject at hand, namely the study of yoga.

CHAPTER II

PRAKRITI OR NATURE

IF ONE were to ask, say, ten cultured men of America whether they had heard the word "yoga", we should receive a few "no's" among the answers. It would be even more interesting to investigate the mental picture this word would call forth in those claiming a fair degree of acquaintance. A few would picture a bearded, emaciated fellow lying composedly on a bed of nails; we might also hear of people sitting cross-legged under the shade of the banyan trees oblivious of what is happening around them. By such an inquiry we should learn that most people hold fantastic notions of yoga, no doubt mixed with certain elements of truth.

Such misconceptions are unavoidable. In the tangled web of Indian thought and practice, the crudest superstitions and the most revolting practices constitute an element of historical tradition. No one could deny that self-immolation is regarded as a method of spiritual salvation in India. The error lies not in believing that such practices exist in India, but in attributing all that is revolting and mysterious to yoga.

What, then, is yoga? The word means "to yoke" (Latin *jugum* is a cognate word meaning the same), which implies the claim that the practitioner of yoga would ultimately be able to unite his soul with the world-soul. In a country where such an ideal was held in high esteem and regarded as the goal of human existence, it is only to be expected that any physical or mental exercises which could allegedly consummate this union would find followers and admirers. Thus in the Upanishadic literature can be found various references to breathing exercises and postures which, in the hands of later authors, became a part of yoga. We shall describe some of these practices in subsequent chapters.

We stated in the previous chapter that the post-Upanishadic period (beginning c. 300 B.C.) saw the beginnings of systematization or schools of philosophy, each pointing, with varying emphasis, the road to salvation. Among these schools yoga took its place some time in the second century B.C. The cornerstone of the system is a book called *Yoga Sutras* (*sutras* means aphorisms) attributed to Patanjali.[1] He did not claim to propound a system of philosophy, but set down valuable instruction to induce certain psychological states. At a time when various systems were competing for recognition in the "philosophical market", mere affirmation or dogmatic assertions would have been of no avail. Doctrines could win general approval only when based on certain critical analyses. Doctrines of yoga assume that the mind, by training, could be made to function at higher levels.

To convince his readers of the possibility of molding the mind, Patanjali has gone into an analysis of matter and mind, their relationship and origin. Not being a pro-

[1] The most readable English translation of the text and of some of the commentaries is the one by Professor Woods of Harvard University (Woods, J. H.—*The Yoga-System of Patanjali*, Harvard Oriental Series, Vol. 17; The Harvard University Press, 1914).

pounder of a new philosophy, he was willing to take over certain doctrines from among those that were current at the time; thus the yogic cosmology and doctrines concerning the evolution of mind and matter were borrowed, with minor modifications, from another system known as *samkhya*.[2] In what follows, we shall attempt a brief exposition of the doctrines of mind and matter and their evolution. Since they are held in common by both samkhya and yoga, we would do well to regard them as samkhya-yoga doctrines.

Every critical philosophy begins with an analysis of experience, and no matter how brilliant might be the attempt of a philosopher in explaining or explaining away matter, or even mind, the antithetical character of the two is a persistent residuum for naïve experience. This is the riddle that has cropped up in every generation and age which has given any thought to deep problems of life. If we separate the two and treat them as belonging to two distinct orders, we are immediately confronted with the problem of knowledge: how can the mind gain experience of the external world when there is no relationship between the two? If we regard both as two aspects of one and the same original substance, we have to give a satisfactory explanation of this differentiation in terms of evolution.

Samkhya-yoga offers a naturalistic interpretation of material phenomena, including in this category mind which, in its various modifications or operations, appears as intellect, will, and feeling. The concept of evolution,

[2] The basic doctrines of the samkhya system are embodied in the *Samkhya Karika* of Isvara Krishna, recently translated into English by S. S. Suryanarayana Sastri; University of Madras, 1930.

common to all systems of Indian philosophy, enabled samkhya-yoga to regard the world as the result of a gradual process of differentiation. By taking the manifold of experience and subjecting it to analysis, we should be able to find certain elements which could not be further reduced without doing violence to felt experience. This is no doubt a process of abstraction, but philosophy is the science of abstraction, accepting the irreducible and rejecting the non-essential and the contingent as unnecessary for the deeper understanding of the totality of phenomena.

What strikes us in samkhya-yoga as the most characteristic feature of experience is the element of change; that which was is no more, that which is will no more be. Everything is in a process of becoming. Nature, both organic and inorganic, is ceaselessly undergoing changes. The particles that make up the inert rock are in a constant state of motion; the process of formation and disappearance ranges over a long period but all objects are momentarily changing from one state to another. It was this theory of flux to which Heraclitus, a philosopher of ancient Greece, called attention when he said that we could never plunge into the same river twice. Buddha, in India, attributed all suffering to this process of becoming. Perpetual motion underlies all phenomena; although, as Alice said in Wonderland, we cannot catch motion at it.

This is equally true of the mental world which can be considered a regular stream of images flowing continuously from moment to moment. Thoughts are born, they grow and disappear; before we can "catch" one, the next one appears on the stage; there is a succession of links in a fleeting chain of dynamic movement. In both the physical and mental worlds, samkhya-yoga found this common feature or element of change and called it *rajas* (energy). Without rajas there cannot be any change or motion, and since the universe of experience, both internal and external, is forever in a perpetual state of flux, rajas or energy is an irreducible substratum.

Side by side with the dynamic nature of phenomena we see a factor of "staticity" whether we call it mass or materiality. This mass-factor could have come into existence only from something which, at any rate potentially, must have contained materiality, for nothing comes out of nothing. Every material object possesses an impenetrability and resistance which no intellectual somersault can take away. It is a datum of experience. The English philosopher Berkeley said that only ideas were real and matter nothing but an illusion, whereupon Samuel Johnson kicked the nearest lamp-post and claimed it was very real. Samkhya-yoga asserts that this common-sense experience of matter could not be dismissed as an illusion. The "stubborn" material object will, no doubt, disappear in the ceaseless flow of change, and the minute particles, whether we call them atoms or sub-atomic constituents, may not be directly experienced, but the coarse impenetrability of matter persists in our experience. At bottom this factor is present in the mind, too, manifesting an inertia or lack of translucence; and while it is predominant in the world of material objects, it is subordinate or latent in the mental world. That which constitutes the most important characteristic of the mind, as we shall see below, is not the factor of mass or inertia; nevertheless its hidden presence may be observed there. This aspect of experience is in samkhya-yoga called *tamas,* which may be translated as inertia, mass, heaviness or resistance.

We may yet infer a third element in the world of experience which, according to samkhya-yoga, can be detected in a highly developed form in the operations of human consciousness. Is there not a quality in the human mind which enables the perceiver to trace relationships between the objects of the external world and consciousness itself? Without this aspect of experience, which creates order and intelligibility in the perceptual field, the world would remain a mad stage for blind actors. Like the shining sun which sheds light on dark corners and hidden crannies, this element enables the human mind to gain knowledge and experience. The shining fluidity of the mind stands in direct contrast to the inertia (tamas) inherent in material objects. Samkhya-yoga calls this element of experience *sattva,* which is best translated as intelligence or mind-stuff, lightness as opposed to the heaviness of matter. The sattva-aspect, although predominant in the realm of the mind, is not absent in the objects of nature, for it lies latent just as the tamas element is latent in the mind. In the lower organism we see the beginnings of sattva in the manifestations of feelings. In the process of evolution sattva gains ascendancy and reduces to a minimum the power of inertia.[3]

These three elements, sattva, rajas, and tamas, which by combining in various proportions constitute the evolving universe (becoming), are called *gunas.* At this stage a very valid question may be asked: what are these gunas? Are they substances or mere qualities? In other words, what is the samkhya-yoga point of view with

[3] *Samkhya Karika,* 12-13.

regard to the age-old question of substance and attributes? It is customary, in philosophy, to make the distinction between primary and secondary qualities. Extension, weight, etc., are primary qualities that are present in the object independently of the perceiving subject. But color and smell, etc., on the other hand, are secondary qualities which have their origin in the observer. They could not be regarded as existing in the object.

The word "guna" has three meanings and one of them is especially significant in connection with the present problem. In this sense guna means quality. According to the second meaning, gunas would constitute a category subordinate to the *purusha* (self or soul). The nature of purusha and its relation to the gunas we shall consider in the following chapter. For the present it may be pointed out that both gunas and purusha are eternal. Thus in a system of two eternal categories it is difficult to understand how one can be subordinate or inferior to the other. This may perhaps be explained from the standpoint of the function of the gunas, since they exist for the experience and liberation of purusha. Although both are eternal, purusha has a pre-eminent position, in that the scheme of evolution, which is made possible by the collocation of the three gunas, becomes meaningful only in the light of purusha's emancipation. In what is yet a third meaning, the three elements which constitute the substratum of the universe, by interpenetration and interweaving, make a rope (guna) or chain to bind the purusha in the meshes of worldly experience. More about this later.

That the word guna, among other meanings, implies

quality is significant, for according to the samkhya-yoga conception substance and quality are identical. Perpetual change is a fundamental postulate; but change is impossible without a substratum that can undergo the change. While the gunas remain the same throughout, the various changes and modifications appear different from moment to moment. Quality is the manifestation of the modification and rearrangement of the gunas. The collocations change and the qualities "announce" these changes.

A glass of water is a particular arrangement of certain particles. Every moment the particles are shifting position with a corresponding change in quality, though such qualitative changes do not come under our vision. If we heat the water the movement of the particles will be increased and at a certain stage, when boiling point is reached, water will be transformed into steam and the changes in quality will be obvious to the observer. Again, by cooling the water to freezing point we could change it into ice. The qualitative differences between ice, water, and steam are sufficiently great from the point of view of the observer to justify three names for three different conditions of the same objective particles.

In the smallest interval of time (*kshana*) the whole world is undergoing change, i.e., a rearrangement of particles. At any particular moment the subsequent changes, as yet unmanifested, exist in a latent form. Similarly, all the past changes of the collocating atoms are not completely lost but exist in a sub-latent form at any particular moment. Without the past the present could not have come into existence; neither could the future arise if it did not exist in the present. The effect is contained in the cause.[4] Evolution, therefore, is a continuous unfolding of the past. The substance or substratum is that which is common to the past, present, and future manifestation of qualities. The power by which the changes are produced is inherent in the gunas. They are the unity of both substance and power.

The basis of the universe is to be sought in the three gunas: sattva, rajas, and tamas. On asking the question why there are only three and no more, we find that the gunas are said to be infinite in number. Each of the three enumerated above represents a type or a class with varying differences of degree. There is, for example, an infinite number of sattva-gunas, each possessing essentially the same quality differing only in degree. Whatever may be the intrinsic difference of gradation between the infinite number of gunas of a particular class (sattva-class, for instance), they are grouped together under one type because of their essential qualitative similarity, in this case lightness or intelligibility which makes them different from the other two, rajas (energy) and tamas (inertia). The triple character of gunas is necessary to account for variety in the manifested modifications of the universe. Let us suppose for a minute that the gunas consisted of one type only, say, tamas; we should then not be able to explain the mind and its intelligibility. If we postulated another class of gunas, sattva, we should still be at a loss to understand the basic and undeniable fact that all phenomena are in constant flux. Hence the three gunas. If it were asked why there are not more than three classes of gunas, the samkhya-yoga philosopher could only answer that these are enough to explain all

4 *Samkhya Karika,* 9.

the differences in the experienced world. When we explore the basic ultimates of experience do we find anything, other than mind, matter and change, that needs explanation?

A consideration of the finite character of some of the productions, as against the all-pervasive nature of others, reveals another aspect of the three classes of gunas. An infinite number of infinitesimals would not explain the all-pervasiveness of some productions like ether (*akasa*) and intellect (*buddhi*). In the chapter on the evolution of categories, we shall see that, although various bodies and objects of nature appear in their finite or limited character before us, certain products of evolution are unlimited, that is to say, they are all-pervasive. It is concluded, therefore, that each class of gunas consists of some that are infinitesimals and others all-pervasive. There are two reasons why they could not all be all-pervasive. First, it would be impossible to account for the finite character of most of the manifested things. Second, motion, which we know to be the essential function of rajas (energy), would be impossible if all the gunas were all-pervasive. The samkhya-yoga philosopher, therefore, concludes that the substratum of the evolving universe consists of three classes of gunas, each in turn consisting of an infinite number of gradations, some of which are limited, which accounts for the finite nature of objects, and others all-pervasive.

At this stage we may introduce a new term, *prakriti*. Once the process of evolution has been started, the reason for which we shall see in the next chapter, the three gunas by combining and re-combining produce the various objects in the universe. Before the beginning of the process of evolution, which has a definite beginning, the gunas must have existed in a state of equilibrium. This is known as prakriti, which may be translated as primordial, undifferentiated matter. It is very important to bear in mind that prakriti is not different from the gunas, but only the gunas before their actualization in evolution.[5] The equilibrium of prakriti is not static but dynamic; because of tension and action among the gunas, prakriti is in a state of balanced motion which does not result in the production of objects. It might be called a type of inner, dynamic movement producing no transformations or modifications—undisturbed perpetual motion. Once the equilibrium is upset we have the beginnings of cosmic evolution which proceeds in an endless series of changes taking place from moment to moment. The various modifications that are manifested in evolution exist potentially in a latent form in prakriti, for effect is only a manifestation of what was already in the cause. The original cause prakriti, consequently, must have contained all the later productions in a latent form. In common with the other systems of Indian philosophy, samkhya-yoga also conceives evolution as a cyclic process. Every period of evolution is followed by dissolution when the universe, after having reached a certain stage, takes a backward course which culminates in the dynamic equilibrium of prakriti. After a time a new cycle would begin, only to end again in dissolution. The reasons for this eternal alternation of periodical evolution and dissolution are not inherent in prakriti, but are to be sought outside, in the nature of purusha (soul) which is independent of prakriti.

[5] *Samkhya Karika*, 15-16.

In the history of psychology, several theories have been advanced to explain the relation between matter and mind; thus we have mechanical, biological, evolutionary, and various other theories of the mind. Among these there is one, the double-aspect theory, according to which mind and matter are two aspects of an unknown original substance. It is worthwhile to point out that, in spite of certain apparent similarities, the samkhya-yoga conception of the mind-matter relation has very little in common with this psychological theory. Prakriti is not a homogeneous primordial substance; it is a dynamic equilibrium of three different, but interdependent elements or gunas. The sattva-gunas which later develop into mind exist potentially in the prakriti. This is equally true of matter and energy. If it were not for the original sattva, no amount of quantitative or qualitative development of the two other gunas, tamas (inertia) and rajas (energy), would produce mind. Mind is not derived from matter nor matter from mind. Nor are they two aspects of the same substance, for they develop from different gunas.

But the interdependence of the three gunas is so close that no manifestation is possible without the three being present. Predominance of any one guna in a particular combination decides its essential nature. Human mind is the highest manifestation of sattva, nevertheless tamas lies hidden in it. Inert matter is predominantly tamas in composition, but here the sattva element lies submerged. Rajas or energy makes motion and change possible in both.

In a land of idealism, it is only to be expected that the greater part of the thought of the various schools would be devoted to the elucidation of the nature of soul and its metaphysics. Samkhya-yoga, however, was not completely swept away by this philosophical predilection; it took the external world as real and proceeded to make as exhaustive an analysis as was possible. The system is a mixture of both idealism and realism. Since the three gunas are eternal and super-subtle elements, the realistic nature of samkhya-yoga stands in contrast to the over-emphasized idealism of the greater part of Indian thought. But the other aspect of the system, its transcendental idealism—the core of Upanishadic thought—comes out clearly in its doctrine of the purushas, to which we may now turn.

CHAPTER III

PURUSHA OR SOUL

THE oft-quoted asseveration that "there is nothing new under the sun" is in a very real sense applicable to philosophy. There is something shop-worn or second-hand about the latest solutions of the persistent problems of philosophy. Most philosophers, and sometimes their formulations as well, can easily be labelled—they are Platonists, Neo-Platonists, Kantians, Hegelians, etc.

Achievements of philosophers look pitifully meager alongside the dazzling discoveries of the sciences. Our conception of matter has undergone a revolutionary change as it has been reduced to mere mathematical fiction, radiations emanating from a center. Matter is no longer a substance, as it used to be, but a series of events that just happen.

Philosophy can boast of no such advance. Old problems, no doubt, are reformulated to incorporate the scientific discoveries of the prevailing age. Philosophic conceptions of the universe current in the time of Galileo and Newton have yielded to those that include Einstein's Theory of Relativity and Planck's Quantum Mechanics. We have today mathematical philosophers like Russell and Whitehead who, using science as a coign of vantage, have built new models of the universe, difficult of understanding even for the enlightened.

Yet the central problems of philosophy, like the concept of the soul, are as debatable today as they were centuries ago. A cursory acquaintance with its history would suffice to convince one that unlike the objectively verifiable formulations of science, philosophy is not above the private values, desires, aspirations and unconscious motives of the individual philosopher. The subject matter and reasoning employed are such that no generally accepted standard of proof can be applied to the problems of philosophy. Professor Alexander has defined philosophy as the "process and expression of rational reflection of experience". Can we say, however, that our individual experiences resulting from the same objective situation are alike? Do we all agree that we see indisputable evidence of a benevolent power in the processes of nature? The answer to all such questions, whether negative or positive, would be greatly influenced by our private prejudices and outlook on life. Philosophical system-builders are endowed with the genius of the potter who can mold the putty in any fashion to suit his tastes. The "will to believe" is common to all, but what we believe is determined largely by what we want to believe. Nietzsche made a remarkable observation when he wrote of philosophers:

They [the philosophers] all pose as though their real opinions had been discovered and attained through the self-evolving of a cold, pure, divinely indifferent dialectic (in contrast to all sorts of mystics, who, fairer and foolisher, talk of "inspiration") whereas, in fact, a prejudiced proposition, idea, or "suggestion", which is generally their heart's desire abstracted and refined, is defended by them with arguments sought out after the event.[1]

The malleable nature of philosophical deductions is a good starting point for a chapter on the yogic theory of the soul. The reader, acquainted even slightly with Western philosophy, will readily see the resemblances between some arguments of yoga and those advanced at different times in the development of Western thought. It should be borne in mind, however, that yoga as a theoretical system of metaphysics is based primarily on certain mystical experiences which, in the eyes of the yogins, are as real and valid as the sense experiences of everyday life. No yogin would ever claim that intellectual arguments by themselves are sufficient to convince critics, who evaluate yoga from the "outside", of the existence of the soul that transcends time and space. The final and clinching argument is the invulnerability of mystical experience.

The prototype of the variants of the doctrine of the soul in Indian philosophy was the Atman of the Upanishadic sages. In its essential aspects the samkhya-yoga soul, called *purusha*, is not very different from the Upanishadic Atman. Similarly, the purusha is independent of the material universe. It is beginningless and eternally unchanging. Even the highest product of prakriti, the mind, has nothing in common with purusha, which is timeless and spaceless, mere sentience and entirely passive. All the products of prakriti are variously characterized by the three gunas; but purusha is devoid of them. It is the eternal seer behind the phenomena of prakriti

[1] Nietzsche, F.—*Beyond Good and Evil*, 9 (tr. by Oscar Levy); The Macmillan Company, 1923.

and its changes. It is without parts and attributes, all-pervasive and subtle. Whatever it may be that characterizes individuality, the empirical "me" is of the essence of prakriti, and purusha contributes nothing to the sum total of personality This inactive, characterless purusha may be put down on the positive side as pure consciousness (*cit*). On analyzing our elements of knowledge we find that it is composed of ideas and images—mental pictures. These various image-patterns are the inevitable accompaniment of all thought-processes, but their constant fluctuations should teach us that they are the work of the sattva (aspect of translucence) element among the three gunas. Motion and activity are characteristic of prakriti alone. But what does this steady flow of the mental stream reveal? Only the content and form of the mind. There is another factor, the pure relating element of awareness (cit), the origin of which, like a distant source of light, remains in the faraway background, shedding luster and glow on, and giving continuity to, the operations of the mental mechanism. This is the transcendent principle of consciousness, purusha, the never-changing soul that makes the content of the mind meaningful. Samkhya-yoga admits that this factor cannot clearly be observed in introspection which reveals only the mental film-roll, but not the light (consciousness) that enables the pictures to be registered. The presence of the purusha as a theoretically necessary principle may be safely inferred from the data of knowledge. One can only wonder at this point if it is Kant or the samkhya-yoga that is speaking.

The emaciated, ghost-like purusha is, in certain respects, less colorful than the Atman; the latter was said to be intelligence, consciousness, and bliss (*ananda*); the purusha, except for the fact that it illuminates mental states, is neither pure intelligence nor bliss. Intelligence as a mental faculty, according to samkhya-yoga, is the work of prakriti and cannot have any relation whatever to the transcendental principle, purusha. Rationality is in the empirical ego. The term "bliss", which was considered an attribute of Atman and later of the vedantic soul, is only a less pretentious name for "pleasure", which cannot be the nature of purusha. Pleasure and pain can be traced to the instincts, desires, and cravings of the ego in the world of experience, but the purusha as a detached spectator is not circumscribed by the limitations of the three gunas. The crucial point that marks the difference between the Atman and samkhya-yoga purusha is the doctrine of the plurality of souls. According to the Upanishads as well as the vedanta, individual souls are only temporal and illusory forms of the cosmic soul, Brahman. In the final analysis individual souls are only appearances; they derive their reality from, and it is their final destiny to become absorbed in, Brahman. Not so in the samkhya-yoga. Each individual soul is here an isolated principle, eternally real and ever the same. Reality, consequently, consists of an infinite number of purushas, instead of the all-embracing Brahman of the monistic vedanta.

Some arguments have been advanced to prove the existence of purushas.[2] The first one is very much like the design or teleological argument that has figured so prominently in Western philosophy, although the conclusion drawn is not the same. The collocation of objects and

[2] *Samkhya Karika*, 17; *Yoga Sutras*, IV.24.

their modifications must exist for the sake and benefit of a principle that is sentient. It is worth pointing out that the conclusion drawn from the design argument is not the same as in Western philosophy. Whereas in the latter God is the designer, the samkhya-yoga points to the purusha which benefits from the design. Nor could this be otherwise. Prakriti, the original ground out of which the material world has evolved, is beginningless and eternal; hence a creator is entirely superfluous.

The second argument is familiar to all students of philosophy; the subject or seer must be free from the perpetual modifications and movements of the physical manifold, a simple, unitary and unchangeable substance. All the presentations and changes are due to collocations of the three gunas, sattva, rajas, and tamas. The seer, therefore, must be free from the limitations of prakriti and its gunas, for none of the products of prakriti can be simple or unitary; and so the actual seer is the purusha which as an unfailing light illuminates the mind, lending meaning and purpose to the cyclical processes of evolution and dissolution. The third argument maintains, as did Kant, that there must be a supreme background without which it would be impossible to coördinate all experiences. In spite of the reality of multiplicity in mental life, there must be a transcendent and unitary principle —the purusha.

The fourth and last argument is drawn from the longing which, samkhya-yoga claims, is present, in varying degrees, in all people. This "instinct" to be free, the desire to escape the impermanence and futility of existence, is, of course, the heart around which the body of samkhya-yoga, as well as the other systems of Hindu philosophy, is built. Desires and cravings and love of life itself may crowd in on us to make living a worthwhile adventure, but a hidden voice, even in those moments when all seems well, might be heard (if we were reflective enough) uttering the language of doubt and despair. A life-tedium overtakes us. This craving for emancipation is interpreted as due to the demand of the purusha to seek release from the meshes of prakriti. That this world-weariness is a real element in our experience has been attested by many great minds. "Would any man of sound understanding," says Kant, "who has lived long enough, and has meditated on the worth of human existence, care to go again through life's poor play, I do not say on the same conditions, but on any conditions whatever?" [3] A materialist or a sceptic might consider this paradox, viz., that we love to live and yet long to escape the weariness of life, as a result of, in the words of Freud, the interplay of life and death instincts. But the samkhya-yoga, believing as it does in the reality of purushas, concludes that the striving for freedom from the limitations of existence points to one that longs for and can effect the release. This is the purusha.

Against monism, which asserts that individual souls are illusory and that only the world-soul is real, samkhya-yoga adheres uncompromisingly to the doctrine of the plurality of purushas.[4] The reasons adduced in favor of this standpoint are drawn from within the framework of the presuppositions of the system, particularly its analysis of the nature of prakriti and its evolutionary devel-

[3] Kant's article, "On the Failure of every Philosophical Attempt in Theodicy," published in 1791. Kant was, in this article, arguing particularly against the optimism of Leibnitz.
[4] *Samkhya Karika*, 18.

opment. Among the various products of prakriti, like ether, mind, etc., which will form the subject of the next chapter, there is one which is the basis of the empirical ego. This, known as *buddhi*, is the active agent in the processes of cognition, feeling, and willing. The various senses are the individual organs of a buddhi. Each buddhi is, therefore, an isolated organism possessing an individuality of its own. We have said that the buddhi is the *basis* of the empirical ego and not the ego-proper, because of the rôle purusha plays in the production of the ego-sense. There is a kind of relationship, best expressed as that of reflection, between the purusha and each individual buddhi. If the purusha did not reflect the light of consciousness in buddhi, there would be no "I" feeling. The "I" sense is the temporal psychological unity produced by the reflection of purusha in the activities of buddhi.

This relationship is important if we are to understand the arguments for the existence of innumerable souls. The samkhya-yoga, unlike the vedanta, is keenly aware of the differences of the individual organisms. The various organisms in the world are neither morally, physically, nor intellectually alike. These differences should indicate that their experiences and perception of the outer world are different. The presiding consciousness, which is due to the reflection of the purusha, must therefore be different for different buddhis. The element of change as well as diversity in the buddhis can easily be understood because the latter are products of prakriti, but the multiplicity of unities (each buddhi is a unity) would demand a corresponding multiplicity of purushas.

On this question samkhya-yoga was faced with the

unrealistic conclusion of the vedanta that the external
world, ego, and knower (Atman) are, in the final analysis, unreal and that Brahman alone is the metaphysical irreducible. But the samkhya-yoga would not and could
not be satisfied with such a sweeping denial of the realities of everyday life. Prakriti is metaphysically as real and
eternal as the purusha, and the latter. although not an
active agent, is the remote knower of the drama of life.
If the world and the ego, that is, life, are unreal, then
what guarantee is there that purusha, also, is not unreal?
Just as there has been a conjunction between an individual buddhi and purusha, there will be, in the fullness
of time, a disjunction of the two. But it must be clearly
understood that while the conjunction lasts, the buddhi
is real and there is no illusoriness about its transformations. As long as prakriti was not the *maya* of the vedan-
tins, samkhya-yoga philosophers, if they were to remain
consistent, could not escape the doctrine of the plurality
of purushas.

Certain considerations are advanced to show the utter
futility and irreconcilable contradictions following from
the assumption of one cosmic purusha. If this were so,
how should we be able to account for the multiplicity of
buddhis, which with their individual experiences and
cognition, would be difficult of explanation? Consistency would demand that we should have one buddhi
instead of many. But this is obviously not the case. According to the samkhya-yoga view prakriti exists for the
emancipation of purushas. If it is a fact that there is only
one purusha, then prakriti would not be working for the
emancipation of purusha but only for the ego which, although real, is only a temporal unity. If the prakriti leads

to the emancipation of only the ego, then its rôle and function as the emancipator of purusha would have to be abandoned. If it is maintained on the other hand that the purusha and not the ego is liberated, then with the emancipation of one, all would be finally released, for there is only one cosmic purusha.

It is very doubtful whether these contradictions alleged to follow from the hypothesis of an all-embracing world-soul are valid enough to lead to the acceptance of a pluralistic theory of souls as preferable. Monists should be, in fact they are, able to find very damaging inconsistencies in a pluralism. Metaphysicians are like subtle lawyers who can make even the camel go through the eye of a needle! Whether we will accept a particular conclusion would depend on how far we are predisposed to believe it. In the case of samkhya-yoga, its realistic attitude regarding the material universe, plus the belief in the possibility of individual salvation by yoga practice, led to the assumption of many souls instead of one.

Among the recurring problems of philosophy is that of the relation between the temporally changing and the eternally ever-the-same. It does not make any serious difference whether it is the relation of the mind to the body or the soul to the body, as long as mind and soul are taken to be different in nature from matter. The interaction or coöperation of the two will always remain an impenetrable mystery to the extent that the dividing gulf between the two orders of existence is broad and deep. Plato tried to bridge the gulf by his participation theory, according to which the material world is real inasmuch as the eternal ideas participated in it. But how are we to understand this participation? Aristotle narrowed down the gulf by his theory of form and matter. There can be no form without matter and no matter without form. His knowledge of biology, his interest in the various sciences, and his consequent realistic attitude towards the world made him think in terms of continuous development from the lowest forms of life to the highest. But in addition to a series of souls of varying grades of significance, the *nous* or noëtic soul (intelligence) stands out as preëminent among free and immortal souls. By calling the soul the "entelechy" (realization) of the body only the name is changed, but the problem remains. Descartes and Locke pronounced it a mystery and helped themselves out of the situation by trusting in God. Kant's conclusion that the Pure Ego cannot be known did not throw more light on the crux of the problem; he only put a damper on the ardor of "soul-chasers".

Samkhya-yoga also had to face this problem. When the mental mechanism and the active elements of cognition, feeling, and willing are all said to be the evolutionary products of prakriti the crucial problem still remains as inexplicable as in any other system, only the relation between the changeable and the unchangeable has been transferred to a different level, i.e., between prakriti or buddhi and purusha. How can purusha, the inactive and colorless soul, have any relation to the non-conscious prakriti? The problem, in fact, is two-fold. First, to ascertain the reason for the existence of prakriti and its relation to purushas collectively, and secondly, to show how buddhi becomes attracted to purusha.

We have already seen the rôle of prakriti in evolving a complex universe by the collocations of the three gunas. While impermanence is of its very essence, it seems to have a direction towards which it is evolving. There is no chaos in nature if we look at it in perspective. It is blind in its activities, following the law of cause and effect even in the minute transformations of simple collocations. There is no place for a "miracle" in nature. While we do not see teleology in isolated parts of nature, samkhya-yoga claims that the evolution of prakriti is, when nature is taken as a whole, adapted to certain spiritual objectives. There is a kind of upward swing from the inorganic to the organic, from the lower to the higher forms of life. This long-range teleology is not due to any conscious purpose within the bosom of prakriti, for it is assumed that prakriti is unintelligent and incapable of conscious reflection. "A strange mystery it is," says Russell, "that Nature, omnipotent but blind, in the revolutions of her secular hurryings through the abysses of space, has brought forth at last a child, subject still to her power, but gifted with sight, with knowledge of good and evil, with the capacity of judging all the works of his unthinking Mother." [5]

Such is the evolution of mechanical prakriti. Although eternal, prakriti plays a secondary rôle. Its reason for existence is its serviceability to purusha. The teleology, consequently, has its origin not within itself but in the nature of the purushas—their demand for emancipation. The samkhya-yoga conception of the evolution of prakriti has many points of similarity with the Leibnitzian view of pre-established harmony. In both the harmonious evolution is the result of an outside agency.

It is possible, therefore, to have a teleology in nature

[5] Russell, B.—*Mysticism and Logic,* 48; W. W. Norton and Co., 1929.

emanating from an outside source. Commenting on the methodology of science, and particularly of physiology, Whitehead makes some very interesting remarks about the upward trend in evolution: "The material universe has contained in itself, and perhaps still contains, some mysterious impulse for its energy to run upwards. This impulse is veiled from our observation, so far as concerns its general operation. But there must have been some epoch in which the dominant trend was the formation of protons, electrons, molecules, and stars. Today, so far as our observations go, they are decaying." [6]

Once we begin to think of the cosmic process in its totality and the reason for its evolution as well as dissolution, the explanation for which modern science does not offer, it is legitimate to seek an answer outside the physical universe. Bergson traces it to an *élan vital*, Lloyd Morgan and Whitehead to God, and a great many minds proclaim it a mystery and let it go at that. Samkhya-yoga calls in the aid of purushas whose necessity for experience and the subsequent demand for liberation from the web of prakriti account for the teleology, evolution, and dissolution in nature. Several analogies are used to explain how the non-conscious prakriti can be utilized for the service of purusha.[7] One of the early commentators gives the following story: Two men, one lame and the other blind, were, each in his own way, seeking a way through the jungle. They agreed to fulfill their duties by mutual coöperation. The lame man climbed on the shoulders of the blind man and by following the former's directions

[6] Whitehead, A. N.—*The Function of Reason*, 19; Princeton University Press, 1929.
[7] *Samkhya Karika*, 21.

both of them reached their destination. The soul could see but not "move"—like the lame man. Prakriti could move, but not see—like the blind man. When they reached their destination, there was a separation. Prakriti ceased to act, for its work was done, and purusha, having reached the journey's end, was free forever after.

The system admits that some questions cannot be answered. To the question as to how the purushas become involved in the meshes of prakriti, there is no clear answer. Since both purusha and prakriti are eternal, and the former free before its entanglement in prakriti, the only explanation is that, as a result of non-discrimination which is beginningless, purushas somehow become entangled. Non-discrimination may have an end and once the purusha attained emancipation, it is forever free from the possibility of further entanglement. This non-discrimination (*avidya*) is common to many systems of Hindu philosophy. What it is we do not know, we can only say that it is.

The conjunction between prakriti and purusha is not one of contact but of proximity. As the magnet moves the iron with its attraction, so the proximity of purusha excites prakriti and guides evolution. But the prakriti is also characterized by the counter-movement of decay or dissolution. Just as the proximity of purushas launched prakriti on the road of development or evolution, the former by inner necessity and united effort seek cessation from the forward movement. This is the beginning of dissolution—the backward movement to reach the original equilibrium of the three gunas. Prakriti thus reaches its original quiescent state. As far as the purushas are concerned, dissolution (*pralaya*) is only a temporary state of cessation from evolutionary activity. It is like a deep slumber in which the bonds that connect the purusha with the buddhi remain intact. Dissolution, in short, is not a state of emancipation but only one of temporary quiescence. The striving of the purushas to seek release exerts after a time "magnetic influence" on prakriti, thereby upsets its equilibrium, and starts it anew on the course of evolution. This alternation of evolution and dissolution, both determined by the transcendental influence of the purushas, will continue until all the purushas find emancipation from the clutches of prakriti.

While the relation between prakriti and purushas is indirect and cosmological, that between buddhi and purusha is more direct and psychological. We pointed out previously certain considerations which inclined the samkhya-yoga to accept the doctrine of plurality of souls. Since buddhi is a product of prakriti, in fact the highest one on the mental side, a detailed treatment of this important problem will be taken up in a subsequent chapter.

Among Western philosophers, one might find a similarity between Aristotle's God or Prime Mover and the samkhya-yoga conception of the purusha. Neither Aristotle's Prime Mover nor purusha is available for religious purposes. They are devoid of those qualities which make a spiritual principle the object of religious dependence. A Prime Mover who is himself unmoved is an aesthetic-contemplative being, with no concern for the detailed running of the universe which is determined by principles within the system. By a kind of attraction the world strives after God; without being an active agent, God's mere presence extends this influence. It is so with purusha too. Its transcendental presence, without in any way affecting or being affected by the transformations of the world, predisposes prakriti to work for its emancipation. It is the metaphysical necessity for a comprehensive understanding of existence that made both Aristotle and samkhya-yoga introduce a non-material transcendental principle—God or Prime Mover and purusha.

It is instructive to point out here the most important difference between the samkhya and yoga. The classical samkhya is atheistic, if by theism is meant belief in a personal God who is either the creator of the universe or the perpetual guardian of its destiny, or both. The samkhya shows a strong bias for rationalism, and anything that could not be rationalistically demonstrated is discarded. Like Kant in a later period, Kapila, the traditional author of the samkhya aphorisms, contends that it is impossible to demonstrate the existence of a personal creator. If God is perfect, then there is no conceivable reason why he should have created the world; if he is imperfect, then he is no God. To say that he is neither perfect nor imperfect is to make all rational argumentation impossible. It is customary to invoke God to reward the righteous and punish the wicked, to play the rôle of moral guardian over the erring ways of mankind. Kapila has no need for a God in this respect, for the law of karma automatically and justly regulates moral retribution.

Prakriti and purushas, says Kapila, are sufficient to explain the universe and its evolution and destiny. Therefore, as Laplace was to maintain later, it is meaningless to assume the existence of God who is neither demonstrable by reason nor necessary as an explanatory principle. Some of the later commentators of the samkhya have tried to introduce God into the system, but their attempts, instead of creating harmony, look like patch-work. Whatever may be the merits or demerits of the system, Kapila's denial of God and his fearlessness in running counter to the current orthodox philosophical opinions deserve admiration.

Although yoga accepted samkhya metaphysics, certain changes were introduced here and there. Practice and not theory is the all-important thing in yoga. So Patanjali, the author of the yoga aphorisms, contends that God as an object of devotion is an aid to the yogin, for he (God) by his kindness might make the physical and mental discipline of yoga easier to bear.[8] Speculative demonstrability or undemonstrability of God did not interfere with Patanjali's reasoning. God is therefore a solicitous creature who is interested in the salvation of souls, but he is not powerful enough to interfere either in the workings of the law of karma or in the evolution of prakriti. God is a special kind of purusha who is ever free. He is not subject to the law of karma, nor has he any direct relation, like purusha, to an individual buddhi. *Avidya* (non-discrimination), consequently, never mars his perfect wisdom and bliss.

One gathers the impression that Patanjali introduced God into the system because he found that concept useful. He must have been an astute psychologist who knew that faith helps. His reasoning could be summarized thus: If belief in and devotion to God help you in your practice, then you may assume that he exists; if this does not help you, you may equally well assume that he does not exist. While yoga was at great pains to defend a meta-

[8] *Yoga Sutras*, I. 23-26.

physic that would justify its practices and aims in the eyes of the public, it allowed for extreme deviations in the matter of philosophical beliefs. The practices were taken over by other schools because of their alleged efficacy to point a way of salvation.

The result is that the passages devoted to the discussion of God (*Isvara*) in the yoga aphorisms are extremely vague and irrelevant to the rest of the system. The arguments are unconvincing. According to Garbe:

> The insertion of the personal God, which subsequently decisively determined the character of the Yoga system, was, to judge from the *Yoga Sutras*, the textbook of Patanjali, at first accomplished in a very loose and superficial manner, so that the contents and purpose of the system were not at all affected by it. . . . The passages which treat of the person of God are unconnected with the other parts of the book— nay, even contradict the foundations of the system.[9]

This liberal and sometimes indifferent attitude towards metaphysical subtleties has been characteristic of yogins throughout the ages. The vedanta has dominated the Hindu mind for so long that today most yogins have grafted the vedanta metaphysics to the yoga practices— Brahman alone is real. It is the adaptability of the system that makes yoga more a philosophy and a psychology than a religion.

The similarity of yogic formulations and Kantian ideas of the soul is close enough to deserve brief mention in passing. Objects, according to Kant, are a manifold of qualities or facts in a set of mutual interrelatedness. But

[9] Garbe, R.—*Philosophy of Ancient India*, 15; The Open Court Publishing Co., Chicago, 1897.

in perception the manifold appears as a unity, which is due to the synthetic way in which the mind handles the manifold. Kant admitted that experience is an essential prerequisite for knowledge, but the way in which we perceive is determined by the mind. The materials of sense-impressions are made to conform to certain categories supplied by the mind. For example, space and time are not objectively real, but our mind is so constituted that we project these on the objects.

The lower faculties retain the object in all its diversity; it is however, the function of the higher faculties, like intuition, apprehension, understanding, etc., to produce unitary perception. The "I think" is the necessary condition of the higher "Unity of Apperception". The consciousness of Self, although implied in all experience, need not always be actually realized; it may remain hovering in the dim background as a potentiality capable of realization. This is the Pure Ego to which he gave the name "original transcendental synthetic Unity of Apperception." Kant, like the yogic philosophers, knew perfectly well the utter futility of any attempt to explore the nature of such a quality-less soul. We could not even know whether it is material or immaterial, simple or substantial. Since it is beyond our introspection, Kant admitted that psychology could gain nothing by this metaphysical entity; instead, the empirical "Me" should constitute its proper subject matter. In the language of yoga, Kant's empirical "Me" would correspond to the individual buddhi and its manifestations. But the Pure Ego of Kant and the transcendental purusha, both dim barren abstractions, look very much like two peas from the same pod. They may be necessary logical postulates for speculative metaphysics but entirely inaccessible to scientific methods.

What has become of the soul in modern psychology? Does it manage to find at least a precarious existence either in psychological books or in its laboratories? It has been humorously suggested that psychology would work with anything but its proper subject, *psyche* (the psychical principle). There is a certain amount of truth in this jocular remark, but at bottom only a confusion and misunderstanding of the modern point of view can lend any substance to this characterization.

Psychology, as any instructed person knows, is the inheritor of two traditions; it has to live up to the one and live down the other. The rise of the evolutionary point of view since the days of Darwin and the scientific approach towards the problems of the biological sciences have made psychology gravitate almost entirely towards science. But for several centuries, in fact, from the beginnings of cultural history, the most important element in the province of psychology, the problem of the mind, whether regarded as an expression of a soul or otherwise, has been conceived in the womb of philosophy and metaphysics. The emancipation took place in the middle of the last century, a period which saw the birth of several new sciences. Contributions in the last century came from men who had their training in both the sciences and philosophy. In their writings one may see both traditions thriving side by side, strict experimental work in the field of mental operations on the one hand and philosophical discussions of the mind on the other. Towards the turn of the century the scientific method and approach gained the upper hand; today the approach to psychology lies through physics, chemistry, biology, statistics, etc., and not through philosophy.

It is only the vagaries of certain enthusiasts that have led psychology to the point of denying the existence of consciousness. The vast majority of psychologists is still working, and will so continue, with the problems of mental life. But their method and approach have changed. The sense of personal identity—and it is for this reason that the soul is invoked in psychology—still constitutes one of the most puzzling problems of this field. But what good purpose is served, asks the scientific psychologist, by the pious affirmation of the existence of a soul about which there is as much evidence as there is for a personal devil? Is anything gained by tracing the unity of mental life to the soul? Nothing. Such a procedure, furthermore, would become a positive hindrance to the development of psychology. If we know nothing about it, then it is an unscientific procedure to bring this concept into a scientific field. Only the maxim "Whatever you are *totally* ignorant of, assert to be the explanation of everything else",[10] can justify the soul in scientific psychology. It would put a premium on scientific laziness. Like the king of England, the soul is a superfluous entity in the government of psychology. For sentimental purposes, just as the Englishman shows an affection for the symbol of kingship, a few psychologists might still offer loyalty to this concept. Motives in such cases would be certainly not scientific, whatever might be the justifications from other realms of life's aspirations. It would be equally unscientific to deny the ex-

[10] Quoted, from H. S. Hodgson, by William James in his *The Principles of Psychology*, Vol. I, 347; Henry Holt and Co., 1890.

istence of the soul, for that would amount to a dogmatic assertion not warranted either by the nature of the subject matter of psychology or the evidence at our disposal. The psychologists would merely maintain that it is a superfluous concept unwarranted and unnecessary as an explanatory principle in a scientific discipline.

Chapter IV

EVOLUTION AND ITS STAGES

THERE has come to us from very ancient times a saying, "There is no knowledge equal to the samkhya, and no power equal to the yoga." One can easily see why yoga was so highly rated, for it was the only system that formulated a discipline to liberate the human soul from the bondage of worldly entanglement. The practices of yoga were accepted on the testimony of the practitioners as desirable for those who sought spiritual development. The method and the life of detachment of its followers held a distinct spiritual charm even for those who could not or would not undergo the strenuous life of a yogin. When one mentions "yoga", it is not its theory that is implied, but a set of exercises that is unrivalled by any other system. At best a philosophy lays down an ethical code as the Stoics and the Epicureans did, or peremptorily demands that its adherents be good without pointing out a positive way of achieving that state as most religions do. Not so yoga. "Do this and this," says the yogin, "and you shall reach higher spiritual levels." In a country where emancipation was not a mere matter for philosophical hair-splitting but the goal of life, yoga, because of its insistence on effort rather than knowledge, won awe-inspiring respect from all and sundry.

But we feel compelled to ask why a unique place should have been assigned to the samkhya. There is sufficient historical evidence that the spirit and the doctrines of the Upanishads had greater following than other systems deviating from its mystical idealism. Absolute idealism has always held a preëminent position in India. Modern vedanta, which is the spiritual inheritor of the tradition of the Upanishads, is unexcelled in its popularity among the cultured of the present generation. In the Bhagavad gita, which is to the Hindus what the New Testament is to the Christians, various schools of philosophy are mentioned, but the dominant thesis is patterned after the idealism of the Upanishads.

The doctrine of the plurality of souls in the samkhya constitutes an uncompromising departure from the monism of the Upanishads, and hence could not have commanded sympathy in the philosophical circles. More problems, in fact, were created than solved by this doctrine. The Upanishadic notion that Brahman was the only reality and that individual souls were mere reflections that would ultimately be merged in the former had so intrenched itself in the minds of the people that no pluralistic position could have made much headway.

What about the concepts of evolution and dissolution found in the samkhya? That the universe is alternately subject to growth and decay, that creation is a myth fit to be believed in by the weak but meant to be despised by the wise, is an accepted doctrine in almost all systems. The concept of God and creation, whenever found in Indian philosophy, may be easily inferred to be a concession to the demands of the finite mind that was never taken seriously by any philosopher. There is a breadth and depth in Hindu philosophies that is a challenge to the unimaginative theistic conceptions of the West. While the evolutionary development of nineteenth-century science undermined to a considerable extent some of the basic doctrines of Christianity, it did not generate even a negligible ripple on the religious consciousness of India. It was subscribed to by the "heterodox" Buddha and the orthodox Sankara. James says:

God as intimate soul and reason of the universe has always seemed to some people a more worthy conception than God as external creator. So conceived, he appeared to unify the world more perfectly, he made it less finite and mechanical, and in comparison with such a God an external creator seemed more like the product of a childish fancy. I have been told by Hindoos that the great obstacle to the spread of Christianity in their country is the puerility of our dogma of creation. It has not sweep and infinity enough to meet the requirements of even the illiterate natives of India.[1]

In this connection it is worth pointing out, paradoxical though it may seem, that Western philosophies are more religious than philosophical, while Hindu religions are more philosophical than religious. Anthropomorphism is the product of the infancy of the human mind and the higher conception of reality should leave behind all personalistic notions, irrespective of the demands of religion—so the philosophers of India have always contended.

If neither the doctrine of the many souls nor the general acceptance of evolution could account for the high

[1] James, W.—*A Pluralistic Universe*, 28; Longmans, Green and Co., 1912.

esteem accorded the samkhya, then we will have to seek the real reason elsewhere. It is to be found in the samkhya speculations concerning the various stages in the evolution of prakriti. It was not enough to say that, under the teleological guidance of purushas, prakriti takes both a forward and a backward course; the various stages in the process of evolution had to be and were mapped out. Reason and logical necessity were the only criteria by which Kapila wished the merits of his speculations to be judged. His thoughts on evolution were in some respects a foreshadowing of the Lamarckian thesis that the need of the self (organism) determines function and that the function generates the organs. The realistic attitude of the samkhya toward the external world demanded more than a vague avowal that all that exists is the product of evolutionary change. Although samkhya admitted that human reason could not penetrate all the mysteries of the universe, it maintained that it should be possible for us to give a rational picture of evolution, the whys and wherefores of it.

Idealistic schools of the extreme variety had paid only very little attention to the real world. True to their central doctrine that the Brahman alone was real, in accounting for the world they explained it away. But the samkhya accepted prakriti as real in the true sense of the word, hence a knowledge of it should be possible and necessary. Herein lies the difference between the samkhya and the idealist thought which called forth the saying: "There is no knowledge equal to the samkhya . . ." The *wisdom* of the Upanishads was, of course, the highest, but the *knowledge* of the samkhya had no equal because it was the boldest and the most rational speculation in the field of natural philosophy. Very probably it is this aspect of the samkhya that made Garbe, a German scholar and life-long student of samkhya and yoga, say that "in Kapila's doctrine, for the first time in the history of the world, the complete independence and freedom of the human mind, its full confidence in its own powers, were exhibited." [2] We can learn very little today about evolution from the ancient speculations of Kapila; we look for evidence in science. But who can deny that the philosophical problems of our age, whether those raised by evolutionism or otherwise, are very similar to those that confronted the ancients? Kapila's answer that the ego generates the function and then the organs would probably not satisfy many critical moderns; nevertheless his thoughts are not uninteresting. Distance in time, furthermore, makes his doctrine the more enticing.

But a hostile critic might ask whether we are justified in using the term "evolution" to describe the thoughts of men who lived twenty-five or so centuries ago. Could these men have meant the same things by that term as we do today, we who are backed by the scientific discoveries of the recent past—say, from the days of Lamarck and Darwin? The most obvious answer is, No. Modern theories are the result of painstaking and careful observation of and experimentation in natural processes; they are contributions from the various sciences. On the other hand, ancient philosophies were mostly vague, lacking in the precision and objectivity that characterizes science. It would be too much of an exaggeration, how-

[2] Garbe, R.—*Philosophy of Ancient India*, 30; The Open Court Publishing Company, Chicago, 1897.

ever, to say that in some cases at least, philosophers of antiquity in Greece and in India did not understand the deep *implications* of evolutionism. The philosophic approach to evolutionary problems, then as well as now, is different from that of the scientific. The former is concerned with questions of origin and end, while the latter considers everything outside the possibility of observation and legitimate inference as beyond its jurisdiction. But the philosophic notions of evolution had to await for their full development the work of researchers in the natural and biological sciences.

One of the early Greek philosophers, Anaximander, claimed that man was descended from the fish. According to some commentators, Aristotle's conception of evolution was not far different from that of today. Heraclitus, more than all the other great men of Greece, contributed to the development of the cyclical idea of the cosmos. The Stoics, who seem to have borrowed this notion from him, thought that "the history of the world and the Deity moves in an endless cycle through the same stage." Pythagoras and Empedocles held traces of this doctrine within their systems. Among recent writers Spencer and Nietzsche may be mentioned. The decline of Greece was also followed by a decline in philosophy and, if the power of the church in the Middle Ages had not demanded of the philosophers strict adherence to credal requirements, Greek speculations would probably have continued and advanced. Perhaps this was just as well. What was needed was scientific evidence and not hypotheses spun out of thin air; evidence for evolution from the various branches of science came to the fore in the last century.

Lamarck and Darwin are the pioneers who established the claims of evolutionism in the field of biology. Various controversies about the details of their arguments and points of view—for example, transmission of acquired characters, natural selection, etc.—are still raging and will continue for years. Here we are only concerned with the influences of the doctrine upon the physical sciences. If the various forms of life, including man, have developed from some crude, primitive life-cell which in turn was the product of purely physical and chemical structures and processes, i.e., if the properties of life are evolved in some yet unknown way from matter, it is only reasonable to conclude that the cosmos as we now know it must have been in some past age subject to evolution. As we shall soon see, the samkhya scheme is interesting for its theory of cosmic evolution. The boundary between the organic and inorganic has never been an insurmountable one to the Indian philosophers. Biological evolution is only a secondary form of the primary cosmic evolution.

The application of the evolutionary hypothesis to the inorganic part of nature originated, at any rate in a limited form, with the French astronomer and mathematician Laplace. Following a lucky guess of Lucretius, Kant had made certain suggestions along the lines of a nebular hypothesis for the origin of the solar system. But Laplace, who knew nothing of Kant's remarks in this field, gave mathematical form to the nebular theory. According to the theory, a nebula, a collection of cloudlike gaseous matter, has been resolved by a process of contraction—by the working of forces and in accordance with laws inherent in the nebula—into a mass which is our present sun, and a number of subordinate bodies, the present planets and satellites. From the gaseous nature of the nebula it may be inferred that it is capable of shrinking; in fact, it has been found that the sun is still shrinking appreciably. The various planets of the solar system revealed various stages of cooling, and the earth before the formation of the crust had passed through a long history: first it was a gas, then a liquid, and finally there was formed the present crust whose temperature was favorable to the development of life.

There was a weak link in the hypothesis from the evolutionary point of view. Where did the nebulae come from? There was no answer except that they consisted of atoms. Atoms (meaning "that which is not divisible"), it was unanimously agreed, were the primary and irreducible units of matter. The different chemical elements had different atoms, and they were arranged according to increasing atomic weights, beginning with hydrogen, in a periodic table. Barring one or two exceptions, the eighty or so elements in the periodic table exhibited remarkable continuity in an ascending series. Was the evolutionary hypothesis to stop at the citadel of the atoms, "the foundation-stones of the material universe, which have existed since the creation, unbroken and unworn", as Clerk Maxwell described them? In that case, evolutionism as a universal doctrine must fail. The discoveries since 1895 have shown that the hitherto indivisible atoms, too, are the products of evolution.

From the beginning of the last decade of the last century, physicists have been pleasantly suffering from a peculiar intellectual ailment, dizziness from a plethora of experimental success. Discovery after discovery enabled them to penetrate the mystery of the atom. The discovery of X-rays by Roentgen, a Würzburg physicist, signallized the beginning of the avalanche. The discovery by Becquerel and the Curies in France that some of the heaviest elements like uranium emitted "particles" or rays which formed the nuclei of helium atoms proved convincingly that atoms are not indestructible and that one element can change into another. After all, the alchemists who believed that elements are transmutable and sought to change lead into gold were not fools!

The understanding of radioactivity cleared the way for the electrical theories of matter. What are called constituents of matter are bundles of energies; protons at the center of atoms represent positive charges of electricity, while the electrons in the outer region of the atoms represent negative charges. We may say, then, that the eighty or so "elements" or energies are reducible to two: the positive and negative charges of electricity. All the physico-chemical phenomena are due to the groupings and regroupings of these two forms of energy. Many physicists believe that all atoms above helium in the periodic table are only various continuations of hydrogen and helium atoms. It is also claimed that helium may be traced to the hydrogen atom.

The case for cosmic evolution has been established on irrefutable evidence, but the various philosophical questions arising out of the new conception have not been satisfactorily ironed out. Certain hypotheses seem more reasonable than others, but there is still room for justifiable differences of opinion. One of the important laws of physics which should have a bearing on philosophy is that of the conservation of matter, first formulated by Lavoisier. According to this, the total quantity of matter in the universe remains ever the same. But the recent developments have shown that matter is merely a name for a transitory phenomenon; and, if we wish to be precise, we should talk of conservation of energy. This principle, associated with the name of Carnot and known as the second law of thermodynamics or the law of entropy, claims that the world is "running down". In every process of nature a certain amount, though small, of energy is dissipated, i.e., it becomes unavailable for further work. Every event is like an engine, it takes up energy but never releases the same amount in forms that might be further availed of. The universe is sinking more and more, slowly but certainly, into a dead level where no event, process, or evolution will be possible. Of all the known laws of physics, this is the most certain. Man may think he is the creator of novelties, he may evolve higher and nobler forms of culture, but he, along with the rest of living forms, is doomed to sink into the anonymity of cosmic death level.

Some physicists, notably Millikan, have contended that the universe might not be a closed one, and new sources of energy might exist not accessible to our present methods of observation. In a sense all laws, including those of physics, are probabilities, and no one is justified in positively asserting that these physicists are wrong. One might point out, however, that such contentions are of the "might be" variety, and not free from the earmarks of wishful thinking. The majority of eminent physicists is agreed that the inevitable destiny of the cosmos is "heat death". Eddington, the English astronomer, thinks that the probability that the universe is "running down" is so remarkably high that the opposite view is, on the basis of our present knowledge, negligible.

Energy dissipates and becomes unavailable for constructive work, but the total quantity remains constant. This is the threshold of philosophical speculations. Ignoring the question of origin for the time being, we may say that, if the world is "running down" at present, there must have been a time when the counter-tendency was predominant. We have substantial evidence, as was pointed out before, that atoms, molecules, stars, and galaxies are not indestructible in their present form, but rather they are the end-products of a long process of evolution.

Although modern physics has reduced matter to energy, the nature of the latter remains a mystery. Be that as it may, we are convinced that, although the form may change, the total quantity remains the same; which is a vindication of the oldest scientific maxim from the days of Thales in Greece: *Ex nihilo nihil fit*, nothing comes out of nothing.

Now what are the possible hypotheses of philosophy to account for the origin of the universe? No one can claim to be impartial and objective, for our wishes and desires are too strong to be unconcerned about the ultimate destiny of the universe. The "tender-minded" would prefer to believe in a personal God who presides over the cosmos; the "tough-minded" in some kind of impersonal spiritual force, like the Brahman, into which everything would be merged in the fullness of time; and the *very* "tough-minded" in physico-chemical processes to explain all that needs explanation.

Our purpose is not to assign a superior place to the samkhya-yoga, but only to show that it is a reasonable theory, perhaps as reasonable as any of the others. Whatever may be the ultimate constituent of energy, we may infer from the conclusions of the second law of thermodynamics that nothing is lost and nothing can come from nothing. May it not be possible that the primordial X, prakriti or what not, is eternal? The theistic notion of a God, standing outside and creating the world at a definite time, is hardly compatible with the law of the conservation of energy. At best, the Deity may be regarded as the All-Sustainer and All-Supporter, to use the words of Goethe.

Or, as the absolute idealists maintain, cosmic evolution and life itself may be a dream, *maya* or a thought in the mind of Brahman. Like solipsism, which maintains that one can be certain of only one's existence and nothing else, this philosophy is logically impregnable. But the vast majority of mankind finds it difficult to explain the universe away.

On the other hand, if the universe, after a phase of evolutionary advance, is lapsing back into the original chaotic changelessness, is it not also possible that it might renew the cycle, evolving and devolving in infinite alternation? The same cause or causes, whatever it may be that initiated the process, may yet again operate after the equilibrium has been reached. As long as the human mind is not able to penetrate the mystery of origins, we may continue to question what the purpose of evolution might be; but that a cyclical universe is a reasonable hypothesis, we have no right to deny. "And thus then is suggested," says Spencer, "the conception of a past during which there have been successive Evolutions similar to that which is now going on; and a future during which successive other such Evolutions may go on." [3]

Some have seriously maintained that the whole thing might be a joke, and that some cosmic mind is being constantly amused by the struggles of the frail human mind to penetrate the veil. Or it may be, as others have suggested, that chance has determined everything; "His Majesty Chance", as Frederick II called it in connection with its intervention in the fate of battles. Samkhya-yoga has cast its lot on the spiritualist side, and finds the reasons for the eternal alternation of evolution and dissolution in the transcendental influence of the purushas that seek emancipation from bondage. This may arouse a sense of futility; lest we forget, it might be also pointed out that many have found consolation and peace in such thoughts. Lotze, in his *Microcosmos*, held that each cosmic period might be an item in a melodious world-drama: "The series of cosmic periods, . . . each link of which is bound together with every other, . . . the successive order of these sections shall compose the unity of an onward-advancing melody." [4] We may now turn to the samkhya-yoga scheme of evolution of prakriti and its different stages.

The name "samkhya" (number) is in all probability derived from the enumeration of the various products, twenty-four in number, that are the evolutes of prakriti. The purusha, which is an independent principle, makes

[3] Spencer, H.—*First Principles*, 482; Williams and Norgate, London, 1862.

[4] Quoted in C. W. Saleeby's *Evolution, The Master-Key*, 315; Harper and Brothers, 1906.

up the total of twenty-five realities (*Tattwas* or "That-nesses"). Prakriti, the original unmanifested basis of all later manifestations, exists potentially as a union, but not an identity, of opposites, in which the three gunas maintain an inner equilibrium which does not culminate in modifications. The transcendental intervention of purushas brings this balanced state to an end, initiating prakriti on the course of evolution. The process of becoming is not a fortuitous one, but works by inner necessity within the limits of space, time, mode, or constitution of things. We cannot understand why a certain product comes first and another later; we can only say that it just happens so. The order is what it is, because nothing else would suit the purpose of purusha.

A significant distinction is made between the unspecialized (*avisesha*) and the specialized (*visesha*) products of evolution. The former are intermediate products that originate further products; but the latter are end-products incapable of initiating new Realities (*Tattwas*). A rough analogy may be invoked from the current distinction in science between the protons and electrons on the one hand and atoms on the other. In fact, as we shall see below, there are two modifications in the samkhya-yoga scheme that are reminiscent of the distinction between sub-atomic constituents and atoms. By the combination of protons and electrons in various proportions atoms come into existence. No one denies that they are a new stage in the evolution of cosmos, for the properties they manifest are entirely new and different from those from which they are evolved. But the atoms, in their turn, are not able to originate new products. Atoms, of course, combine among themselves to produce the different substances, but no new unit or state of existence is formed. This is approximately the contention of samkhya-yoga. Unspecialized products are, therefore, both effects and causes, but the specialized ones are only effects. There is, no doubt, a haziness about these subtle distinctions. The chief contention is that the properties of the new products are so different from the original that, whatever may be the intrinsic re-shuffling or synthesis that brings about these changes, it deserves to be considered a new stage. Thus the twenty-three Realities, which are all ultimately differentiations within the homogeneous and ubiquitous prakriti, are new existences or stages of cosmic evolution. A new existence exhibits new properties which were, at any rate, not manifest in the old. This is the dialectic of nature. Evolution is from the subtle to the gross, resulting in the phenomenal world of atomic matter which serves completely the purpose of purusha.

The first product of prakriti is *mahat*, sometimes called *buddhi*, or the Great.[5] We have already explained at length that prakriti is the unity of the three gunas, sattva (the basis of mental life), rajas (activity), and tamas (non-activity or inertia). Mahat is characterized by the preponderance of the sattva guna. No evolute of prakriti is free from the three gunas, but in some there may be more and in others less of a particular guna. The sattva predominance in mahat, therefore, means that it is primarily mental stuff, or, to use the language of Western psychology, the stuff of consciousness. There is a theoretical reason why the stuff of consciousness should be the first product of evolution. Purusha is the

[5] *Samkhya Karika*, 22.

real and ultimate source of pure consciousness. This potential source can manifest itself only by a kind of "magnetic relation" of "contact" by proximity. Since the sattva guna is the nearest in likeness to purusha, only where there is a predominance of sattva can the remote purusha come into relation with prakriti. The logic of the situation, therefore, demands that, if purusha is to guide the thread of evolution, the sattva should preponderate in the first evolute. Perhaps, here as well as in many other places in our exposition, an analogy would clarify our understanding. A piece of rock and a crystal are both composed of atoms, but the latter can reflect the rays of the sun while the former cannot. Sattva, as against the other two gunas, has that something in its nature which, although different from purusha, makes the reflection of the latter possible. When mahat is spoken of as consciousness-stuff, this is all that is meant; it is that existence of matter which can come into "contact" with purusha and act as the basis of the mind and discursive intellect.

The gulf between the subject and the object, the perceiver and the perceived, is an acute problem to all those who have pondered over it. Many philosophies with idealistic preferences have found it necessary to consider the two as having a common origin, unfolding in the course of evolution into what appears as two mutually irreconcilable opposites. The samkhya-yoga had to face the same difficulty. Mahat is that evolute of prakriti in which there is no differentiation between subject and object. It is neither subject nor object but subject-object, a vast ocean of cosmic consciousness. It is both mind-and matter-stuff. From the subject-object point of view, all the modifications after the mahat stage are either subjects or objects but not both.

Buddhi (meaning "intellect") which is a synonym of mahat indicates that, in addition to the cosmic aspect, there is a psychological (individual) sense in which the term is used. In life, we know that mental operations take place in organisms; mental faculties, in short, are individual and not collective. Buddhi is the faculty by which we perceive and distinguish objects. This is the vital distinction between consciousness and self-consciousness; hence buddhi (self-consciousness) is the psychological counterpart of mahat in the organism. It is the contention of samkhya-yoga that individual buddhis passively exist in the mahat. Quite naturally, the two terms, buddhi and mahat, are used interchangeably, depending on whether the cosmic or psychological sense is referred to. Here it may be pointed out that, until the time of emancipation when there is a cessation of evolution, the bond between purusha and buddhi holds good. It exists potentially as seed-force in an unmanifested condition. It follows, consequently, that the same relation should exist in the mahat stage. The germs of rebirth are the spiritual residue of experience which has its location in the buddhi. In the prakriti as well as in the mahat stage the experiences exist in seed-form, with this difference: that in the former the relation is unmanifested and in the latter manifested. Buddhi is the storehouse of all memories.

The passivity of buddhi in the mahat stage is what makes it one with cosmic consciousness. Although each buddhi is potentially the principle of individuation, which later becomes the mental apparatus and basis of intellection, there is no complete differentiation in the mahat.

Terms like self-consciousness and ego are very often used in psychological literature without a precise definition or limitation of meanings. But in samkhya-yoga, the distinction is relatively clear. Self-consciousness is that phase of the experience of the organism existing passively without the "I" sense. This is buddhi. Ego may be put down as passive self-consciousness (buddhi) plus the "I". Thus the "I" is a later product, coming into existence when the buddhi transforms itself into the ego —the second stage in cosmic evolution.

This second stage in which buddhi evolves into the ego is technically known as *ahamkara* (self-sense).[6] From the passive buddhi (mahat), self-sense arises by the preponderance of rajas (activity). Since mental functions like perception, reasoning, etc., are all due to the modifications of buddhi, the activity of self-sense (ahamkara) is a limited one. It appropriates to itself the rôle of agency. It is the sense of "I" that is the source of much confusion in individual life. The true Self, the eternally real, is the purusha; but our intellectual life is so preoccupied with the external world that we associate our experiences, sorrows and joys, which are merely the changing state of buddhi, with the eternal purusha. Through the mediation of phenomenal "I", agency is falsely attributed to the purusha, which is at all times free. Non-discrimination is the cause of this, and only the right knowledge can put a stop to the illegal and fatal marriage of self-sense (ahamkara) and purusha.

[6] *Samkhya Karika,* 24.

Ahamkara is the source of yet another cause of human suffering. It is the father of self-love. The desire for emancipation is, more or less, in inverse proportion to self-love. Whatever self-love may mean in the abstract, concretely it means a desire to continue the pleasurable experiences of life. But experiences, pleasurable or painful, are of the very essence of prakriti; and continuation of them would only mean deeper and deeper entanglement in the chain of existence which is to be avoided if the wheel of rebirth is to be broken.

There is yet another point which needs clarification—the relation of self-sense to the principle of individuation. The intricacy of samkhya-yoga psychology reaches its height when we are told that the phenomenal "I" (ahamkara) has nothing whatever to do with individuality. It is the mental life as a whole, rather than the crust "I", prominent though it may be, that should constitute individuality. Buddhi is the mental substance; it is, therefore, also the basis of individuation. What is the organ that coördinates mental life? It is a well-known fact that our impressions and sensations, although mediated by the different sense organs, develop a unitary phase. Here also the self-sense plays no part, coördination being the rôle of a later product yet to be described. After this organ has coördinated experience, the "I" sense may relate the unified whole to the purusha.

There are undoubtedly some conflicting accounts of ahamkara in the ancient books. One may safely say, however, that its function is essentially practical rather than cognitive. It merely takes part in the false attribution of individual experience to the purusha, the real self.

Throughout the ahamkara as well as the buddhi stage, tamas, the inertia or non-activity factor dominant in matter, exists in a suppressed state. In our waking life the "I" sense becomes real in opposition to the external world. In short, how can the "I" exist if there is nothing other than the "I"? If there is no material world as yet, then there can be no mental content for objects. In answer to this, we are told that the gunas contain in themselves the germs of subjectivity and objectivity. Through rajas (activity) the ahamkara comes into existence and continues to function abstractly, making itself its own object. Although primarily subjective, it remains as an energizing activity, awaiting the development of the tamas-dominated external world for concrete expression.

In the next stage of cosmic evolution after the production of self-sense (ahamkara), the gunas evolve through different lines, one of the three gunas preponderating in each.[7] The sattva side develops into the five cognitive senses—hearing, touch, sight, taste, and smell; the rajas side produces the five conative senses or organs of action—speech, hands, feet, and excretory and generative organs. The tamas side generates first matter potentials (*tanmatras*), which in turn evolve the five gross atoms (*paramanu*) of ether, sound, light, water, and earth. The predominance of a particular guna along one line of development does not preclude, of course, the presence of the other two gunas in a latent stage. Of particular importance is the rôle of rajas as a common denominator, furnishing the power of movement.

[7] *Samkhya Karika,* 25-26.

It is the need of the organism that generates function and the preponderance of a guna determines the nature of the function. Cognitive function could not develop from tamas (inertia), nor a material atom from sattva (the translucent guna). The conative organs like hands, etc., are called forth by the need for action; hence rajas (activity guna) plays the chief rôle in these functions. There is, however, a clear distinction between function and the organ of function. An organ is made up of the grosser products of matter evolved along the tamas (material) side; but the function or sense is the subtle need which has its genesis in the ahamkara (self-sense). The gross, material sense organs are, so to say, the vehicles of the five faculties.

In addition to the five cognitive senses, the sattva side of evolution produces, also, the coördinating sense called *manas* (mind).[8] Each sense is specifically suited to take in only a particular kind of sense data; hence there must be a faculty and its organ to synthesize and arrange the chaotic impressions that come streaming in from the outside world. If the senses are the doors, mind (manas) is the doorkeeper. This is what we meant above when we said that the "I" or the ahamkara was not the coördinating sense. In fact, the "I" is prior to the mind. Though chiefly associated with the cognitive side of mental life the mind is also related to the organs of action, hands, feet, etc., arising out of the rajas (energy) side. A full life is not a life of synthesis and reflection alone, but one of action too. In voluntary as well as involuntary actions there is interplay between the synthe-

[8] *Samkhya Karika,* 27.

sizing mind and the executing organs. Manas (mind), therefore, is said to partake of the nature of both the cognitive senses and the organs of action.

From the ahamkara ("I") stage on, the development of the material world takes place through the preponderance of tamas (element of inertia). The suppressed tamas develops into homogeneous, inert, and characterless rudiments of matter called *bhutadi*. These are infinitesimal units of mass or quantum, devoid of physical and chemical characters. This is only a development within the ahamkara.

With the operation of rajas (energy) these rudiments or quanta (bhutadi) evolve into the five potentials (tanmatras).[9] These are sound, touch, light, taste, and smell potentials, the differences being partly due to unequal aggregation of the original units of bhutadi and partly caused by the unequal distribution of energy (rajas). Being sub-atomic potentials, they are partly specialized but do not possess chemical properties like the gross atoms. They are subtle, vibratory, and pregnant with energy; some of them possess power of impact, others penetrability, still others power of cohesive attraction, and so on. The name "tanmatra", which means "mere thatness" signifies its nature. They cannot serve as sensory stimuli, however, since this is possible only after they have undergone further evolution into gross atoms. These sub-atomic potentials, therefore, may be taken as the indeterminate state of matter, their essences being indistinguishable one from another as far as manifestation of effects are concerned.

How do these sub-atomic potentials (tanmatras)

[9] *Samkhya Karika*, 38.

evolve into the gross atoms? In spite of the divergence of views on certain matters of details, atoms (paramanus) may be said to arise through the compounding of the potentials with the addition of the original units of mass (bhutadi). The order of the evolution is as follows:

sound potential + bhutadi = ether (akasa) atom
sound potential + touch potential + bhutadi = air (vayu) atom
sound potential + touch potential + light potential + bhutadi = light (tejas) atom
sound potential + touch potential + light potential + taste potential + bhutadi = water (ap) atom
sound potential + touch potential + light potential + taste potential + smell potential + bhutadi = earth (kshiti) atom

Each succeeding atom possesses one more quality than the preceding one because of the extra addition of one more potential. The ether atom, for example, has sound for its manifest quality, the air atom sound and touch, and so on down the line to the fifth, the earth atom which has the qualities of sound, touch, color, flavor, and odor.

It is needless to point out that atoms, since they are formed by the compounding of potentials (tanmatras), have parts. In the true sense of the term, only the gunas are partless. Atoms, by definition, are the smallest indivisible particles which possess the properties of the compound. An atom can act as a sensory stimulus, although it has to unite with others to form objects of the sensible world. The trend of evolution, as we have said, is from the subtle to the gross; atoms reveal greater differentiation than the potentials (tanmatras) and the potentials still more than the rudimentary units (bhu-tadi). Since the atoms constitute the last stage in evolution, we may now represent the scheme by the following diagram:

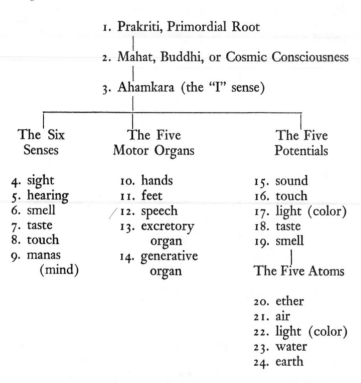

1. Prakriti, Primordial Root

2. Mahat, Buddhi, or Cosmic Consciousness

3. Ahamkara (the "I" sense)

The Six Senses	The Five Motor Organs	The Five Potentials
4. sight	10. hands	15. sound
5. hearing	11. feet	16. touch
6. smell	12. speech	17. light (color)
7. taste	13. excretory organ	18. taste
8. touch	14. generative organ	19. smell
9. manas (mind)		

The Five Atoms

20. ether
21. air
22. light (color)
23. water
24. earth

Purusha, when added to the above twenty-four principles, makes up the twenty-five Realities (Tattwas) of the samkhya-yoga. The distinctions between the non-specialized and specialized products of prakriti should become more clear with the above diagrammatic representation of evolution. Mahat, ahamkara, and the five tanmatras are both causes and effects, for they are evolutes of previous existences and capable of producing further effects; hence they are non-specialized. The five sense organs and manas and the five motor organs and the five gross atoms are end-products incapable of further differentiation. Since it is eternal, prakriti is the uncaused root-cause, and purusha, being transcendent, is neither cause nor effect.

Primary evolution comes to an end with the gross atoms. The underlying principle is that when new properties come into existence we have an instance of primary evolution. The various products of the material world are all due to the shuffling and re-shuffling of the five basic atoms which form their constituent units. This is a case of development or secondary evolution. According to the samkhya-yoga, therefore, mutation of biological species is only a case of secondary evolution. Inorganic, vegetable, and animal kingdoms are only three phases of the same development. The same atoms are constituents of the bodies of plants and animals as well as of the inorganic compounds. The different qualities in the products are to be traced to the different arrangements of the atoms.

The samkhya-yoga classification is a qualitative appraisal based on the senses. Every atom that displays the qualities of heaviness, roughness, obstruction, etc., for example, comes under the earth group, while those that possess subtlety, softness, clearness, etc., belong to the water group, and so on. In the formation of chemical compounds atoms of one group may combine with those of the others. In plants there is a predominance of earth and water atoms in varying proportions. In the bodies of man and animals there is a large aggregation of earth atoms, and the largest accumulation of light atoms is to be observed in the sun. Matter can exist in three states, potential, atomic, and as gross substance. The first two are the products of primary evolution. The last is a case of secondary evolution. All the changes and developments in the world of perception are due to the combining and re-combining of atoms.

Before bringing this chapter to a close, the samkhya-yoga conception of time and space must be briefly described. Everything in the world appears as change and the empirical mind relates these changes to time and space. Considered independently time and space are abstractions. Time order is merely another way of representing a series of changes. If the atom is the smallest "indivisible" unit of matter, then the time taken by one atom to change, i.e., to leave one point and reach the next, would constitute the smallest indivisible unit of time—a moment (*kshana*). Objectively there is a continuous succession of changes and moments. This does not give us the right to believe that there is a continuous time. Our empirical knowledge of an infinite continuum is not objectively true; hence this perception must be the mind's method of schematizing the objective world. Time, therefore, is discrete; our perception of infinite time has no metaphysical reality. The present is a single moment during which the whole world is undergoing change. In the present the past is no more and the future is not yet. The effect of the preceding change is latent and the future is potentially hidden in the present. The present moment alone exists, the past and future are relative to it.

Space as position is the relation of the finite objects to the all-pervasive *akasa* (ether). Without the object limiting the all-pervasive medium, there could not be relative position. While change and objects are real, space as position is only relatively real; it is illusory and has no external existence. But space is also considered as extension. A thing is gross because it occupies space. In this sense it cannot be reproduced in infinitesimal units of position and hence is existentially real.

We have already seen that two causes, material and efficient, are recognized. The efficient cause is the teleological influence of purusha, for whose service the whole of prakriti evolves in a particular direction. Outside of this remote relationship, purusha has no bearing on the cause-effect sequences of the material phenomena. That the effect is pre-existent in the cause is a central doctrine; hence in the final analysis evolution is the continuous transformation of energy from one form into another. It is a process of greater and greater differentiation with integration, both taking place in prakriti. None of the products are in opposition to prakriti; they are only prakriti in a changed form. Mahat, or any other product of evolution, is different from prakriti in the sense that the latter has become, or differentiated into, mahat. To use the words of Dr. Seal: "The process of evolution consists in the development of the differentiated (*vaishamya*) within the undifferentiated (*samyavastha*), of the determinate (*visesha*) within the indeterminate (*avisesha*), of the coherent within the incoherent." [10]

[10] Seal, B. N.—*The Positive Sciences of the Ancient Hindus*, 7; Longmans, Green and Company, 1915.

Potentially all things are alike, for they are only manifestations of the same gunas. We may compare evolution to the flooding of lower levels due to the breaking of barriers holding back water on a higher level. Although effect is contained in the cause and fundamentally there is no difference between the two, certain concomitant conditions limit transformation of potentiality into actuality. Otherwise, all manifestations would appear at once. The marble may contain the image, but the sculptor must work with the chisel to manifest the hidden form. Plants do not grow from stones, nor does the form of man rise from that of a deer. The concomitant conditions that limit the course of evolution are place, time, form, or constitution. A plant will not shoot forth from a stone because the form of the latter, or the arrangement of the atoms, stands as an obstacle to this development. Potentiality, like stored water ready to flow forth when the obstacles are removed, is ever in readiness to manifest fully in actuality; but the barriers restrict the speed and course of this process.

The samkhya-yoga presents evolution as actualization of power or energy. There is no ultimate difference between substance and quality; hence gunas are both substance and energy. Just as evolution is explained on the basis of conservation and transformation of energy, dissolution too is accounted for by the same principles. The teleological reason for the backward march of the evolved universe we have already seen. The epoch of dissolution is determined by the collective influence of the purushas which seek respite from evolution. Then the prakriti would resume a counter-march, atoms would disintegrate into tanmatras (potentials) and so on all along the line. There would be a temporary cessation of activity when the prakriti has reached its original state, to be resumed again to satisfy the demands of purusha.

Chapter V

YOGA PSYCHOLOGY: THE PROCESS
OF KNOWING

IN THE mind of the modern psychologist, trained as he is in the quantitative appraisal of experimental results, the samkhya-yoga analysis of the mind would perhaps evoke the same sense of intangibleness and of futility as have the soul-psychologies of the Greeks and of the Middle Ages. The modern terminology, ideas, approach, and experimental temper of the laboratory are far removed from the qualitative observations of the ancients. There is an irreconcilable gulf between conditioned reflexes, physiological gradients, and the intelligence tests on the one hand, and the *nous*, soul, and vital spirits of the earlier period on the other.

In this respect Hindu systems are not unlike those of the ancient Western world. They are empirical rather than experimental; they are products of observations and reflections on experience. Attention, will, imagination, etc., were treated as manifestations of *a mind*, emphasis being chiefly centered on the interrelationships between these aspects of mental life rather than on their bodily basis. The subtle distinctions of the indistinguishable nuances of the mental processes in the Hindu treatises, particularly those of the Buddhists who developed psychological analyses to a high degree, might appear to some today like trying to split a hair in the dark. Changes in the mental stream at every turn in the progress of concentration are elaborately described. There is a special word for the state of concentration when the name of the object alone is in the mind, another when the object is thought of with its predicate relations, still another when it is merely a point, and so on. It is significant that more words for philosophical and religious thought are to be found in Indian literature than in the Greek, Latin, and German languages combined. This fact has been recognized by one of the modern investigators of Indian culture, Count Hermann Keyserling.[1]

There was an impelling reason for these empirical observations. Like all other philosophies, yoga was directed towards a particular goal or salvation. Unlike the other systems, however, yoga discovered a practical method of mental training; hence the study of the mind was not a matter of philosophical diversion but a practical necessity. Yoga improved on the metaphysical contributions of the samkhya by offering a feasible method of mental development. This, by the way, is another important difference between the samkhya and the yoga. The former contended that an intellectual understanding of the nature of purusha and prakriti was enough to emancipate the individual from the woes of rebirth. One who truly grasped the eternal nature of purusha and the fact that ignorance of the true nature of things was the cause of pain and suffering in the world, said the samkhya, would not permit himself to be swayed by a false set of values. Reason alone was sufficient to bring

[1] Keyserling, H.—*The Travel Diary of a Philosopher;* London, 1925.

about this transformation. Yoga, on the other hand, was not satisfied with this philosophical complacency. Without denying the samkhya contention that the wise may attain emancipation by philosophical reflection of the nature of things, it formulated a scheme of systematic training to guide the individual. Reason may help all those who are naturally equipped to climb the sublime heights of philosophy; since such men are always few, however, yoga specialized in a method and a way of life that would be within the reach of all who could put forth the necessary effort.

Thus, in a sense, yoga may be called "cosmic therapeutics", and its analysis of the mind is colored by this underlying aim. The popularity of psychoanalysis in recent years may be traced to its appreciation of the quite obvious truth that there can be a mental cure for mental illness. In a subsequent chapter we shall devote some thought to the close similarity between certain phases of psychoanalysis and yoga. Here we shall be content to point out that whatever may be the limitations of therapeutic psychology—which are undoubtedly many—they are bound, by the very nature of their approach to the problems, to throw extremely valuable light on the nature of mind, its motivation, its alleys and labyrinths. And so we should not only be able to appreciate yoga psychology but also to see it in concrete perspective.

Every act of knowledge is a three-cornered affair; an object of the external world that is known, the knower or the subject that knows, and thirdly the process that makes knowledge possible. In the samkhya-yoga the problem is very complicated because purusha, the real self and element of pure consciousness, is the knower without being an agent. Prakriti and all its modifications are non-conscious, but some evolutes, because of the predominance of the sattva gunas (element of translucence), are able to reflect the light of purusha. By "contact through reflection" knowledge becomes possible. Evolution is greater and greater differentiation within prakriti. While for functional purposes the various products, like buddhi, ahamkara, etc., may be said to fulfill different purposes, all evolutes on the mental side collectively serve to acquire experience for the purusha. These are: buddhi, ahamkara, the five cognitive senses and the mind (manas or mind is sometimes claimed as the sixth sense), and the five motor organs. The thirteen modifications of prakriti may be said to constitute, collectively the psychic apparatus. While the samkhya uses the term buddhi also in the sense of psychic apparatus, yoga shows a bias for the word *citta*. Hereafter we shall use the word citta in its traditional collective sense (psychic apparatus) and reserve the word buddhi for contexts in which intellectual operations of the mind are meant to be emphasized.

Thus knowledge, which is not possible for either citta or purusha if each were to exist alone, becomes possible by the reflection of the transcendental purusha in the non-conscious citta.[2] Being non-conscious, citta cannot experience or apprehend; purusha, therefore, is the real experiencer. The modification that takes place in the citta following perception is "caught" by the purusha. We may say, then, that simultaneously with the modification in citta, purusha "catches" a glimpse of what is

[2] *Yoga Sutras*, I.4.

happening and thereby gains experience. This association between the two results in an apparent interchange of functions—citta appears, as it were, conscious, and purusha appears active; while in reality purusha is eternally passive and citta mechanical and non-conscious. If it be asked how the purusha can be the experiencer and still not change, we are told that such an experience is a modification that does not result in new qualities. Any entity is always the same if it does not produce new qualities. Purusha's experience is of this kind.

Let us try to clarify this analysis in another way. If we forget for the moment the sense impressions that come from the outside world, every perception is a blend of two factors: the modification of the citta (*vritti*), which assumes the shape of the object, and the element of awareness which is caused by the reflection of purusha. This reflection follows or imitates the modification of citta and results in apprehension (*jnana*) by the purusha. The apparent identity of the two is compared to the "red-hot iron ball". The formless glow appears spherical, and the cold iron, hot. In order to gain experience for purusha, through the evolution of the mental series prakriti has adapted itself to the needs of the former. It is the citta that comes in contact with the material world, but the experience belongs to purusha. Thus the transcendent purpose of purusha is achieved. The apparent union of buddhi and purusha and a lack of understanding of the true nature of their connection are the source of pain and suffering. The road to liberation lies in severing this bond. The yoga claims to be able to do this by gradually steadying the mind through practice.

There is a cosmic as well as an individual aspect to citta: citta as cause (*karanacitta*) and citta as effect (*karyacitta*). We saw in the preceding chapter a similar distinction between the individual buddhi and the cosmic mahat. The underlying reason for this cosmic-individual differentiation is to find a theoretical basis for the so-called "miracles," like telepathy, clairvoyance, etc., which are claimed to be genuine experiences in the higher stages of yoga practice. In the organism citta appears as effect pervading the whole body. But citta as a cause is cosmic and all-pervading. By concentration, according to yoga, it is possible to turn the limited mind into the cosmic mind-stuff and thus establish contact with other minds. This may be compared to the relationship between space as limited by the four walls of a room and cosmic space in which all objects inhere. Only the four walls divide the room-space from cosmic-space. Individual citta (karyacitta) is limited by the organism, but it is not separate from cosmic mind-stuff (karanacitta). Citta as effect, which undergoes modifications in perception, is only a limited manifestation of citta as cause.

In everyday life we are concerned only with organismic citta. We perceive an object when the citta assumes the form of the object. It may come as a rude shock to some that thoughts, according to yogic theory, are things and that they occupy space. Both matter and mind are only parallel developments of prakriti, the ultimate elements in both being the three gunas. Tamas (inertia) predominates in gross matter, while sattva guna is uppermost in the mental series; hence both mind and matter occupy space. When it is said that citta modifies itself and assumes the form or shape of the object, we should take it not metaphorically but literally.

While the citta, the psychic apparatus, collectively operates in perception, the sense organs, ahamkara (the "I" sense), etc. perform different functions. If we take the visual sense, for example, we find that it establishes contact with the external object only under certain conditions: when the distance between the object and eye is neither too great nor too small, when the object is not too small, when the visual organ is not defective, when the object is not lost in its own medium (as when a drop merges in a volume of water), etc. At the first moment of contact we have a case of indeterminate (*nirvikalpa*) perception—raw, unverbalized perception, to use the language of James. This stage is characterized by a vague awareness of something without an understanding of the nature of the object or its relation to other objects. The second stage is that of determinate perception (*savikalpa*) where the object takes "shape and form". The manas (mind), which we described in the last chapter as the coördinating organ, imposes determinateness on the indeterminate sense data. One might say that the work of mental analysis and synthesis takes place in the manas. In the third moment perception becomes individualized when it is appropriated by ahamkara (the "I" sense). Finally, buddhi decides the course of action that should follow perception. Buddhi, here, may be taken as the organ of deliberation and will.

While this is the general picture of the various moments in perception, it must be pointed out that there are, here and there, minor differences of detail among the commentators. It is contended by some, for instance, that

determinate perception takes place simultaneously with
the modification of the sense organs without the intermediation of the manas (mind). These commentators
have naturally subordinated the rôle of manas. It may
also be pointed out that the sequence described above
need not chronologically follow in any and every case
of perception. As an example, the fear of a man when
confronted by a tiger is very realistically described; the
various moments accompanying such a perception are
said to take place simultaneously. Here one is vaguely
reminded of the modern theory of reflex action as an
automatic process.

No perception is free from subjective factors. Since
the mediation of the senses is essential we never perceive
things as they are, only as they are modified by the
senses. If the sense organs are defective, our perceptions
become distorted. At no time is our perception complete,
for we see things only partially. Spatial position of things
in relation to other objects is included in the data that
the sense organs gather from the outside, but the temporal order is a construction of the citta.

The problem of memory and recognition deserves
mention. Every experience leaves a trace or potency
(*samskara*) in the citta which is a great storehouse of all
past experiences. They lie as seeds awaiting activity at a
favorable opportunity. A present perceptual image would
resuscitate, by internal relationships, all the potencies
that are in any way related to it. Thus the modifications of
the citta to assume the form of an object are invariably
due to the conjoint influence of two sets of factors: sense
impressions coming from the outside and the previous
potencies that were already in the citta. It is not only

the individual differences of the senses alone that modify our perception, but also the memory factors as well. The potencies are carried over from previous births which are constantly modifying our mental life. The details of the mechanism through which these potencies are carried over from one life to another and the influence of the subconscious we shall take up in a later chapter.

Like a flame that is constantly bending in all directions, the citta is perpetually undergoing modifications. In internal perception, as in dreams, imagination, etc., psychic process is the same with the difference that the coöperation of the senses is not required. Memory is the function of only three evolutes of prakriti—buddhi (intellect), ahamkara (the "I" sense), and manas (the organ of synthesis and assimilation) which are called, collectively, the "inner-organ" (*antah-karana*). If it were not for the proximity and "attachment" of purusha to an individual citta, these perceptions and consequent modifications would remain non-conscious. Prakriti is blind and non-conscious, and no matter how fine the citta may be as against the gross matter of the external world, it cannot be the source of consciousness. It is the purusha that intelligizes knowledge by its reflection in the citta.

The mechanism of auditory perception and verbal cognition was a subject of great interest to grammarians and philosophers of ancient India. Several theories were current in different schools. Patanjali's theory, in his *Yoga Sutras*, was different from that of the samkhya. He maintained that the basis of sound is the sound-potential (*sabda tanmatra*), the first evolute on the material side through ahamkara (the "I" sense). While these potentials objectively constitute the nucleus of sound, the medium in which it takes place is the cosmic ether which is all-pervading. But the subject becomes aware of sound only through the movement of air which is composed of gross atoms. Sound could be generated in the absence of air but, in that case, we would not hear it. When the moving air atoms touch the organ in the ear the sensation of sound is produced.

Each letter of the alphabet potentially can reveal an infinite number of meanings in combination with other letters; individually, however, they have no significance. Take the word "man" with its three letters, *m*, *a*, and *n*. Only when the three letters are uttered in continuous succession do we become aware of its meaning. But the *m* and *a* could combine with *t*, producing the word "mat", which has an entirely different meaning. Temporal intervals between the letters are important, otherwise sounds would not register as a word.

It is further argued that there is no unity between word and its object. All that the sense organ registers is a succession of sounds. The word becomes complete only after the last sound has been heard, but by that time the previous sounds have perished. The sense of hearing has no power to hold together the sounds that vanish as soon as they are registered in the ear. Letters may act as a kind of stimulus to generate the comprehension of the complete word which takes place by modification of the citta. The image produced in the citta is called "notion" (*sphota*). The important point about the "notion" is that, unlike the letter-forms produced by sounds, it is an inseparable and unified whole, possessing connotation and denotation. As long as the letters are heard in a particular order, they arouse the notion-forms. Great importance is attached to these citta-notions, as against letters which are considered insignificant. The full word is comprehended by the citta and not the sense. The relation between the word and its meaning, i.e., the object implied, may be traced to immemorial custom and tradition. The word is a sign of the thing signified. Thus three stages are distinguished: the letter sounds that are heard by the ear; the unitary perception of the completed word (sphota) which is the work of citta; the external object which the notion (sphota) signifies. Ordinarily there is a confusion between all these three stages, but analysis should show that there is no unity between any two or all three.

Two kinds of inference are accepted as valid. The first is that of positive concomitance or from cause to effect, as when we infer from the cause, clouds, the effect, rain. We may reverse the process and infer the cause from the effect. Inference is also possible on the basis of similarity. In all these cases, however, the necessity of isolating the relevant from the irrelevant causes is emphasized. The syllogistic form of reasoning is accepted where the premises are derived from valid inductive reasoning. Testimony of trustworthy and skillful observers are also accepted as a source of valid knowledge.

We have explained the essential nature of sensory perception as a form of cognitive knowledge. Perception, inference, and reliable testimony constitute one of the five kinds of the modification of the citta.[3] Of these we have described, so far, only the first. The other four are: unreal or illusory knowledge in which the modification

[3] *Yoga Sutras*, I.7.

of the citta is different from the real form of the object; abstract imagination; sleep; and memory.[4]

We walk along the beach, see a shell, and immediately come to the conclusion that it is silver. Where is the source of this illusion? Every apprehension is the result of the coöperation of two factors, the individual bias of the perceiver and the object seen. Citta, being the seat of impressions of previous experiences of silver and similar objects, brings to bear on the present object certain factors that are peculiar to the perceiver. The source of error lies in the power of the citta to interfere with the object, or, rather, the error might be traced to the subject's peculiar mental twist. We never see any object in its completeness, only that much of it that is in keeping with our mood at the time. Every illusion, therefore, is the result of incomplete observation. A relatively complete examination of the shell would show that it is quite different from silver. The way to amass correct knowledge is to appraise everything from all sides. In the case of the shell the error was due to mistaking part for the whole. Error is not a positive wrong knowledge, but a lack of complete knowledge. While errors result basically from this deficiency of knowledge, they may appear, of course, in various forms. Thus a white crystal which appears red by the side of a red flower is a case of illusion where two objects are involved. It is one of non-discrimination, for the moment we realize the distinction between the two there is no longer any error. But non-discrimination implies that we failed to investigate the situation fully. Complete knowledge would have shown

[4] *Yoga Sutras*, I.8-11.

that the white crystal and the red rose were two distinct things.

We have attempted to give only one of the several views on the psychology of error found in the samkhya-yoga books. All the discussion on this subject is aimed to show that the pain and suffering of the empirical life is itself due to non-discrimination (*avidya* or ignorance) which is the confusion or mistaken identity between the empirical self (buddhi) and the true self, purusha. A complete understanding of the distinction between the two, claims samkhya-yoga, would dispel this fatal ignorance.

The third modification of the citta takes place in abstract reasoning or imagination, where language symbols are employed to express relations between parts of the real world. For practical purposes, the knowledge derived through this source is valid to the extent that it enables discursive intellect to proceed with its rational operations, to broaden our understanding, and to convey meaning to others. They represent an indispensable tool of thinking. The symbols, however, do not convey the relations in the world as they are. They produce symbolic knowledge which is valid by common consent.

When philosophers say that the "true nature of purusha is consciousness" they attribute, by the inevitable demands of symbolic thinking, consciousness to purusha. In reality purusha is nothing but consciousness; but to make its nature clear philosophers have divided a unitary thing into two and established an attributive relation between two imaginary parts. Again, what do we mean when we say "Chaitra's cow"? In the real world there is no relation between Chaitra and the cow, but in our imagination we have established a relation. Through language we falsely attribute diversity to things that are identical, and identity to things that are diverse. The purport of the whole discussion is to point to the questionable nature of most of our thinking. The concepts and names with which we build our syllogistic propositions may have an instrumental value in furthering a limited kind of knowledge. But they cannot be a valid source of knowledge, for they are only partial representations of processes in nature. Abstract thinking cannot be carried on without the aid of symbols, but we should constantly be watchful lest we identify symbolic knowledge with real knowledge.

Dreamless sleep is a kind of modification. The sense of inactivity accompanying sleep should not mislead us into thinking there is no fluctuation at all in the mind-stuff in this condition. No doubt, the citta is in a state of relative quiescence, there is neither perception nor reflective thinking; consequently the citta does not assume the form of objects in sleep. This quiescence of the citta in sleep only shows that the usual predominance of sattva (the element of translucence) characteristic of citta in its waking hours, and which constitutes the essential difference between matter and mind, has sunk into relative insignificance. Instead of sattva, tamas (inertia, the guna conspicuous in matter) dominates the psychic apparatus and the purusha remains inwardly conscious because there is no modification of citta into the form of an object. This conclusion is supported by the evidence that on awakening, we are able to reflect: "I have slept well and my mind is calm," "I have slept poorly and my mind is dull," etc. These reflections would be possible only if we had some vague experience of a cause in sleep. Also, we would not have the memories based upon these experiences if sleep were not a peculiar modification of the citta.

The yoga method demands that, in order to attain the highest stages in concentration (one-pointed mind), it is necessary to suppress all five kinds of modifications of the citta.[5] It is also true that the highest state thereby reached is a condition of thoughtlessness. One might argue from this that there is a similarity between such a state (*samadhi*) and sleep, for in the latter the citta is relatively suppressed. This would be an erroneous conclusion because in concentration sattva is predominant and in sleep tamas is. As a matter of fact the progress through concentration to the highest stage of "modificationlessness" is in a direction completely contrary to that of sleep. Only by steadying the citta, by increasing the power of sattva and suppressing the tamas, can we improve our concentration. In sleep we are nearer the "thoughtlessness" of "inert" matter, for in both tamas (inertia) is uppermost.

The fifth and last kind of modification is memory (*smriti*). It is the peculiar nature of citta that it can retain percepts in the form of impressions. In this hidden state they lie latent. Like the seeds that come to life when the necessary conditions, like watering the soil, etc., are fulfilled, these impressions or potencies change from an unphenomenalized into a phenomenalized form in accordance with certain association laws. Thus we have a revival of a previous experience known as memory. Every time a memory is revived, the potency of the cor-

[5] *Yoga Sutras*, I.12.

responding experience is further strengthened. No memory is ever wiped out; it is ever ready to be phenomenalized, to take advantage of favorable opportunities.

The difference between perception and memory is this: the former gives rise to something new, whereas the latter cannot go beyond the limits of previous experience. Every perception is in a very real sense a new one. Memory may correspond with the whole of the past experience or with part of it, but it never adds anything to the old. The dream state is a kind of memory depending on previous experiences and not on real objects as in perception. It is admitted that what may look like a new experience may occur in dream. For example, one's deceased parents who have been experienced in one time and place are brought into relation with another time and place not previously experienced. The answer to this is that there are two kinds of memory: that in which mentally-construed (imagined) things are remembered, and the memory in which only real things are remembered. Of these two, yoga contends, the latter alone has the right to be called memory proper. The other is like illusory perception described above. If it be argued that the distorted dream experience is real as long as it lasts, it might be pointed out that this is equally true of illusory knowledge. The shell *is* silver, until discrimination reveals the error. So it is with distorted dreams.

In addition to the production of knowledge, the feeling side that accompanies every kind of modification of the citta deserves emphasis. Knowledge and feeling are inseparable as the obverse and reverse side of a medal. All life is suffering and it is the feeling side of mental and emotional life that gives the urge to live its dynamic motivation. The cardinal feelings are three, pleasure, pain, and ignorance. The doctrine of the universality of suffering which is an axiom in all Indian philosophies leaves no room for choice between pleasurable and painful feeling. All experience is tinged with pleasure and pain, the former being inevitably followed by the latter. It is impossible to acquire knowledge which is not tinged with feeling and in suppressing the modification of the mind-stuff we shall eliminate both knowledge and feelings. It is foolish to expect to gain emancipation by increasing knowledge.

Although seldom attained by men, there is a state in which the citta could be free from all fluctuations where neither knowledge nor its twin, feeling, could exist. This state can be reached by slowly steadying the mind through exercises in concentration. Citta is like a river that runs in both directions, one leading to a continuance of the present existence and resulting in strengthening the tie of life, and the other leading to release from the chains of rebirth. To be successful in the latter venture, it is necessary to redirect the natural course of the mental life. By slow practice and training, yoga claims, it is possible to effect this redirection.

Chapter VI

YOGA PSYCHOLOGY: ETHICAL PREPARATION

In the previous chapters we have dealt with the philosophical foundations of yoga which are essentially those of the samkhya; and to emphasize the relation the compound term "samkhya-yoga" was used throughout. This usage would have no justification when dealing, as we propose to do in this and the following chapters, with the practical side of a yogin's training, from the ethical preparation to the higher stages in which mental modifications are suppressed. This method and its development are a contribution of yoga alone, samkhya having very little to say in the matter. In the rest of this book we shall use, therefore, the word "yoga" instead of "samkhya-yoga".

Life at every stage is an attempt to make a harmonious adjustment to the environment. This growing adaptability of the organism is what makes life possible. In the course of the struggle of man to mold the environment for his own advancement, a new factor emerges—a conscious attempt to regulate conduct. Ethics, the science of conduct, presupposes the existence of a cleavage between the ideal and the natural inclinations of man. But the nature of any system of ethics would depend upon what we believe to be the purpose and meaning of life itself. If life is an accident and mere sensuous pleasure is the goal toward which we are striving, then a conscious attempt to pattern life after a transcendental ideal would be misguided heroism.

On the other hand, for those who, like yogins, take a spiritual view of life, progressive self-development is an inevitable requirement. More than any other school of spiritual interpretation of life, yoga regards the so-called joys of life as at bottom the source of our suffering. Only when each individual becomes weary of life and all its attractions will yoga become real to him. Even after one has convinced himself that worldly life will lead to greater pain and suffering, the instinctive propensities may yet continue to operate, leaving the individual at the mercy of the current of life.

If we forget metaphysical theories for a moment, we shall see that the first requisite of contemplation is a withdrawal from the hazards and responsibilities of a life of action. Superficially this may appear to be an escape from reality. But if we penetrate deeper, we shall find that the real motive that impels most men to substitute solitude and contemplation for action is the positive conviction that security and happiness may be gained only by spiritual emancipation. The life of a yogin will itself bear testimony to the fact that the path of spiritual progress is not a bed of roses. So far as our instinctive tendencies are concerned, it is very much like making the river flow backwards, or, to use Bergson's language, a remounting of the natural slope of our minds.

Yoga has recognized this need for remolding the mind and reversing the natural trend of our propensities and inclinations to achieve the ultimate objective by prescribing a long program of step-by-step progress towards the goal. It is a comprehensive plan beginning with moral preparation and ending with *samadhi*, the highest mystical state. The various stages in the yogic discipline are: [1]

1. Yamas (negative ethical code)
2. Niyamas (positive ethical code)
3. Asanas (postures)
4. Pranayamas (breathing exercises)
5. Pratyahara (withdrawal of the senses)
6. Dharana (meditation)
7. Dhyana (contemplation)
8. Samadhi (isolation)

The first two, which we shall deal with in the present chapter, are aimed to wean the neophyte away from the social world and to reconcile him to a life of retirement and seclusion. Since what is desired is a well-rounded development, the mind and body are both taken into consideration.

Our normal life, says the yogin, is one of confused thinking; we never see clearly the motives of our actions nor the consequences of our deeds. Automatism is characteristic not only of our body but also of our mind. We follow the line of least resistance, seeking pleasure and avoiding pain. We are the victims of habits developed in early childhood which are aimed to make living more efficient and successful. But how many of us stop to ask whether these habits, which constitute our character, are desirable from a spiritual point of view? If one were to sit down at the end of a day and recapitulate all that he

[1] *Yoga Sutras*, II.29.

had done from morning until evening, he would find that
very little was undertaken after conscious deliberation.
Mental energy contains thoughts directed towards the
perpetuation of worldly experiences as well as those
pointing to the higher ethical ideal of liberation. In the
confused rush of life the latter group of thoughts and
desires, which are as few as pebbles in an ocean of sand,
is lost sight of. But with the unveiling of our mental life
and the motives that prompt us to action, we should be
able to identify these desirable moral urges and then develop them. The plasticity of the mind and the habit-
mechanism are both ethically neutral; hence by conscious
redirection and effort it should be possible to destroy the
old habits and build new ones in conformity with the
yogic creed. Looked at from the point of view of our
normal trend this may be, no doubt, a reversal of our lives
but we should not therefore think it unnatural, for
what is being done is to strengthen the "voice" of liberation which, yoga claims, is already there, only tempo-
rarily relegated to oblivion by the strangling hold of a
crowded but confused life.

We must penetrate a little deeper into the causes of the
confusion of empirical life if we wish to conquer them
in the long run. The main cause of all our troubles, yoga,
as well as other Hindu philosophies, calls ignorance
(*avidya*). All the other obstacles to a correct understanding of the true realities of life, however much they
might appear as instinctive to all life forms, are the offspring of this all-embracing ignorance.[2] The precise
meaning of this conception is unfortunately not fully
conveyed by the English translation. Ignorance is recti-

[2] *Yoga Sutras*, II.3-4.

fied by amassing knowledge, but not so avidya which is
a general cloak operative in our whole empirical life,
from the most abstract reasoning to crude, instinctive
acts. It is, like prakriti, eternal and effective for souls in
the flux of life. In fact, as we have already mentioned in
a previous chapter, avidya is the basic cause that brought
the soul into the maelstrom of evolution. But it is difficult
to see how the transcendental purusha could be inveigled
into the thralldom of natural existence by this magic
wand of cosmic ignorance. Yoga, therefore, maintains
that we shall never know the true nature of this confusion. The moral urges of empirical life can only convince
us of the firm hold and reality of avidya, but not its
metaphysical nature nor its *raison d'être*. For practical
purposes avidya may be thought of as that tendency
which inclines us to mistake the real for the unreal and
vice versa. What is meant here is the innate instinct of
man to seek sensuous pleasures, and thus drive the nexus
of our enslavement more deeply into the complex whirl-
pool of prakriti. If life itself is the cause of our suffering,
then it cannot be an isolated error or confusion, but only
a generalized ignorance affecting all the activities of
mind, that can induce us to cling to the pleasures of life
—a doubtful good no better than the cooling shade of a
cobra's outstretched hood. Instead of making haste to
retrace our steps, instead of realizing that the highest
pleasure is tinged with pain, we allow ourselves to be
victimized by avidya. The supreme ethical task of yoga,
therefore, is the uprooting of avidya; and this is accomplished by steadying the discriminatory knowledge that
arises in the beginning in scattered moments of insight.
There is no guarantee that avidya can be completely

overcome in finite life, but energetic application to yoga should enable us to reduce its hold and accelerate the progress towards liberation.

Avidya, then, is the generating cause of all misery. Again this in its turn leads to results which may be treated as the immediate sources of the confusions of life. The foremost of these is egoism or self-esteem.[3] We have the metaphysical origin of egoism in the mistaken identity of the power of knowing (purusha) and the instrument by means of which one knows (citta or the mindsubstance). Could we but know that the citta is only a transitory unity of changing elements and that purusha is the real self, egoism and the resultant misconception would have no hold on us. Sorrow, joy, vanity, feeling of power and ambition are all tentacles by means of which egoism increases our dependence on life. Who wants to be lost in the race of life? In everything we do, consciously or unconsciously, the ego has a place. But the more we allow ourselves to be influenced by this feeling of personality, the farther away we get from the real self.

Take the development of egoism in early childhood. The child begins to identify itself with all the things that give it enjoyment: mother, playthings, etc. The ego thus slowly expands, until at last it includes a greater part of the environment. When any of the objects to which the child has become attached is taken away the result is a genuine feeling of despair and agony. While the adult may have outlived the ego-world of the child, he in turn begins to build a new one—friends, ambition to outstrip others, desire to be a social success, and so forth. All these

[3] *Yoga Sutras*, II.6.

demand continuous effort leading to a craving for the experiences of life. It is the feeling that certain things are *mine* that leads to identification of the ego with them. While egoism is necessary for the successful continuance of life, yoga contends that it is an obstacle to the realization of the higher self. Egoism and yoga are mutually incompatible. For the former dulls spiritual vision, keeps the victim in a state of perpetual subservience, and helps to evaluate the values of life in wrong perspective.

The subjective element through which egoism builds an attachment between the individual and life is the desire for the perpetuation of pleasurable experiences. All our cravings, from that for food to the higher aesthetic appreciation of art, are tainted with this desire. It covers the whole realm of emotional life. Like the bird in the gilded cage, we are held captive in the net of enticing pleasurable experience. A little introspection is enough to show how imperceptibly and unconsciously, and almost as if by an unerring instinct, we seek those activities which would offer the maximum pleasure. Yoga claims that these desires can be "tamed" by inculcating in the mind of the neophyte the thought that they are extraneous to his true inner self. We shall show in a later chapter that the method by which this is accomplished is different from what we usually understand by the word "repression". Here it may be pointed out that the chief aim is neither to ignore nor deliberately to suppress them, but to treat such experiences as external or as having nothing to do with the individual. Everything must be consciously appraised from a detached point of view, never allowing the subject and the experience to become one. It is possible, says the yogin, to have an emotion and yet be neither *in it* nor *of it*. Only because we feel that we have something to gain or lose if a certain situation develops one way or the other do we become identified with the emotion; and this develops into a passion. It is a true insight that has made poets and artists depict love and anger as blind passions. A man at seventy, who had been the victim of a blinding passion in his youth, looks at his previous experience in a very different light. He is able to objectify it and even smile at himself for having taken certain things so seriously. By a conscious effort of the will we should be able to detach ourselves from emotional experiences. In the case of the yogin a long period of training is necessary before he achieves a relatively important degree of success.

Opposed to the above are aversion and the feeling of hate which, although not of the same intensity as desire, are emotions and, as such, manifestations of citta. Both desire and aversion are effective only as long as we pay unreserved homage to the ego. It is the natural instinct in all living things to withdraw from pain and to hate those who might injure them. But for a yogin who is expected to develop detached brotherliness towards the whole of creation such emotions are a serious handicap. One should learn to be unmoved and unaffected by painful situations. This can be done by conquering them and not by withdrawal.

The last undesirable quality in the list is the will to live which is so strongly embedded in life that it characterizes the stupid and the wise.[4] In the language of Western psychology this is the familiar instinct of self-preservation. While granting that this instinct is neces-

[4] *Yoga Sutras*, II.9.

sary for the prolongation of life, yoga maintains that fear of death or clinging to life, which are two aspects of the same motive, prejudice all human thinking. However unpleasant it may be, yogins should, therefore, learn to be fearless of death which is only just another incident in the long round-of-rebirths. The more we fear death, the greater the crop of worries and anxieties we develop; hence an unruffled mind which is a prerequisite of yoga and fear of death are incompatible.

One conclusion which yoga has drawn from the universal presence of fear of death in all living creatures is interesting, for it shows an attempt to explain instinct in terms of the subconscious. Even in the case of a new-born worm there is a disposition to withdraw from pain and death. The same is true of the new-born infant. But knowledge is acquired through three sources, perception, inference, and verbal testimony, none of which can account for this fear in the infant. It would be meaningless to conclude that such a universal reaction is a mere accident. We may conclude, therefore, "from this peculiar quivering the child infers the nearness to himself of the experience of death and is found to be afraid of it." This fear is not any different in the case of the wise man, i.e., one who realizes that death is only an episode in the chain of rebirths and that eternal existence is isolation of the purusha from phenomenal evolution. From all these considerations we can draw only one legitimate conclusion: that in a previous life the organism must have experienced the pain of death. The memory of this painful experience of the past life, since it persists in the subconscious, is the cause of this universal fear. By practice, the yogin should uproot even the subconscious impressions. One can imagine the austerity of a discipline which demands the eradication of a primary instinct like that of self-preservation.

The five modifications described above are the important obstacles in the path of successful consummation of yoga. Of these avidya or ignorance is the root-cause of the last four—egoism, desire, aversion and hate, and the will to live. Certain other hindrances, though not so deep-seated or fundamental, are also mentioned. They are: "sickness, languor, doubt, heedlessness, worldliness, erroneous perception, failure to attain any stage of concentration, and instability in the stage when attained." In the course of the progress toward the ultimate ideal of yoga, these might arise as sources of doubt and despair, and by guarding against these from the beginning one might be better able to overcome the obstacles of the second group.

It is one thing to point out habits that are inimical to a yogin's progress and another to devise a workable method to overcome them. Without denying the possibility of achieving liberation by rational understanding, as, for example, maintained by samkhya, yoga claims that its discipline consisting of eight stages is, for those who are willing to go through with it, a satisfactory method to reach the goal. Yoga points to a difference between the distant and immediate goal of its discipline. The former is, as has been pointed out several times, isolation of purusha and escape from the bonds of rebirth. But this can be achieved only by calming the mind-stuff, that is to say, going beyond the mind. All the elaborate preparation, ethical, physical and psycho-physiological, is aimed to serve this one purpose: the control and then the elimination of mental processes.

The first of these eight stages, *yamas*, may be called abstentions or negative ethical code, corresponding to the "thou shalt not's" of any practical religion. The yogin is asked to refrain from causing injury to any living thing, falsehood, theft, incontinence, and acceptance of gifts. The first one, abstaining from injuring others, is considered the most important and a proper fulfillment of it will, it is said, automatically take care of the rest. Every time, for example, we tell a falsehood we are injuring some one. Interpreted thus, this moral principle, familiarly known in Indian philosophy as the doctrine of *ahimsa*, demands of the yogin a spirit of friendliness to all living creatures. It is not a conditional principle making allowance for exceptional situations. Not even self-defence, nor differences of age, sex, or circumstances can justify murder. The yogin should go through life bearing malice towards none. By observing these obligations, yoga claims, it is possible to develop an attitude of mind which will remain unruffled in the face of situations both pleasant and painful.

If the first set of ethical precepts is negative, the second, known as *niyamas* (observances), constitutes positive directions concerning what the yogin shall do to develop a serene frame of mind. They are: cleanliness, self-discipline of body and mind, and resignation to life.

Cleanliness includes regulations concerning diet, clothes, and other requirements of the body as well as those dealing with the mind. In the matter of food, a yogin is not allowed to undergo extremes of privations.

On the other hand, he should eat only just as much as is necessary to keep fit. In these matters a golden mean is what is desired; overeating and undernourishment are equally ruled out.

Anyone who has recognized that the development of the will goes hand in hand with the breaking up of old habits can also recognize the significance of the second precept, self-discipline of body and mind. The neophyte who takes yoga practice seriously has to give up many of his old standards of comfort and luxury. This can be done only by bodily austerities. Here, as elsewhere in yoga, extremes are prohibited. The impression most Westerners have gained that yoga means self-mortification and torturing of the body is true only of those cases in which men, despairing of insufficient spiritual progress, mistakenly lend themselves to incredible physical tortures. Such aberrations are not countenanced by yoga. In fact, the practitioners are explicitly warned against these malpractices. In our investigations we have had the privilege of coming in close contact with several who had dedicated their lives to the discipline of yoga, but at no time did we find any instance of self-mortification. What they aimed at was eradication of the desire or craving for comfort which is the curse of one who has devoted himself to a spiritual life. This mastery is gained by deliberate effort of the will and a corresponding determination to undergo the discipline. Thus the immediate goal is self-control and not self-torture. One of the aphorisms describes perfection of body as "beauty and grace and power and the compactedness of the thunderbolt."

But the psychologist has also to face the fact that in the history of mankind a desire for spiritual perfection has spontaneously led in many cases, both in the East and the West, to the most tormenting kinds of self-castigation. The writer has seen men lying for hours on a bed of nails, others gazing steadily at the bright sun, others piercing the body with nails, and others rolling on dusty streets under a scorching sun for miles and miles. The West, too, has many instances to offer. The lives of Heinrich Suzo, St. Bernard, and St. Teresa are enough to convince one that self-immolation of the utmost severity was characteristic of a leading group of Western mystics also. Commenting on the severity of Suzo's exercises, Leuba says the following: "One could wish this tender soul might have been spared the repulsive pains of extreme asceticism. But the destruction, by torturing the body, of the evil tendencies of the flesh and of the pride of the spirit was an established tradition. By him, as by others, voluntary suffering was regarded in addition as expiation for sin and as visible token of utter devotion to God." [5] All that we wish to point out here is the futility of lumping together, as some writers have done, all these phenomena (steady discipline, ethical preparation of yoga, and extremes of physical torture) in one grand category and then dismissing the whole thing as manifestations of psychopathic traits.

With regard to disciplining the mind in the early period of a yogin's life, it is necessary to find something that would absorb his time and attention. The previous interests, of course, have to be discarded; hence reading of books that treat of spiritual life and problems is prescribed. By developing this habit one is weaned away

[5] Leuba, J. H.—*The Psychology of Religious Mysticism*, 61-62; Harcourt, Brace and Co., 1925.

from old mental attitudes and the interest in the new life is developed.

The third prescription is directed to destroying the self-will, the feeling that "I" am doing things. It is desirable, therefore, to feel that whatever the yogin accomplishes or does is for the sake of and by the will of another. Most often, *Isvara* (God) is the being to whom the yogin succumbs his will, in some cases the teacher (*guru*) takes the place of God. It is a fact of religious life, even of the institutionalized kind, that one who attributes both deed and consequence to God gains a sense of relief by this act. The individual ceases to be responsible no matter what happens. The result is that those petty little worries and anxieties that haunt us as long as we remain the agent of action no longer adversely affect the mental serenity of a yogin who has resigned his will to one higher than himself. Subjection of the individual will and transference of responsibility would lead to that detachment of spirit which would make the yogin a spectator rather than a participant even of his own actions. Passionlessness (*vairagya*) or freedom from attachment to objects or the consequences of one's own deeds, as the yogins call this mental attitude, is a prerequisite for success in exercises of mental concentration.

We may now summarize the first two stages as the ethical code of yoga by which a moral transformation, involving important psychological changes or redirection of mental set, is brought about, marking the beginning of a veritable uphill climb in mental training. We should like to point out that this ethico-psychological preparation has been recognized and utilized by mystics as well as pietistic religious groups in the West. The central aim everywhere has always been to emasculate the over-whelming strength of the pull-back of instinctive life. Until this is accomplished, it is impossible to develop personality around a spiritual mental set. The process takes various forms but the target is invariably egoism or self-will. Whatever may be the academic psychologist's theories about instincts, whether they can be sublimated or not, there is no doubt that by their practice mystics are able to harness all their energies and direct them along one channel—towards a new life. Leuba, who has studied Western mystics very extensively, is clear on this point: "According to their theory and practice," says Leuba, "the fundamental psychological condition of Union is *passivity*. It is only when the human will ceases to strive and surrenders to the divine Will that it becomes possible for God to communicate himself." [6] That psychological conditions are primary and intellectual beliefs relatively unimportant in spiritual progress has been well recognized by men who have penetrated beyond the crust of institutionalized religions. According to Underhill:

This need for the conversion or remaking of the instinctive life, rather than the achievement of mere beliefs, has always been appreciated by real spiritual teachers, who are usually some generations in advance of the psychologists. Hence they agree in finding the "root of evil", the heart of the "old man" and best promise of the "new". Here is the raw material both of vice and of virtue—namely, a mass of desires and cravings which are in themselves neither moral nor immoral, but natural and self-regarding.[7]

[6] Leuba, J. H.—*The Psychology of Religious Mysticism*, 156; Harcourt, Brace and Co., 1925.
[7] Underhill, E.—*The Life of the Spirit and the Life of Today*, 70; London, 1922.

It is the precise care with which yoga has been presented in systematic form that marks it as different from all other treatises on mysticism. Ethico-psychological preparation is only the beginning. As we shall see in succeeding chapters, various other exercises have to be practised before the individual can reach the higher stages.

If while trying to establish the new habit and mode of life, the yogin finds that he is assailed by thoughts of his old life, desires and cravings, what is he to do? When such resistance is very great, he is asked to think of what the consequence might be were he to leave the path of yoga. This is known as contrary production in psychoanalysis. The language in which the opposite thought is formulated is often very strong.[8] If the thought of wanting to hurt any creature comes to mind, the yogin is asked to think the following: "Baked upon the pitiless coals of the round-of-rebirths, I take my refuge in the rules for yoga by giving protection to every living creature. I myself after ridding myself of perverse considerations am betaking myself to them once more, like a dog. As a dog to his vomit, even so I betake myself to that of which I had rid myself."

[8] *Yoga Sutras*, II.33-34.

CHAPTER VII

REBIRTH

THAT death is not the end of life is a universal belief of mankind. It probably had its origin in the primitive animistic religion—the belief that the world is full of spirits and that the disintegration of the material organism does not mean the annihilation of the spirit. Belief in any kind of immortality goes hand in hand with a corresponding belief in some kind of union between that which is immortal and the body. Various imaginative pictures have been employed to make this connection understandable. Thus the body, for example, has been conceived of as the prison or tomb of the soul.

But if one were to press the believers for a precise statement of the kind of immortality they believed in, one would surely be faced with conflicting answers. Some would subscribe to conditional immortality, others to personal immortality; some would be pleased at the prospect of absorption in the oneness of Brahman and many others would passionately believe in some kind of rebirth. In this chapter we shall consider the doctrine of rebirth, a central doctrine of yoga which it shared with all the other systems of Indian philosophy. While it may have originated in the superstitious beliefs engendered by primitive psychology, later on it was very seriously considered by philosophers in Greece as well as in India. For the materialist the problem does not exist. The scientist is not concerned with metaphysical truths. And the vast majority of Western philosophers has been very much concerned with the fate of the soul after death, but not before birth.

The present attitude of most western thinkers to the doctrine of pre-existence is curious. Of the many who regard our life after the death of our bodies as certain or probable, scarcely one regards our life before the birth of those bodies as a possibility which deserves discussion. And yet it was taught by Buddha and by Plato and it is usually associated with the belief in immortality in the far east. . . . My conclusion is, then, that any demonstration of immortality is likely to show that each of us exists through all time—past and future—whether time is held to be finite or infinite.[1]

McTaggart points out that the general antagonism of Western philosophers to the doctrine of transmigration is due to the uncompromising attitude of the Christian religion towards any deviation from its particular doctrine of immortality.

The commonest Greek word for rebirth is *metempsychosis;* some of the modern equivalents are re-incarnation, re-embodiment, transmigration, etc. A fierce battle is raging among Orientalists and Greek scholars about the origin of this doctrine in Greece, whether it was an indigenous growth or an importation from India. While there is no doubt of the cultural contact between ancient civilizations, there is no reason to believe that a doctrine like the present one, the premises of which existed in

[1] McTaggart, J. M. E.—*Some Dogmas of Religion*, 112, 115; London, 1906.

every culture, could not have independently arisen in the metaphysically-inclined minds of the Greeks. The cult that grew around Orpheus, the bard of Thrace (about sixth century B.C.), contained the germs of the doctrine. To men who were caught in the wheel of inexorable rebirth Orpheus preached the necessity of self-purification and an ascetic life as the means of deliverance. Among those in the direct line of Greek thinkers, the doctrine is particularly associated with Pythagoras. He speaks of the body as the transient habitation of the soul, death severing the connection only to unite with another body.

Empedocles carried the doctrine further. He conceived the possibility of human souls migrating to sub-human organisms or even plants:

Thus, in former lives, I have been a boy and a girl, a bush and a bird and a fish without speech in the depths of the sea.

This extreme position was taken for the first time in Greece by Empedocles. Two traditions have existed both in India and in Greece: that which confined the soul's migrations to the human level and that which extended it to cover all nature.

Plato believed that the human soul could migrate to animal bodies, but he diverged from many of the thinkers by introducing a novel idea. Those who had devoted any thought to the original fall of soul had maintained that it was caused by an ancient guilt; consequently the soul was banished to the earth. Plato, on the other hand, rejected this conception, maintaining that the soul became involved in earthly existence by its own mistake, by the failure of the intellectual element to master its own passions. These passions induced a craving for the pleasures of life, and hence release can come only through philosophical enlightenment. The reader may notice the close similarity between this and the yogic conception of *avidya* (ignorance) as well as the samkhya conception of philosophic discrimination.

Plato further maintained that the self-sufficient law of moral growth determined the choice of a body. Thus the character the soul had acquired by deeds and experiences would decide whether it should rise or sink lower in the next birth. Emancipation would come, therefore, only through self-development. This Platonic conception is also the same as that of yoga. Neo-Platonism grew around the mystical and intellectual thoughts of Plato. Plotinus, who was the chief figure in this movement, was himself a mystic and a great admirer of Plato's system. *Dionysius Areopagita*, a book of anonymous origin and the fountain of Christian mysticism, was directly influenced by Neo-Platonism. But in this book the transmigration of souls was ignored, undoubtedly through the growing opposition of the Church.

In the Renaissance period, with the revival of Greek philosophy, metempsychosis was introduced into European thought. Marsilio Ficino, in addition to translating Platonic and Neo-Platonic works, wrote a treatise on the Platonic doctrine of immortality. Giordano Bruno expounded the various ramifications of the doctrine in his writings. Emanuel Swedenborg, the founder of the "New Church of the Heavenly Jerusalem", gave partial support.

If these were only sporadic movements, one may say

that re-incarnation came to full fruition in the classical period of German literature. Goethe's references to it were more than casual; he even explained deep attachment between individuals on the basis of friendships developed in previous births. He says to Frau Von Stein:

> "Ah, in the depths of time gone by
> Thou wast my sister or my wife,"

Other minor intellectuals, like Lichtenberg and Johann Georg Schlosser, brother-in-law of Goethe, wrote essays and dialogues on the subject. One of the greatest figures of this period, Lessing, came to the defense of this theory. He expressed the idea eloquently:

Why should I not come back as often as I am capable of attaining fresh knowledge, fresh skill? Do I bring away so much at once that it does not repay the trouble of coming back? Not on that account. Then because I forget I have been here already? The recollection of my former state would permit me to make only a bad use of the present. And what I must forget now, have I of necessity forgotten for ever? Or because too much time would be lost for me? Lost? And what have I then to miss? Is not a whole eternity mine? [2]

It is significant that David Hume, who destroys several illusions of philosophers, contends in his essay, "Of the Immortality of the Soul," [3] that metempsychosis is the only theory of its kind deserving of attention by philosophers. Schopenhauer, although he stood in the German

[2] Lessing, G. E.—*The Education of the Human Race*, §§97-100.
[3] Hume, D.—*Essays: Moral, Political, and Literary*, 404 (ed. by T. H. Green and T. H. Grose); Longmans, Green and Co., 1875.

tradition, was deeply influenced by the Upanishads. He made the astute observation that the doctrine was a myth, but a myth which contained great philosophical truth. The present-day revival of the subject in philosophical, religious and popular circles has undoubtedly been considerably influenced by Hindu thought which began flowing into the West on a large scale since the middle of the last century.

Any theory of immortality when carried to extremes can be made to appear as a caricature. This has been particularly true of metempsychosis, with its dark and sometimes comic picture of the same soul passing through the body of man, animal, and stone. It is, therefore, quite easy for unsympathetic critics to paint a ludicrous picture of this doctrine. But if we were to judge any doctrine at its highest level, as it was held by sympathetically critical minds, we should find that it answers, granted that materialism is not the final world in philosophy, some of the important questions that man has always raised.

In India, metempsychosis has always been supplemented by the doctrine of *karma* which is nothing but the law of cause and effect in the mental world. There is an unbroken continuity between the early habits and thoughts of the child and the later adult. What a man does at any particular time will be determined by his past. Life is a continuous growth, a desire and aspiration for completeness, which is suddenly interrupted by death. This feeling of inadequacy, a hidden thought that we might have done differently or even better had we had another chance, is probably the mainspring of this doctrine both in the East and the West.

At this point we may notice a fundamental difference between the Western theories and that of yoga. According to yoga, that which migrates is not the soul but the *citta*, which is the congealed and concentrated essence of all the previous experiences gathered together in an individual mental substance. At the end of all rebirths, that which is destined for immortality is the purusha which, once it has been liberated from the round-of-rebirths, is all-pervasive and hence incapable of migration from one body to another. On the other hand, Western philosophers, most of them at any rate, attribute mental faculties to the soul and quite naturally we have the expression "transmigration of the soul".

It has been urged that metempsychosis leads to a conception of distribution of reward and punishment which is not in keeping with a belief in an all-merciful and omnipotent power. This argument only goes to show how difficult it is to outlive the magical belief in a capricious and unpredictable God. For, first and last, rebirth assumes a moral law according to which effects follow causes as automatically as in the physical world. If we believe in a spiritual world, we can have two alternatives: regulation of spiritual life by the law of karma, or a God who capriciously decides to save some and damn others. It is not an accident that adherents of rebirth have either completely ignored or pushed the conception of a benevolent, omnipotent God into the limbo of oblivion. At least, as in yoga, he could be an aid to concentration, but never powerful enough to interfere with the law of karma. If our character is what it is because of our past deeds, we can see in it evidence of a just law rather than the existence of an external power who retributively dispenses justice, rewarding the good and punishing the wicked. The adherents of rebirth think in terms of personal responsibility rather than attribute their misfortunes to an avenging God.

This criticisim, furthermore, entirely ignores the very reason which has inclined people to take this doctrine as an answer to the problem of human existence. It has been advanced to explain the inequalities among men in mental and moral capacity and inclinations. The responsibility for our fate has been sought in our own actions and not traced to the whims of an Almighty God. Conceived in this spirit the doctrine is an incentive toward aspiring for a higher goal.

Some have insisted that this conception leads to fatalism—a belief that we are victims of fate and nothing that we can do will alter our condition. This is the age-old and tattered question of free will and determinism. It would be presumptuous on our part to enter into a discussion of any phase of this problem on which volume after volume has been written. We can only urge that the whole spirit of yoga is against a fatalistic acceptance of life. Each individual holds the future in his own hands, with freedom to rise or fall. In either case, he alone is responsible for his state. This should not be construed to mean that yogins do not appreciate individual differences and the ease with which some could respond to spiritual influence or urges from within. Greater effort and long practice would be necessary for such persons to destroy the heavy store of past influences. But the freedom and opportunity, although limited, are there for all who will make the necessary sacrifice. It is only a superficial view that could characterize yoga as pessimistic, for

underneath its outspoken rejection of the life of the
senses may be seen a deeper and more emphatic joy, that
the changeless and eternal souls, one and all, will regain
their pristine purity after much travail and agony.

Is metempsychosis at variance with what little we
know of heredity? Those who have advanced this argument fail to see that rebirth is itself a theory of heredity.
Let us see how this is. That the child inherits physical
features of the parents is so well established that it would
be accepted by all. As for mental traits evidence is not so
incontrovertible. We may accept, however, the strong
possibility that the offspring inherits also a mental predis-
position, though not actual traits, from its parents. Yoga
maintains, as if in anticipation of this objection, that
every organism has a gross and a subtle body (*linga
sarira*). One might, if it would lead to a clearer understanding, call the latter the psychical body. Karma or
the dispositions and tendencies which we develop in
any life is, in a concentrated and congealed form, de-
posited in the psychical body. After death, this psychical
body in conjunction with the purusha is ready to re-
embody itself in a gross organism. Quite naturally, the
psychical body seeking rebirth would accord only with
that gross body which will be "symmetrical", to use
Plato's expression, with its mental potencies. The psychical body, therefore, selects its own physical form for
rebirth, thereby establishing a harmonious reciprocity
between the physical features and the mental predisposi-
tions of the gross body manufactured at birth, on the
one hand, and the potencies (*vasanas*) of the ego seeking
re-embodiment, on the other. The soul, being eternal
and all-pervasive, is ever in relation with the buddhi (the

principle of individuality) through the innumerable number of rebirths. We inherit our parents! The psychical or the subtle determines the selection of the gross or the physical, although, as we have already seen, both are manifestations of prakriti.

Again, if we set aside the materialist contention that the complexities of indvidual differences and mental life can all be explained on the basis of physico-chemical combinations, we are justified in asking if the differences between the parents and the offspring are not too great to be explained away by heredity. There is too much of a tendency sometimes to trace what is inexplicable to some remote ancestor. Until we know more about what is at present partially a mystery, those who believe in rebirth would seem justified in seeking an explanation from the doctrine of transmigration for inequalities among men in respect to mental and moral capacity.

Now when we look at the natural characters of men, we find that in many cases they possess qualities strongly resembling those which, as we learn by direct experience, can be produced in the course of a single life. One man seems to start with an impotence to resist some particular temptation which exactly resembles the impotence which has been produced in another man by continual yielding to the same temptation. One man, again, has through life a calm and serene virtue which another gains only by years of strenuous effort. Others again have innate powers of judging character, or of acting with decision in emergencies, which give them, while yet inexperienced, advantages to which less fortunate men attain, if they attain to them at all, only by the experience of years. Here then we have characteristics which are born with us, and which closely resemble characteristics which, in other cases, we know to be due to the condensed results of experience. If we hold the doctrine of pre-existence, we shall naturally explain these also as being the condensed results of experience—in this case, of experience in an earlier life.[4]

The problem of child prodigies is, to say the least, a baffling one. In recent days the subconscious has been invoked to account for these phenomena. If the subconscious is a development of the present life and not inherited, then the paradox remains unsolved, for the child certainly did not have a chance to develop these special gifts in its infancy. Our conception of heredity may be enlarged to include the subconscious. This thought seems to underline Jung's theory of the "collective unconscious". The "collective unconscious" is a possible alternative explanation. But the advocates of rebirth, since they base their belief on certain moral considerations, such as individual responsibility, will not be inclined to accept the Jungian view of the inheritable unconscious for the contents of which, whether good or bad, the inheritor is not liable.

Is there not something weird and ghostly about these psychic bodies "floating around" trying to find suitable bodies to migrate to? Yoga claims that just as there is attraction and repulsion between certain bodies among natural objects, as for example, between iron and magnet, in like manner rebirth is adjusted by some kind of force that may be called psychic gravitation. Each subtle body, by this law, is attracted towards its most natural gross body. If chemical affinity may be invoked to explain some of the phenomena of nature, why could we

[4] McTaggart, J. M. E.—*Some Dogmas of Religion*, 122; London, 1906.

not conceive of some such law to bring about the necessary connection between the subtle and the gross body? Analogies are, no doubt, vague and misleading, but we should not forget that the adherents of any other view of immortality would have the same difficulty in picturing a union of the immortal and the perishable. If this union takes place by an act of God, as many theistically-minded folks would have it, it is neither more clarifying nor less miraculous, however more pleasing it may be than the yogic analogy.

We may make use of another analogy from daily life. The hat each man wears fits him perfectly not because of any causal connection between the two but due to the fact that the wearer selects the right one from among several that might be near-fits. The head was not made to fit the hat nor the hat to fit the particular head. Yet, among a large number he has found one that looked as if it were made for his head. The shape and size of the head determined the selection but not the production of the hat. In a similar way the psychical body would gravitate towards that organism most suited to its re-embodiment.

The lack of memory of experiences of past lives has been advanced in recent times against metempsychosis. This too was the burden of Epicurus' argument against Pythagoras. As far as the feeling of identity is concerned, I feel as though my life began at birth. Even if I have lived several times before, there is no conscious identity connecting my past lives and the present. Am I to be held personally responsible for what I cannot remember? So runs the argument.

Pythagoras was not able to offer a satisfactory answer to this objection. With the theory of the subconscious in so much prominence today, the reader would easily see that this objection is no longer relevant. Yoga, centuries—rather, about two millennia—ago contended that all the experiences of past lives are conserved in the subconscious as traces and impressions influencing our life at every turn. The crux of the matter is the important point concerning whether we can have a continuity of mental life without a corresponding memory of experiences. Yoga answers in the affirmative and modern psychoanalysis religiously confirms it as far as the experiences of the present life are concerned.

It has been unanimously admitted by psychologists that the early years of infancy are the formative period of life. No one would question the influence of these years on the adult life. But do we have a memory of these early experiences? We cannot recall them even if we wish to. The situation is not very different in respect to those habits which are developed later in life. I have an intense liking for a particular type of food which is the cumulative result of having eaten it on several occasions. Quite naturally and automatically, I shall in all probability order it again the next time I am in a restaurant. Every time I order it I do so because of an inclination developed in the past, without consciously having before me a memory of the circumstances in which I ordered it before. That I could recall some of these occasions if I cared to does not alter the case, for every time I order I am behaving in continuity with the past without being aware of these experiences.

So the lack of memory of the past is no bar to continuing our life along a mental groove that was developed previously. Consciousness and memory help the organism to adapt itself to the environment in its fight for survival. And think for a minute what a positive hindrance it would be if we remembered all our past including previous lives! Yogins have claimed, it may be noted here, that in certain stages of yoga practice memories of previous lives might be revived!

We may throw more light on this problem from a group of psychological phenomena known as *amnesias*, in which the individual as a *result* of some intense emotional experience or injury to some part of the brain, forgets all or part of the memories of the past. These memories have sometimes been recovered, which would show that they were not lost once and for all. During the period of amnesia the individual may not be able to recall the experiences, but he will act on the basis of his past habits. He may have forgotten, for example, that he was a storekeeper, but he is able to open a new store and make use of his past experiences.

Death is a crucial break, contends yoga, a time when all our experience gathered in the course of life undergoes a sudden transition, giving a sudden twist to the psychical body. The traces of these experiences continue to exist as seeds in the subconscious which determine the new birth and influence the new life. Our subconscious has a long past and will continue through several new births. There will be no liberation until the cumulative experience of the past, which is exerting its influence through the subconscious, has been eradicated through yogic practice.

Does rebirth follow immediately on death? Or is there a strange interlude after death and before the psychical body finds its appropriate corporeal apparatus? There is no unanimity of opinion on this point. Some contend that "as the caterpillar, when it has reached the tip of a leaf, lays hold of another and draws itself over to it, so the soul,[5] after it has cast off the body and [temporarily] abandoned ignorance, lays hold of another beginning and draws itself over to it." [6] Others hold that a period of time may elapse before re-embodiment, comparing this state of the psychical body to that of deep sleep.

As has been pointed out in the chapter on "Purusha", scientific psychology may rightly balk at problems of immortality and at theories of metempsychosis. These subtle bodies and souls are all beyond the grasp of science. Yogins, while making a reasonable case for this theory, have held that human reason would not be able to comprehend these transcendental mysteries. But our reach is greater than the grasp, and a deep yearning has made some great minds, widely removed in time and place, seek peace and spiritual consolation in metempsychosis. "A theory," says George Foote Moore, "which has been embraced by so large a part of mankind, of many races and religions, and has commended itself to some of the most profound thinkers of all time, cannot be lightly dismissed." [7] If we were to make an agenda of the most puzzling and as yet unsolved riddles of human experience, we should be justified in assigning an honored place among the various items to the doctrine of rebirth. Even those who will frown upon any

[5] Unlike the yoga, this passage, being Upanishadic, follows the tradition that it is the soul that migrates.
[6] *Brihadaranyaka Upanishad*, IV.4-5.
[7] Moore, G. F.—*Metempsychosis*, 67; Harvard University Press, 1914.

conception of immortality cannot fail to see the poetic magnificence and cosmic grandeur of a theory that regards our phenomenal existence, extending through several lives and regulated by the workings of a law, as a temporary phase of an eternal and changeless purusha.

Chapter VIII

YOGA AND PSYCHOANALYSIS

NIETZSCHE used to say that the mind is a "horned" problem. If the system built by Freud means anything it confirms this view. Discarding the restraints and cautiousness of the laboratory psychologist, his ways of measuring and weighing, Freud has approached the problem from a new angle. There is something of an accident in the origin of psychoanalysis itself. Beginning in the medical clinic as a cure for neuroses, especially hysteria, it has become a system of psychology and a theory of the mind. Step by step, Freud was led to building a colossal edifice on the findings of the clinic. Although based on the observations of the abnormal, the doctrine has come to be applied to the normal. In influence, one might say that psychoanalysis has deepened our understanding of the social sciences more than any other intellectual movement of the last three decades. The result is a new way of looking at history, religion, social evolution, literature, and of late even politics.

The laymen might well be puzzled by the variety of psychologies which all attempt to explain the same phenomena. The mind is so elusive that it cannot be explained in its entirety by any one of several approaches, biological, philosophical, environmental, or therapeutic. The tolerant person, therefore, should be appreciative of every new attempt to explore this "horned" problem.

Many factors have contributed to the repugnance of the academic psychologist to psychoanalysis. Its dogmatic tone and "nothing else but" complex have alienated the sympathies of many fair-minded scientists. Freud, and to a still greater extent his disciples, has failed to pay any serious attention to the incontrovertible findings of the experimental psychologist and other workers in allied fields. Psychoanalysis rolls on its own wheels, somewhat like a religious cult. While Freud has argued that the opposition emanates from the moral bias and sex taboos of the academic world, it is difficult to believe that the vast majority of intellectuals is so prejudiced that it could not appreciate the basic theories of psychoanalysis even if they were as well established as Freud claims. The truth of the matter is that psychoanalysis is an unpardonably one-sided theory of human motivation. Its unsubstantiated speculations have scandalized many, amazed others, and made them smile at Freud's claim that every one of his conclusions is based on sufficient observation.

Psychoanalysts claim that their work is scientific. Certain abstractions and postulates no doubt constitute the foundation stones of every scientific edifice. In the present condition of our imperfect understanding of the ultimate nature of both matter and mind, such formulations are unavoidable and even necessary. For this reason Freud's attempt to build a science on the concept of mental energy alone, if it leads to clarification of fundamental problems, is commendable. It is not, therefore, the psychoanalytic concepts that are at fault, but rather the inclination of psychoanalysis to speculate sky-high in the name of science. The published results of dream interpretation are enough to convince one of this.

Whatever may be our conception of science and scientific procedure, Freud has, his sins of omission and commission notwithstanding, distinctly furthered our understanding of the ways of the *psyche*. But what kind of understanding? Certainly Freud has not contributed anything of value to the elucidation of the mind-body relation, acquisition of learning, and various other questions of a like nature on the agenda of every laboratory psychologist. But for those who take seriously the old Greek maxim, "Know thyself", Freud has furnished an interesting line of thought. By making sexuality the central theme of human motivation, he has put forth a unitary picture of the psyche and its devious ways. In presenting this thesis, Freud has had to make several subsidiary excursions into the unconscious, developing an extremely interesting theory of instincts which is not very different from that of yoga. In fairness to him it must be said that he is aware of the speculative nature of some of his conclusions and has appropriately grouped them under the name "metapsychology".

Were we to judge Freud by his system, we would fail to obtain a correct appreciation of his contributions. He would have us all accept him whole or not at all, but we are not obliged to do so. Many unverified assumptions are intertwined with some refreshingly original reflections of a kind of which only men of high intellectual order are capable. It is the latter that have made sympathetic minds among the academic scientists speak approvingly of Freud. McDougall's estimate that "Freud has done more for the advancement of psychology than any student since Aristotle",[1] may perhaps contain some pardonable exaggeration; this appraisal, however, is nearer the truth than the unrestrained condemnation and derision of some. There are dogmas aplenty in psychoanalysis, but the approach is materialistic and naturalistic. Some people thought that Freud would probably turn out in the end to be a "mystic" and philosopher. But his book, *The Future of an Illusion*,[2] has revealed him as a consistent materialist and, for that matter, a hard-boiled one. While he is unable at present to base his psychology on a physiological foundation, he leaves no doubt that this will be accomplished by future workers. As the biological sciences advance further, it is reasonable to expect that the valuable material from the structure of psychoanalysis will be fitted neatly into the sum total of knowledge. Until then much of it will remain loose and even rootless.

How can there be any similarity between the materialistic psychoanalysis and the spiritual yoga, two disciplines which were born in different ages and bear the marks of different cultures? Underlying a multitude of differences of both theory and practice, there lies a therapeutic thread that is manifested in both. As Jung has pointed out, psychoanalysis is not only an achievement but a psychical symptom of our times. Man seeks relief from the ever-mounting problems of civilized life. He is like a reed wafted by every passing breeze, assailed by

[1] McDougall, W.—*Outline of Abnormal Psychology*, Preface, viii; Charles Scribner's Sons, 1926.
[2] Freud, S.—*The Future of an Illusion* (tr. by W. D. Robson-Scott); The Institute of Psycho-Analysis, 1928.

doubts, victimized by his own uncontrollable passions, often "lived" by urges and strivings that do not add credit to the crust of rationality with which we are supposed to be endowed. How often it is heard: "If only I could understand myself." The scientist, from his Olympian heights, might prefer to look with disdain on the "petty" worries and fears of the layman. But this does not alter the fact that to the layman himself the illness is acutely real, ignorant though he may be of its origin and true nature. What he is looking for is a "soul-cure" and psychoanalysis fills the need. What we have said so far about yoga will, we hope, convince the reader that it too is a way of life, a "prescription" for mental ills. Both these approaches, divested of theoretical formulations, are in the final analysis therapeutic systems. To be sure, yoga goes much further than psychoanalysis, for even fear of death, which is an underlying cause of a mild neurosis in many people, does not assail the yogin. Psychoanalysis, on the other hand, makes its appeal to those whose concern is with a successful adjustment to social life. Analysis enables them to evaluate their own motives, to know themselves.

The psyche may be one thing according to some, and another according to others, but in every case neuroses arise out of the complications of the psyche and a cure is possible only through it. Theosophy, Christian Science, and the varieties of occultisms, which have only to be mentioned to find followers, offer a way of life to their respective adherents. But the intellectual crudities of these movements are too glaring for the modern man, educated as he is in the spirit of science. He wants something in keeping with his intellectual self-respect and capable of deepening his psychological understanding. This purpose is admirably served by psychoanalysis.

We have mentioned the psychotherapeutic value of yoga and psychoanalysis to explain their wide popularity. But the fact that both systems are not only therapeutic but psychological gives justification enough to the examination of a few of the basic theories that are common to both. After this we shall turn our attention to points of similarity in practice.

It is not that mental life may be divided into what is conscious and what is unconscious that makes psychoanalysis unique, but rather that the unconscious is the determining factor in life. The conscious is a thin superstructure definitely at the mercy of the deep cravings and urges originating in the unconscious. Several psychologists and philosophers before Freud had used the concept of the unconscious, but none of them had made it the pivot of psychology as Freud has done. Consequently, one may rightly say that Freud's point of view is a novel departure in Western thought.

The unconscious is likewise the basic proposition of yoga. Its practice from beginning to end is a long-range plan to get at the unconscious by various methods and to destroy its generating power. As long as the unconscious retains its potency, the yogin does not consider himself to have made any progress. The essential part of mental life in both psychoanalysis and yoga is, therefore, the unconscious.

The rôle of the conscious in both systems is also the same. Its content is transitory and changing, "like the flame that bends in all directions". Freud compares the conscious to a sense developed to meet the demands of the external world. We have already pointed out in a previous chapter how yoga also treats the conscious part of the mind as the sixth sense, assigning to it an assimilative function. Consciousness or awareness is not the whole of mind; it is only a quality or property—an insignificant one at that—of mental life which in its totality includes all the past experiences of the individual. There is a difference between the two systems as to how far back the influences of the unconscious extend. We shall come to this soon.

The logical reasons for assuming this existence of the unconscious have been put forth clearly by Freud, as well as by other psychologists who, while not accepting Freudian theories, have found it impossible to account for certain occurrences, like slips of speech, loss of memory, etc., except by means of a dynamic unconscious that extends far beyond the conscious. It is claimed that, for those who approach the psychological problems independently of physiology, Freudian arguments are logically compelling to warrant the postulation of the unconscious.

The more one studies the controversies concerning the use of this concept of the unconscious in psychology, the greater becomes one's conviction that the larger part, at any rate, of the differences is a mere matter of terminology. Some have argued that, since we might distinguish various gradations of intensity and clarity in consciousness, and since it is also possible to bring the fringes to light by paying more attention to them, it is a matter of difference of degree between the center and the margin of consciousness; hence, they argue, the term unconscious serves no useful purpose. Freud has answered these critics in forceful language:

The reference to gradations of clarity in consciousness is in no way conclusive and has no more evidential value than such analogous statements as: "There are so many gradations in illumination—from the brightest and most dazzling light to the dimmest glimmer—that we may conclude that there is no such thing as darkness at all"; or, "There are varying degrees of vitality, consequently there is no such thing as death." Such statements may in a certain sense have a meaning, but for practical purposes they are worthless. This will be seen if one proceeds to draw certain conclusions from them, such as, "it is not necessary, therefore, to strike a light," or "therefore all living things are immortal." Further to include "what is unnoticeable" under the concept of "what is conscious" is simply to play havoc with the one and only piece of direct and certain knowledge that we have about the mind. And after all, a consciousness of which one knows nothing seems to me a good deal more absurd than an unconscious mind. Finally, this attempt to equate what is unnoticed with what is unconscious is obviously made without taking into account the dynamic conditions involved, which were the decisive factors in formulating the psychoanalytic view. For it ignores two facts: first, that it is exceedingly difficult and requires very great effort to concentrate enough attention on something unnoticed of this kind; and secondly, that when this has been achieved the thought which was previously unnoticed is not recognized by consciousness, but often seems utterly alien and opposed to it and is promptly disavowed by it. Escaping from the unconscious in this way and taking refuge in what is scarcely noticed or unnoticed is, therefore, after all only an expression of the preconceived belief which regards the identity of mental and conscious as settled once and for all.[3]

[3] Freud, S.—*The Ego and the Id*, 14-15 (tr. by Joan Riviere); The Institute of Psycho-Analysis, 1927.

The last sentence is significant in that it shows that the arguments of the critics were based on a confusion of terminology. Neither psychoanalysis nor yoga would admit that conscious and mental are identical. But it is true that the overwhelming tradition of several centuries and the terminology of academic psychology have used these terms interchangeably. Since there is no indubitable evidence to prove the identity of the two, the adherents of the doctrine of the unconscious are quite justified in treating the conscious as a property or manifestation of the mental. Once the distinction has been grasped, arguments of this kind should become invalid.

Another group of criticisms, more basic than the previous ones, has been advanced by the biological sciences, particularly by naturalistic psychology. The essence of this criticism is that a scientific concept of the unconscious, if it is to become compatible with the already established knowledge, should have a biological foundation. Although our present knowledge is pitiably meager, we have sufficient evidence for the close relationship between the manifestation of consciousness and the nervous system. The inference that there can be no idea without a corresponding change in the brain is, while not conclusively demonstrable, a logical conclusion from available evidence. Any theory of the unconscious that does not root itself on firm physiological foundations, therefore, will run counter to the traditions of science. What we need is a cerebral unconscious.

Rivers, who was anxious to find an organic basis for the unconscious, has furnished a clue in the distinction between *protopathic* and *epicritic* sensibility. He concluded that there is a nervous basis for the crude, vague sensation as against the clear and easily recognized one. In the lowly organisms we may trace the protopathic system which, in the higher species, especially man, has been submerged by the epicritic (discriminating). In short, according to Rivers we may find a correlate for the unconscious in the protopathic or primitive element of the nervous system.[4]

Freud thus becomes a dissenter, doing his own excavation and building on his own foundations. Is he justified in running counter to well-established tradition? Our answer would be determined by our belief as to whether psychoanalysis could develop a line of thought on concepts different from those of academic psychology. Freud seems to think that the intriguing ways of the mind can be better understood by such concepts as libido, unconscious, complexes, etc., than by the strictly physiological ones. There is a dim obscurity in the foundation of every science. The classic example is physics, which is daily making use of concepts like atoms, energy, electrons, etc., concerning the basic nature of which we know very little. In an analogous fashion Freud is building a system in the language of mind alone. The ultimate test of any such scheme is its usefulness in deepening our knowledge. While a political complex is inexplicable in physiological terms, none of us would deny its reality in mental life nor the fact that it can lead to observable changes in behavior. Consequently, the Freudian concepts, in so far as they lead to a satisfactory explanation of psychic changes,

[4] Rivers, W. H. R.—*Instinct and the Unconscious;* Cambridge University Press, 1920.

may be taken as working principles; a dynamic theory of the mind is forced to lay its own foundation stones.

The unconscious of psychoanalysis, with which we are chiefly concerned here, is such a working principle. Our incorrigible habits of thought find it difficult to conceive of this working principle in any except recognized physiological terms. Behind the substantive there always looms the substance, with the consequence that even an energetic concept of the unconscious, as that of psychoanalysis, is thought of as amenable to localization. The language of Freud and his followers would often lead one to think that the unconscious is some kind of subterranean cavern where various ideas are waging a life-or-death battle to seek an outlet through the conscious. Whatever may be the impression we receive from such language or the picture we form of the unconscious, Freudian concepts are meant to be nothing more than working principles to explain the psyche in psychic terms alone. Since the physiological terms do not help us in this procedure, they are left alone.

Yoga has also been confronted with the same difficulty in formulating the unconscious. The speculative schemes of the evolution of prakriti and the underlying thought of the same basic energy manifesting itself in different forms, as mind and body, have enabled yoga to conceive of the mind (*citta*) as a subtle material entity which is the depository of thought life. The unconscious ideas are said to exist in the citta as traces, potencies, or impressions (*vasanas*). They are active and ever able to influence the conscious. The important point in connection with the yogic theory is that the mind, being a substance, can retain all the past ideas as traces. The theory of transmigration made necessary the continuity of a material individual mind that could pass from one organism to another. In both psychoanalysis and yoga an unconscious idea means an idea which is "latent and capable of becoming conscious". When we advance beyond this working assumption, every theory of the unconscious, including the physiological theory of Prince, appears full of glaring contradictions—one more evidence that the mind is a "horned" problem. The difficulty of picturing the unconscious in physiological terms seems to have been felt in the two systems. Freud prefers to talk in terms of energy, working principles, and clinical realities. Yoga, having been born in a pre-scientific age, worked out a cosmic scheme of evolution, with transformation of energy as a basic concept and matter and mind as special developments. In spite of much speculation that is involved in Freudian thought, one might wonder how much further it would have gone if it were not for the restraints of science which are bound to exert a remote control even on psychoanalysis!

A word about the content and origin of the unconscious. If the conscious exists to meet the demands of life, the unconscious is, in many ways, its opposite. One need not, therefore, be surprised to find a contradiction between the attributes of the two in psychoanalytic literature. Says Freud: in the unconscious "instinctual impulses . . . exist independently side by side, and are exempt from mental contradiction. . . . There is in this system no negation, no dubiety, no varying degree of certainty. . . . Its processes are timeless, they are not ordered temporally, are not altered by the passage of time, in fact bear no relation to time at all . . . their fate depends only upon the degree of their strength and upon their conformity to regulation by pleasure and pain." [5]

All these attributes tend to emphasize the "dynamicity" and the "blindness" of its urges as against the dull conformity of the conscious to the needs of the factual reality which demands consistency, moderation, and resignation to immediate pain in the interest of deferred pleasure. This picture of the nature of the unconscious is shared by yoga as well. The conscious, according to yoga, is ever at the mercy of the volcanic rumblings of the threatening unconscious, which knows neither reason nor sanity. Its demoniacal nature is unalterably opposed to the ways of the timid conscious, and pleasure is the goal of all its strivings. While yoga would agree with psychoanalysis that pleasure is the guiding principle of the unconscious, it makes a slight exception in favor of those strivings which, although feeble, do exist to remind the individual of the utter futility of an endless pleasure-chase. This muffled voice, diametrically opposed to the dominant trend of the unconscious, speaks a different language and shows the way out for those who, like the yogins, are willing to subdue the clamor for experience in the interest of emancipation. In his earlier works, Freud recognized nothing except the pleasure principle. Since the publication of *Beyond the Pleasure Principle*,[6] he has consistently placed emphasis upon the existence of a different motive which, to the

[5] Freud, S.—*Collected Papers*, Vol. IV, 119; The Institute of Psycho-Analysis, 1925.

[6] Freud, S.—*Beyond the Pleasure Principle* (tr. by C. J. M. Hubback); The International Psycho-Analytic Press, 1922.

consternation of those who have accepted the supremacy of the self-preservatory instinct, he calls the instinct of death. More about this when we come to the Freudian and yogic views on instincts.

In the beginning of his investigations, Freud's emphasis on the repressions of childhood led to the impression the unconscious has an infantile origin consisting mainly of sexual impulses. The zeal with which his followers, like Jones, upheld the sexual nature of infantile life only confirmed the apprehension of critics. Theoretically, however, Freud had left a loophole. All repressed experiences were in the unconscious, said Freud, but not the whole unconscious was repressed. What else was unconscious other than the repressed? This problem the master ignored. With greater clinical work, it would seem, Freud came upon certain phantasies which, because they all assumed a typical form, could not be traced to the actual experiences of infancy. The unconscious, therefore, had to be extended to include racial inheritance, and Freud began to explain "primal phantasies" on the basis of phylogenetic possession:

I believe that these *primal phantasies* . . . are a phylogenetic possession. In them the individual, wherever his own experience has become insufficient, stretches out beyond it to the experience of past ages. It seems to me quite possible that all that today is narrated in analysis in the form of phantasy, . . . was in prehistoric periods of the human family a reality; and that the child in its phantasy simply fills out the gaps in its true individual experiences with true prehistoric experiences.[7]

[7] Freud, S.—*A General Introduction to Psychoanalysis,* 324; Liveright Publishing Corporation, 1935.

Among other things, Jung diverges from Freud on this point and places only little emphasis on the infantile origin of the unconscious. Nor has he much use for Freud's concepts of repression, sexuality, and several others. He has broadened the unconscious to include a superpersonal or collective inheritance phylogenetically acquired. "In every individual, in addition to the personal memories, there are also . . . the great 'primordial images', the inherited potentialities of human imagination. They have always been potentially latent in the brain structure." [8] These "dominants" and "archetypes" which are projected on the analyst in the form of divinities, saviours, and magical demons are explicable on the basis of a racial level in the unconscious. To the question, whether these ideas are inherited as representations, Jung answers: "I do not hereby assert the transmission of representations, but only the possibility of such representations, which is a very different thing." [9]

We need emphasize here only one fact: both Freud and Jung believe the unconscious contains something more than the personal experiences which, whatever be the difficulties in explaining, could be possible only through inheritance. Here again, yoga would agree with the psychoanalytic belief in the superpersonal content of the unconscious, but the emphasis placed upon it and the way of accounting for it are quite different.

Yoga believes that the unconscious contains the individual experiences of all the past lives and will continue to be effective until the passion for life has been

[8] Jung, C. G.—*Collected Papers on Analytical Psychology*, 2d ed.,. 410; Moffat Yard and Company, 1917.
[9] *Ibid.*

forcefully conquered by "burning the seeds of the latent deposits". The "primal phantasies", "dominants", and "archetypes" attributed by Jung to a collective unconscious and by Freud to phylogenetic inheritance can equally well be explained on an individual basis if the yogic theory of a subtle mental substance, which might constitute the principle of individuality, is accepted. Freud has pointed out that a childhood experience after having been long forgotten, might manifest its effect in later life. Why should not the same apply to the experiences of earlier lives? Theory of rebirth and a subtle mental substance in which the latent experiences could inhere are fundamental to the yogic concept of the unconscious. Not so in psychoanalysis because it lays particular emphasis on the ontogenetic unconscious, recognizing the superpersonal element of this unconscious just enough to admit a phylogenetic basis for it.

Just as psychoanalysis shows a bias for polarities and antitheses, as for example, pleasure-pain, life-death, love-hate, activity-passivity, etc., yoga too has shown a predilection for dualities. The most important of these linked opposites are love-hate, the seer and the seen (purusha-prakriti), passion-aversion (pleasure-pain), and life-liberation. The last duality, life-liberation, is not very different from the Freudian life-death antithesis, except that what yoga interprets as the urge for emancipation, cessation from life, Freud calls the instinct of death. Although admittedly speculative, the new Freudian theory of instincts has enough in common with that of yoga to deserve a slightly detailed treatment.

The use of the word "instinct" with various shades of meaning in the biological sciences is nothing short of a scandal, since each writer has made his own list. Terms like "drives", "urges", "impulses", etc., are so difficult of precise definition that they are understood and interpreted differently by various writers. Freud, however, is quite consistent in his use of the word "instinct". He reserves the term for primary innate trends, those which are irreducible. As an instance we may point out that the herd-instinct, which is found in many psychological classifications, is traceable, according to Freud, to a more fundamental and irresolvable innate trend. He thinks of instincts in terms of energy, as a constant psychic upswelling from within, demanding satisfaction. In this sense "urge" would be an appropriate synonym. Freud admits, however, that the source of instincts is to be sought in the bodily processes.

The earlier Freud distinguished two groups of instincts, the sexual and the ego-instincts. Although the term "sexual" was used in its most comprehensive connotation, like Plato's "love", it was given a pre-eminent position. The energy derived from the sexual instinct was called "libido"; but there was no corresponding energy-representation for the ego- (self-preservative) instinct. In recent years he has concluded that at least in part the ego-instincts originate from the same source as the sexual instincts, i.e., libido. All these, therefore, are brought under the term "Eros" or life-instincts.

The manifestation of destructive tendencies—masochism, sadism, etc.—did not receive satisfactory explanation in the earlier dualism of sexual and ego-instincts. In the new formulation of the theory the destructive impulses are grouped under a new concept, the death-instinct. In place of the old duality, we have, in the new theory, two different groups of instincts: life-instinct and death-instinct. The former represents the universal urge to maintain life: the uninhibited sexual impulses, the sublimated impulses and the self-preservative impulses. The death-instinct stands for the tendency to lead organic matter back to the inorganic state from which all life sprang.

All psychoanalysts have not agreed on the presence of a death-instinct. Freud admits that, since the death-instinct is very elusive, it is seldom found in its pure state; on the contrary, it manifests itself by fusing with the life-instinct. And so we have the peculiar phenomena of sadism and masochism which throw light, also, on ambivalence—the strange feeling of love and hate towards the same object. The life-death instinct theory has led to a modification of at least one fundamental thesis of psychoanalysis: that pleasure, as Freud had thought in the beginning, is not the only goal of human activity. Even before Freud had come upon his new theory of instincts, Barbara Low, one of the early popularizers of psychoanalysis, very appropriately termed the desire for annihilation "nirvana principle". Freud incorporated this suggestion into his writings, but maintained that it still conformed to the pleasure principle. With the development of the new instinct theory, nirvana principle has been linked with the death-instinct.

To the student of yoga, the antithesis between the life-death instincts is a very familiar one. Just like Freud, yoga has maintained that all the manifestations of self-preservation, fear of death, destructive impulse towards those who might thwart one's life, etc., may all be derived from the supreme will-to-live. Yoga has not shown any inclination to treat at length such subsidiary impulses as the desire for sexual gratification, parental love, and so on. It would seem, therefore, that the importance Freud assigned to sex, in the broad sense in which he uses the term, is inconsistent with his latest formulation of the instinct theory. Which seems more primary, the will-to-live or the desire for sexual gratification? We might quite correctly say that sexual impulse is one among the several impulses which make continuance of life pleasurable. The will-to-live must naturally base itself on certain impulses and sex is only one among them.

Another deep urge, according to yoga, is the instinct of liberation, a deep yearning for passivity or cessation from life. Might it not be that Freud's death-instinct is only a variant of this urge which yoga says is inherent in all life?

The arguments by which Freud establishes a death-instinct are, to say the least, questionable. It should be possible to explain much of the destructive impulses, from which the death-instinct is derived, as merely a way of overcoming the obstacles in the path of the will-to-live. Adaptation to the conditions of life is not accomplished always in the same way. Under certain circumstances destruction is quite understandable as the ideal method for preserving oneself. Masochism may then be understood as the turning inward of the impulse for outward aggression and destruction.

Granting that psychoanalytic arguments are sufficiently valid to warrant the postulation of death-instinct, yoga might well ask a very pertinent question: if an instinct for liberation were to exist in life, could it manifest itself in any way other than by self-destruction?

Obviously not. It is, therefore, not impossible that Freud has misinterpreted the instinct of liberation as the death-instinct. Freud points out that the concept of death in its literal sense is not present in the unconscious, and hence the organism instinctively strives for passivity rather than complete annihilation. Nirvana, of which we spoke above, does not signify death, although Freud seems to have attached that meaning while incorporating the term into his body of thought. It means only release or liberation from the wheel-of-rebirth, existence. It is by no means an entirely negative concept like death.

Both yoga and Freud agree that two antithetical and qualitatively different groups of instincts exist in life. The clamor of life-instinct is too noisy to let the voice of liberation (death, according to Freud) be heard. Some followers of Freud have shown a hesitation to accept the speculative conclusions of the master, claiming that at any rate the death-instinct has no significance in clinical work. Others hold that it is a discovery of cardinal importance destined to influence the theoretical development of psychoanalysis in the future.

Be that as it may, it is a matter of unusual importance that these two systems of psychology, both built on the concept of the unconscious, have also advanced a nearly similar theory of instincts. What psychoanalysis interprets as death, yoga claims to be the urge for release—two interpretations one might legitimately expect to follow from the contrary assumptions of the two psychologies, one materialist and the other spiritualist. Since both interpretations are speculative and beyond the reach of scientific method, one might say that both alternatives are tentatively justified. However, it might be advanced for the consideration of Freudians that in every age and culture several individuals have manifested life-weariness and an urge for passivity which would be better understood by the yogic theory of striving for liberation than by the negative concept of death or complete annihilation. Is it possible that this elusive instinct in its pure form leads to orderly withdrawal from the craving for life's experiences, as the lives of yogins and other mystics show; and that, when it is fused with life-instinct, it also leads to the dramatic destructive impulses which form a sad chapter in the history of mankind?

Apart from the above points of similarity in theory, certain aspects of practice in both systems are worth noting. Freud has always maintained, and it has been confirmed by practice, that to be effective analysis must have the coöperation of the patient. Unless it dawns on the patient that he is the victim of mental maladjustment which could not be set right by his own skill, psychoanalysis would be ineffective. A feeling of self-dissatisfaction accompanied by a willingness to change and accept new standards is an essential prerequisite for successful treatment. "It [psychoanalysis] is also not to be applied in persons who are not prompted by their own suffering to seek treatment, but subject themselves to it by order of their relatives." [10] What is expected of a yogic disciple is also about the same. It is understood by yogic teachers that no one could be persuaded to accept their discipline by philosophical argumentation or logical reasoning. The seed of dissatisfaction could not be

[10] Freud, S.—*Selected Papers on Hysteria and Other Psychoneuroses*, 181 (tr. by A. A. Brill); The Journal of Nervous and Mental Disease Publishing Co., 1909.

planted from the outside. It has to grow from within to such proportions that the individual would begin to entertain doubts about his pretended security. The old values must crumble before one can accept new ones. There is an old tradition among yogins that the aspirant who does not find his own teacher would probably not succeed in yoga. That is to say, if his dissatisfaction with life is acute enough, no obstacle will stop him from finding a *guru* (teacher) who could study his case and impart the necessary instruction.

Freud has insisted from the very beginning that the analyst should not assume the rôle of a director or guide. He should refrain from imposing his own view on the patient as to what the latter should or should not do. Many of his adherents, on the other hand, think that there are patients who even after a successful analysis would need guidance. Such schools of analysis actively interfere with the life of the patient. To keep him from lapsing into the old ways, the patient is made to take up some study or occupation of absorbing interest, painting, clay-modelling, etc. This is a well-recognized device, found in all systems of psychotherapy, to break up the old habits and automatisms and initiate new ones. As far as yoga is concerned, every disciple is made to apply himself "intensely to some one thing", usually the study of the Scriptures. During the first few years of yoga practice this in an absolute necessity.

The relation of the patient to the analyst and of the disciple to his guru (teacher) brings us to an element common in both systems. The phenomenon known as *transference* is well attested to by the experience of all analysts. As the hidden complexes are unearthed and as the analyst penetrates deeper into the hidden experiences of the psyche, the patient begins to objectify his emotions on the physician. He is sometimes loved and at other times hated, a phenomenon which has no parallel in yoga. This may be due to the difference in the approach to the patient. The yogic disciple, while not in intimate bond with the guru, is always under his watchful eye. But in analysis a session lasts for not more than an hour during which period the analyst makes a concentrated effort to get at the psychic complexes either by letting the patient relate his own story or by interpreting his dreams.

It is apparent, however, that the analyst and the guru are in a very real sense confessors. Whatever may be the law underlying this phenomenon, a psychic tension is at least partially relieved when related to an "understanding soul". It has the effect of a mental purge—a fact well recognized by the Catholic Church. The dependence on and devotion to the guru are vastly more important in yoga than in any other system of psychotherapy.

In conclusion it might be pointed out that therapeutic similarities exist between psychoanalysis and only the earlier phases of yoga. The higher stages of yoga are reached by psychophysical and mental exercises for which psychoanalysis has no parallel.[11] Freud's "depth-psychology" would not be considered deep enough by yoga. The repressions of childhood and their uprooting by psychoanalysis may equip a man to meet success-

---

[11] We are not to be understood to imply that there are no fundamental conceptual differences between psychoanalysis and yoga. On the contrary, such differences are many. The concept of repression, for example, which is central to the dynamics of psychoanalytic conflict is conspicuous by its absence in yoga.

fully the problems of life. The method may be sufficient for the goal. But the spiritual objective of yoga, a release from the chain of existence, is attained only by a contrary procedure, the extinction of life-instinct itself. Can there be any two ideals more mutually opposed?

Chapter IX

YOGA AND PSYCHIC RESEARCH

Yoga is a product of the East and psychic research belongs to the West. In between the two we have a few eclectic movements that have a flavor of both—theosophy, occultism, anthroposophy, Christian Science, etc. Whatever may be their doctrinal differences, the latter have one thing in common, a caricature of Eastern thought and Western science. "Mahatmas" and "astral bodies" of the Orient are brought together with the "mental radiations" and "psychoplasms" of the Occident. Psychic research, as the name implies, is carried on in the name of science, sometimes with the active support and encouragement of a few men in that field. Not infrequently "official science" is condemned for its lack of interest in certain alleged supernatural phenomena.

While the supernatural forms the kernel of such movements, in yoga it is merely a superficial crust kept alive by the weight of popular recognition. The yogins themselves are reticent about these miracles. The tradition connected with yoga continues to perpetuate the belief that the practitioners can "do things" which defy the known laws of nature. If our task were merely to narrate facts, that is, if we had come across phenomena that could not be accounted for by normal means, the answer could be given in one word, "no". But the problem is not as simple as that. A critical examination of some of the claims of yogins might reveal that the mind under certain conditions is capable of reacting in strange ways. One might see apparitions, hear strange sounds, and smell fragrant odors. Most of the yogins know them to be hallucinations and accordingly advise the new disciples to ignore them.

Not so the theosophists and such experts in "psychism". They point to yoga with the same feelings that a devout Muslim has for the birthplace of the Prophet. They insist on treating the fictions of their imagination as realities, mixing philosophy and science, abdicating reason and fact to wishful thinking. Our experience and long conversations with yogins have convinced us that they have a greater appreciation of logic and reason than the mystery-seekers and spirit-chasers. "There are more things in heaven and earth than are dreamt of in our philosophies" is the watchword of the supernaturalist. Strangely enough, this is the fundamental assumption of science as well, for only one overpowered by the delusion of omniscience can say that he knows all there is to be known. If the above assumption is common to both science and psychic research, why is it that "official science" considers it beneath its dignity to investigate the supernatural? When the phenomena are well-attested and have been properly investigated, they are incorporated into the body of accredited knowledge. But scientific method stops short of glorifying human foibles as scientific facts. The debunking of séances demonstrates this more than any other supernatural epidemic of the present day.

Whatever may be its emotional value, the word "supernatural" has no special meaning for science. When the investigator is faced with new kinds of phenomena, his first task is to establish relationships. Let us take the alleged phenomena of telekinesis, which refers to the alleged movement of objects by some mysterious non-physical force. The conclusion of the supernaturalist is that the movement is produced by some spiritual agency. The scientist, on the other hand, first attempts to see if any concealed apparatus not visible to the naked eye has had any part in the manifestation. He also likes to know if the limbs of the medium have been in any way free to operate a string, rod, or anything else that might indirectly cause the movement of the distant object. If, by patient investigation, it is found that some hidden apparatus has been responsible for the movement, the phenomenon is easily explained. It is assumed that the conditions in the séance-room are favorable to a thorough investigation.

If, on the other hand, it were found that objects move around without being in touch with some physical medium, the investigator would no doubt be left baffled. He would know of no way in which this could be reduced to the known laws of science. If such phenomena do recur a sufficient number of times, then he will be able to make further observations. Sooner or later he will be able to lay down the law or laws that operate in such phenomena. When thus formulated the supernatural becomes natural, the mysterious no more glamorous.

There is still another possibility. Even after the most exhaustive analysis and investigation, the phenomenon may elude our grasp. In plain language, we would not know how and why it occurs, nor when it will occur again. Here the word "supernatural" turns out to be a high-sounding term for our ignorance. If it is a well-established fact that yogins could levitate and that ectoplasmic materializations are not due to the fraudulent practices of mediums, and if these phenomena cannot be accounted for by science, there is no reason why one may not believe that they are caused by discarnate spirits, devils, or angels. Any being that imagination can conceive of may be made to "do the work". Science cannot disprove this hypothesis because it knows nothing about disembodied intelligences. But the cautious man will not go to any such extremes, for he knows that the supernatural is a doubtful luxury certain to become natural tomorrow or the day after.

Science claims neither infallibility nor omniscience. Its conclusions are invariably tentative, and its premises are subject to revision and correction. Its cautious and undramatic manner of experimenting and its critical attitude may not satisfy those who, from motives of faith and belief or fear of death, would like to believe that the universe is what they wish it were. Wishful thinking is out of order in the house of science. While the student of science knows these things and conducts his research accordingly, the lay public, which is easily deceived by the claims of psychic research, theosophical caricatures of yoga, etc., is not equally appreciative of the difficulties of the problems involved. What may seem impeccable proof to the layman might be shown by the scientist to be an elaborately though cleverly arranged fraud. For those who have a scientific interest in yoga, it is important to know the pitfalls of supernaturalism. "What is fiction and what is fact" should be asked at every turn. Most of the alleged "miracles" of yoga will, on scientific investigation, turn out to be fictions which may be pleasing to the imagination but of no moment for science. The history of psychic research demonstrates this more than any other movement.

The group of problems known in the English-speaking countries as psychic research is called "metapsychics" in France and "parapsychology" in Germany. One of the important characteristics of psychic "events" is that a specially gifted person, known as a "medium", is necessary for their production. Although every country has produced its quota, America may claim first place for both the quality and number of its mediums. It was discovered in the middle of the last century, March, 1848, that the two Fox sisters, Margaret and Catherine, of Hydesville, New York, could produce raps at will. The sisters were separated but the raps still followed them. An excited public and pious clergymen attributed the phenomenon to the supernatural. Shrewd observers pointed out that the raps were caused invariably by the cracking of the toe-joints. This was confirmed by more than one scientific commission. But the public stood by the supernatural theory. In August, 1888, Margaret showed before a large audience in the Academy of Music in New York how she had fooled an international public for several years. The toe-joint theory was right. "That I have been chiefly instrumental in perpetuating the fraud of spiritualism upon a too confiding public," said she, "most of you doubtless know. . . . The greatest sorrow of my life has been that this is true, and though it has come late in my day, I am now prepared to tell the truth, the whole truth, and nothing but the truth,—so help me God!" [1]

Thus ended the first "supernatural fraud" perpetrated on a gullible, international public. The scientists, whenever they got a chance, exposed the impostors, but the "will-to-believe" proved stronger than the power of reason. The errors of observation that even an impartial investigator of unrivalled merit might make when dealing with the supernatural are a matter of great importance to science. Sir William Crookes, an eminent chemist, had the following to say of Margaret Fox: "With a full knowledge of the numerous theories which have been started, chiefly in America, to explain these sounds, I have tested them in every way that I could devise, until there has been no escape from the conviction that they were true objective occurrences not produced by trickery or mechanical means." [2] To Locke's saying, "There is no error to be named that has not its philosophers," might be added "and scientists".

Margaret Fox was only a novice compared to Signora Eusapia Palladino, said to be an ignorant Italian peasant. She was "dragged through all Europe and half America" followed by a galaxy of savants and commercial agents. With her table she made history—a history that has taught the wary investigator many useful lessons. The table moved, it rose, it levitated for seconds. From her seat in the half-dark séance-room she moved objects at a distance, some of them floating through the

[1] Coover, J. E.—"Metapsychics and the Incredulity of Psychologists", in The Case for and against Psychical Belief (ed. by Carl Murchison); Clark University, 1927.

[2] Crookes, Sir William—Researches in the Phenomena of Spiritualism, 87; J. Burns, London, 1874.

air and resting on the heads of "scientific sitters", apparently to establish irrefragable proof. She too got her share of "scientific" testimony, gushing tribute, and plain cash. The believers in turn had their faith confirmed.

She escaped detection in Europe. But a séance in New York in April, 1910, proved to be her ruin. Two observers, dressed in black and unknown to Eusapia, had managed to crawl under the transcendental table. They had their eyes close to her left foot, which they had suspected was the cause of levitation. Here is their report:

A foot came from underneath the dress of the medium and placed the toe underneath the leg of the table on the left side of the medium, and pressing upward, gave it a little chuck into the air. Then the foot withdrew and the leg of the table dropped suddenly to the floor. . . . I was lying with my face on the floor within *eight inches* of the left leg of the table; and each time that the table was lifted, whether in a partial or complete levitation, the medium's foot was used as a propelling force upward.[3]

Other famous mediums, like Home and Margery, were exposed several times, but the pestilence still continues. The fraud is not always confined to the happenings of the séance-room. For an appropriate payment, spirit-photographs are produced. In case of doubt spirit fingerprints may also be had. This novel idea, it seems, was introduced by the American medium, Margery. Sir Arthur Conan Doyle claimed that he had in his possession genuine pictures of fairies—human figures with

[3] Jastrow, J.—*Wish and Wisdom*, 145; D. Appleton-Century Company, 1935.

wings like those of a butterfly. Abundant evidence has been adduced by Dr. W. F. Prince, Research Officer of the American Society of Psychical Research, that all spirit and fairy photographs are fraudulently manufactured. Some of the various methods of producing such photographs have been described by Houdini.[4] Sir Arthur, however, preferred to ignore such unpleasant thoughts.

An important point to remember in connection with séances is that the conditions are not favorable for scientific investigation. In a genuine investigation, the experimenter controls the conditions. The medium, in psychic research, dictates the conditions. Usually a very dim red light is all that is allowed. If it is too bright, the phenomena either do not appear or change their nature. If the medium suspects that there are investigators in the room who might be too critical, then the "spirit" does not condescend to perform. Errors of malobservation and non-observation play a large part to confound the investigators. A semi-hypnotic lethargy induced by the monotony of gramophone records or vocal singing and religious atmosphere are enough to warp the human critical acumen. Aldous Huxley says, in a magazine article,[5] that after thirty minutes under séance conditions, he would not trust his own testimony. In the fortieth volume of the *Proceedings of the Society for Psychical Research* (London) the results of an interesting experiment, carried out by Theodore Besterman, to test the reliability of trained and untrained witnesses at

[4] Houdini, H.—"A Magician Among the Spirits", in *The Case for and against Psychical Belief;* Clark University, 1927.

[5] Huxley, A.—"Science Views the Supernatural", *Forum,* Vol. 93 (Jan.–June, 1935).

séances, are given. Of a possible total of 100 marks the highest on record was 61 and the lowest 5.9, the average was 33.9. It has often been remarked by metapsychists that the mediums have to be in a semi-unconscious state before the phenomena begin to appear. This may be doubted, but it would seem there is no doubt of the state of the "sitters", judging by the above results.

One wishes to be as charitable as possible toward men like Sir William Crookes, Sir Oliver Lodge, and a host of other intellectuals who have an abiding faith in the genuineness of psychic phenomena. Even to think for a minute that such men are capable of deliberately misleading the public is preposterous. They themselves have exposed many a fraud, and, where they failed, conjurors have succeeded. But the scientists are not immune to unconscious wishful thinking. In such matters as psychic research, evidence may be found in abundance if our impulse is to believe. Professor Boring of Harvard has related a very interesting incident in the *Atlantic Monthly*.[6] Mr. Code, one of the investigators of Margery, had agreed to produce all the phenomena by trickery. At the séance Professor Boring occupied an important position holding Mr. Code's left hand. The demonstration was a success; things happened as mysteriously as if Margery were the medium. But once in the red light Mr. Code attempted too much and Professor Boring saw how the trick was done. According to previous arrangement he was to have immediately reported any fraud into the dictaphone, but he did not. He wanted the séance to be a hundred percent success; hence he did not

[6] Boring, E. G.–"The Paradox of Psychic Research", *The Atlantic Monthly*, Vol. 137 (Jan.–June, 1926).

"see" the fraud. His desire to have Mr. Code succeed was at the moment stronger than the impulse to fulfill what was demanded of him as a scientific investigator. Professor Boring, in mentioning this incident, draws the obvious conclusion that persons, no matter how eminent, who are inclined to believe in psychic phenomena do not make good investigators. An amusing story of how the celebrated electrician Ampère tried to "cheat" a scientific committee is on record. He was giving an electrical demonstration before the committee, but at the crucial moment the galvanometer needle failed to move, whereupon he gave it a mild push with his finger. At the second trial he said triumphantly, pointing to the needle, "This time it goes of itself!" [7]

The mediumistic spirits, like cockroaches, seem to prefer darkness, in addition to a cabinet and plenty of apparatus. The scientist can at least drag the unwilling cockroach into broad daylight, but he is helpless before spirits. If there is a law that spirits can manifest their power only in the dark and only under conditions in which séances are staged, then "official science" can do no more than reiterate that every investigation conducted so far has gone on record against the pretenses of mediums.

Sometimes the advocates of spirits use a strange variety of logic. "It is true that mediums use trickery and deception. But it is possible that genuine occurrences also take place." Would this reasoning be accepted in a court of law? One might as well say that, where no investigation was carried on, the phenomena were real. This kind

[7] Richet, C.—*Thirty Years of Psychical Research,* 458; The Macmillan Company, 1923.

of logic takes advantage of the scientific axiom that a universal negative can never be proved. Proof is by its very nature positive. If one were to say that the book before me has the vicious habit of rising from the table every time I was not looking at it, I could not annihilate the argument. I would have to be omniscient to be able to affirm positively that such an occurrence is impossible. One can only say that a judicious mind would not be persuaded by such negative logic.

Another argument is somewhat as follows: There are very many things about the universe of which we are ignorant. We know the ultimate nature of neither mind nor matter. What we previously had thought was impossible has turned out to be possible today. We should be humble before the mysteries of the universe, etc., etc. Here again there is a fallacy, the fallacy of not recognizing the essential difference between a scientific fact and what we would like to believe about the unknown concerning which science has nothing to say. Science neither denies nor asserts that there is a spirit world. "Official science" only says that it is not a scientific fact. The void of the unknown may be populated by angels, demons, fairies, gods, and three-horned incorporeal serpents. But when one claims that their existence is a well-established fact, it is very important to draw the distinction. Like nature, mind also abhors a vacuum; hence we build our philosophies and seek satisfaction through belief. We saw in a previous chapter on what an ingenious and, to many, satisfying scheme of evolution the theory of yoga is built: an attempt is made to find a satisfactory explanation of the persistent questions confronting life. Whether we abhor some types of philosophy and accept others, they are all merely speculations. None of them can be proved or disproved. But to mix philosophy and science is to do violence to both.

It must be admitted, however, that a group of phenomena, on the borderland of psychology, has received attention in the laboratory. The most important of these are telepathy and clairvoyance. The claim is made that some persons possess a faculty of knowing the thoughts of others and seeing distant events and objects without the intermediation of the senses. When the perception is of mental conditions, it is known as telepathy and when of physical objects or occurrences, clairvoyance. It is well known that belief in telepathy and clairvoyance has been current among all races from remote times. The first effort at gathering data along this line was made by Gurney, Myers and Podmore in England. Their two-volume book, *Phantasms of the Living*,[8] has recorded several interesting cases of spontaneous telepathic occurrences. A more recent book by Osty, *Human Experiences*, also contains a properly classified report of many cases. It may be of interest to point out that most spontaneous telepathic phenomena deal with messages received from the dying, or from those suddenly confronted with danger to life. Sometimes the message is revealed through a hallucinatory vision, dream, etc. Does the experience of death, a state of "collapse into immediacy", to use an Hegelian phrase, create a state of mind favorable to "sending out" telepathic messages? These and many other questions could be answered only after we have had enough experimental evidence under all

[8] Gurney, E., Myers, F. W. H., and Podmore, F.—*Phantasms of the Living*; Trübner and Company, London, 1886.

possible conditions. The above books were responsible for initiating serious work in the field of telepathy.

The earliest experiments were those of Mr. and Mrs. Henry Sidgwick.[9] The material used in the transference consisted of simple numbers and words. This was followed by a series of experiments in European countries as well as in America. From the vast mass of these early attempts no clear conclusion one way or the other was possible. The most extensive of these experiments, those of Pierre Janet in France in 1885 and 1886, are striking but not convincing.

What appears to be an impressive piece of work was reported in 1921 by Dr. Brugmanns at the First International Congress of Psychical Research. The experiments were carried out by three professors in the psychological laboratory of Groningen, Netherlands. The materials, as in the Sidgwick experiments, consisted of letters and numbers. Three professors took turns as "senders" of the message. The conditions for excluding sensory cues were nearly perfect. The sixty successes out of 187 trials were far above chance expectation of 4.5 successes according to the theory of probability.

Professor Coover's [10] experiments in the psychological laboratories of Stanford University constituted a distinct mile-stone in American investigation. They were as well controlled as might be wished. Out of 10,000 the successes were 294, only 44 above chance expectation. The difference is not sufficiently great to constitute positive evidence for telepathy. But Dr. Rhine has pointed

[9] *Proceedings of the Society for Psychical Research*, Vol. 8, 1892.
[10] Coover, J. E.—*Experiments in Psychical Research*; Leland Stanford University Publications, Psychical Research Monograph No. 1, 1917.

out that, if Professor Coover had continued the tests with those who succeeded best the first time instead of continuing with "good" and "bad" subjects, he might have obtained satisfactory results. This is a very legitimate criticism, for we have no right to believe that all people are equally endowed with the "telepathic faculty". It is possible that such gifts, if genuine, may be possessed by only a few; hence it is desirable to repeat the tests with promising subjects.

Harvard, too, has done some experiments in telepathy. Professor Gardner Murphy, who held the Hodgson Fellowship in Psychical Research from 1922 to 1925, carried out experiments with undergraduates *en masse*, as well as with individual subjects who claimed special telepathic gifts. His conclusions may be summarized in his own words: "The great bulk of my telepathic work has yielded results closely comparable to those of Dr. Coover; that is to say, the vast majority of subjects give results which offer no difficulties of explanation in terms of coincidences. Some rather marked exceptions remain unexplained." [11] His successor, Dr. Estabrooks,[12] continued the work using the average college student as subject. The conditions for excluding sensory cues were an improvement on Professor Murphy's. The results are extraordinarily consistent, showing that out of 20 trials the first 10 yielded better results than the last 10. This would indicate a progressive diminution of the "telepathic faculty".

The most recent, and by far the most impressive and

[11] Murphy, G.—"Telepathy as an Experimental Problem", in *The Case for and against Psychical Belief*, 273; Clark University, 1927.
[12] *Boston Society Psychic Research Bulletin V*, 1927.

exhaustive, work in the field is that of Dr. J. B. Rhine of Duke University. Although the work is still proceeding he has already published the results of the first three years in a little volume, *Extra-Sensory Perception*.[13] Dr. Rhine, if we judge his work by the precautions taken to control the sources of error, has amply profited by the mistakes of his predecessors. He has taken care to distinguish telepathy and clairvoyance, which in previous experiments had often been lumped together. Material consisted of cards with the following symbols: circle, rectangle, plus, star, and wavy lines. Instead of repeatedly experimenting with large numbers of students, he concentrated his efforts on a few who showed signs of promise.

Rhine's results and conclusions are convincingly positive. Seven out of the eight major subjects have shown a remarkable ability in both telepathy and clairvoyance. The lay reader will find impressive, if not spectacular, evidence for believing that the same general function, whatever that may be, underlies telepathy and clairvoyance. Both are affected in the same way by drugs. Rhine's statistical methods and experimental procedure have been severely criticized by Willoughby.[14] These criticisms have in turn been met by Stuart.[15] Since the

[13] Rhine, J. B.—*Extra-Sensory Perception;* Boston Society for Psychic Research, 1935.

[14] Willoughby, R. R.—"A Critique of Rhine's 'Extra-Sensory Perception'", *Journal of Abnormal and Social Psychology*, Vol. 30, No. 2, 1935; "Prerequisites for a Clairvoyance Hypothesis", *Journal of Applied Psychology*, Vol. 19, No. 5, 1935; "The Use of the Probable Error in Evaluating Clairvoyance", *Character and Personality*, September, 1935.

[15] Stuart, C. E.—"In Reply to the Willoughby 'Critique'", *Journal of Abnormal and Social Psychology*, Vol. 30, No. 3, 1935; "The Willoughby Test of Clairvoyant Perception", *Journal of Applied Psy-*

discussion in the technical journals has only begun, it is as yet too early to conclude that extra-sensory perception has been scientifically demonstrated. Most psychologists, we believe, would say that Dr. Rhine's experiments are by no means conclusive, but that they are interesting and important enough to warrant further investigation.[16] More research is in order and no doubt his work will attract many psychologists to the field in the near future.

We have gone into this short review of experimental work in telepathy to point out that, where there is reasonable evidence for some phenomenon yet to be understood, scientists are quite prepared to launch investigations. The rank and file of scientific psychologists have every right to hold their opinions in abeyance until further experimental results are available. In an important problem like that of telepathy, where practically nothing is known as far as the basic laws are concerned, a large block of evidence gathered under various conditions is a prerequisite for reliable conclusion, especially for positive affirmation.

Experiments in telepathy and clairvoyance, if thoroughly established, will lead to some radical changes in our theoretical conception of the mind. Most of the theories of psychology in the West have been built along lines which do not take into consideration telepathic manifestations. It is, therefore, worthwhile to point out that yoga has held that such phenomena are not only possible, but also that they have been confirmed by the

chology, Vol. 19, No. 5, 1935; "A Reply to Dr. Willoughby", *Character and Personality*, September, 1935.

[16] Kellog, C. E.—"J. B. Rhine and Extra-Sensory Perception", *Journal of Abnormal and Social Psychology*, Vol. 31, No. 2, 1936.

experiences of yogins; and so yoga makes the distinction between the individual mind and collective mind (*karanacitta* and *karyacitta*). The mind under certain psychological conditions somehow seems able to "make connection" with other minds, without at the same time losing its identity. Each mind is an isolated organism in one sense, and at the same time it exists in a cosmic whole. This is the yogic contention. If and when extrasensory perception is established beyond any doubt, theoretical considerations would probably lead to an hypothesis not very different from the yogic theory.

What is the mental state that makes telepathy possible? None of the scientific workers doubts for a moment that it is a mental process, but they all claim that it is in many respects, if not all, different from the attitudes and qualities of mind demanded in meeting the ordinary problems of life. Judging by external observations, it would seem that the percipient (one who "receives" telepathic messages as contrasted with the "agent" sending them) has a blank, vacant look. The subjects themselves have described their experience as one of "detachment", "abstraction", "relaxation unknown in the waking life", and the like. The critical faculty of discrimination, a highly prized quality of intellectual life, is the opposite of the mental state of the telepathic percipient. In that most popular book on telepathic episodes, *Mental Radio* by Upton Sinclair,[17] Mrs. Sinclair, who was the percipient, relates from her experience what she considers to be essential conditions of telepathic reception. Among them are complete bodily relaxation, a blank mind and an

[17] Sinclair, U.—*Mental Radio;* T. Werner Laurie Ltd., London, 1930.

inward turning of the mind, i.e., withdrawal or turning away from the ordinary stimuli of the external world. The reader will do well to bear these observations in mind while reading the succeeding chapters, for this is exactly the mental condition the yogin claims to strive for in the early stages of his mental exercises. The term "concentration" should not mislead us. Circumscribed concentration leads to a state of blankness sooner or later as against intense application to a particular topic, which is what we usually mean by the term in popular language. Yoga, of course, has evolved a technique to produce the "telepathic state of mind". Western experimenters and yogins would both agree that "a vacuous mind" is essential for these unique experiences. If telepathy is a genuine experience, we might reasonably expect yogins to make admirable subjects.

In discussing the borderland-phenomena of psychology, critical students usually separate the grain from the chaff, those that deserve experimental attention from the hallucinatory experiences. But the popularizers and supernaturalists, by the natural inclinations of their spiritual propensities, are wont to attribute the same degree of reality to all. Yogic "miracles" constitute an ever-recurring theme in the repertoire of such writers.

Anyone who looks into the history of mystics of all countries and ages may satisfy himself that hallucinations are common at certain stages. They see "flames", colors of unexcelled beauty and brilliance, pearls of various shapes and sizes, apparitions, and ghostly forms. Hyper-aesthesia may spread to fields other than that of vision; smell of strange perfumes and sounds of soft voices are also common. In an introduction to a mystical treatise of probably the 12th or 13th century, Evelyn Underhill, commenting on the hallucinatory experiences of the anonymous authors, says:

> Psychic phenomena, too, seem to have been common: ecstasies, visions, voices, the scent of strange perfumes, the hearing of sweet sounds. For these supposed indications of Divine favour, the author of the *Cloud* [the name of the book] has no more respect than the modern psychologist: and here, of course, he is in agreement with all the greatest writers on mysticism, who are unanimous in their dislike and distrust of all visionary and auditive experiences. Such things, he considers, are most often hallucination: and, where they are not, should be regarded as the accidents rather than the substance of the contemplative life—the harsh rind of sense, which covers the sweet nut of "pure ghostliness".[18]

Another phenomenon often referred to as a miracle is the impression of levitation. A very satisfactory history of this experience among Western mystics is given by a French author, A. De Rochas, in his little book, *Recueils de documents relatifs à la lévitation du corps humain*.[19] The experiences of yogins are in no essentials different from those of their spiritual comrades of the West. In some instances those who are able to relax themselves have experienced a feeling of "floating" or levitation. In an experiment in which relaxation was naturally produced, Lydiard H. Horton [20] reported that out of 20 subjects who retained consciousness after they had completely relaxed, eight testified they had experi-

[18] Underhill, E.—*The Cloud of Unknowing*, 22; John M. Watkins, London, 1922.
[19] Leymarie, Paris, 1897.
[20] Horton, L. H.—"The Illusion of Levitation", *The Journal of Abnormal Psychology*, Vol. 13 (1918–19).

enced levitation. One of them, a woman, gripped the chair in the momentary belief that she was floating away!

While most of the experiences of illusion and hallucination of yogins as well as other mystics may be traced to psychical causes, we have very satisfactory evidence that they may also be produced by drugs and other physical means. Ancient civilizations had many hymns in praise of intoxicating drinks and drugs. One of the four Vedas consists of many hymns praising the divine value of *soma*, a juice drunk to experience ecstatic visions. The drinking ceremony was associated with the Delphic mystery religions of Greece. Among drugs, mescal (a product of the branches of cactus of the Melocacteae group) known until recently to Mexican and American Indian tribes only, and hasheesh are unexcelled in producing hallucinatory experiences. Of the visions produced by taking mescal, Havelock Ellis says, "On the whole, if I had to describe the visions in one word, I should say that they were living arabesques." [21] One of his subjects felt his self had been released from the body. Under the influence of hasheesh time and space judgments are seriously affected and the experiences are "indescribably exquisite". In experiments with nitrous oxide, Leuba [22] was told by one of his subjects of his experience that "the ego is a definite and indestructible unity". Three gases that give the strange and sublime feeling of severance from physical bonds of the body and the consciousness of pure selfhood are ether, chloroform, and nitrous oxide.

[21] Ellis, H.—"Mescal: A Study of a Divine Plant", *The Popular Science Monthly*, Vol. 61 (May–Oct., 1902).
[22] Leuba, J. H.—*The Psychology of Religious Mysticism*, 272; Harcourt, Brace and Co., 1925.

The conclusion that hallucinatory experiences may be induced by physical as well as psychical means is obvious. My acquaintance with the yogins has convinced me that they do not use drugs. One of the aphorisms of the *Yoga Sutras*, admitting that "supernormal experiences" may be induced by intoxicating liquors and drugs, strictly prohibits their use. The point we wish to emphasize is that yogins who have the spiritual ideal before them pay very little attention to these "psychic phenomena". One encounters them in the course of his practices, but they are merely distractions to be overcome. They are not gifts but obstacles. Barring the pretensions of the professional marvel-seekers, there is no basis for the popular impression that the "supernatural" centers around yogins and yoga. They would merely laugh such claims out of court provided they were at all willing to discuss the subject.

CHAPTER X

POSTURES

IN THE progressive development of a yogin special attention is paid to the building of a healthy body. The third
of the eight stages of the yogic discipline deals with a
series of gymnastic exercises which are meant to improve
the various parts of the organism.

Although yoga consists of eight stages, the reader
should not consider the yogin as mechanically progress-
ing from one stage to the next. The *guru* or teacher
determines, as we have already indicated in a previous
chapter, the requirements of a disciple and prescribes the
necessary exercises in line with his capacity and needs.
There is no uniform formula that is applicable to all.
This important point should be borne in mind in reading this and the following two chapters. While in theory
these physical exercises are available for those who may
benefit by them, one may directly proceed to the mental
exercises, ignoring this stage altogether. It is assumed that
in such cases the individual does not need, from the yogic
point of view, any development of the physical side
other than that which he already possesses. Nor is there
any definite regulation about how long a time one may
devote to a particular kind of exercise. Here, also, the

BOW POSTURE

PLOUGH POSTURE

DIAPHRAGM-RAISING EXERCISE IN TOPSY-TURVY
POSTURE

SEMI-MATSYENDRA POSTURE

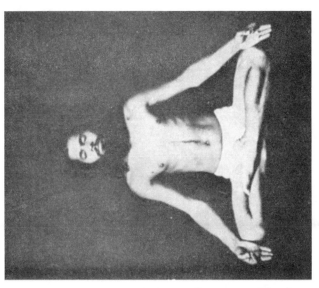

ONE OF THE FOUR MEDITATIVE POSTURES

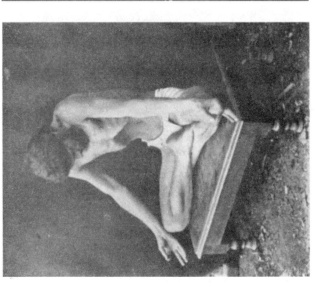

CHIN LOCK

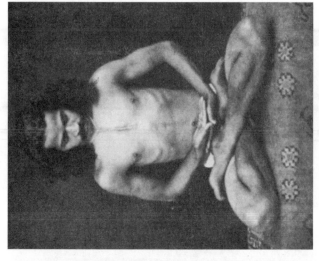

LOTUS POSTURE
(One of the Four Meditative Postures)

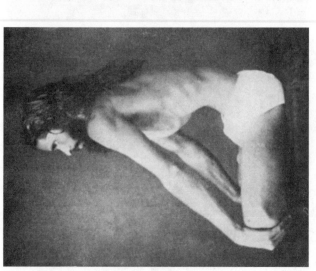

DIAPHRAGM-RAISING EXERCISE IN SITTING
POSTURE

PEACOCK POSTURE

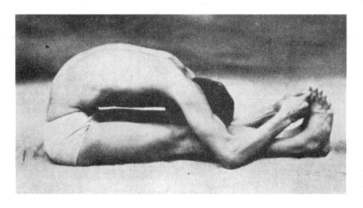

POSTERIOR-STRETCHING POSTURE

ISOLATION OF THE RIGHT
RECTUS ABDOMINUS

ISOLATION OF THE LEFT
RECTUS ABDOMINUS

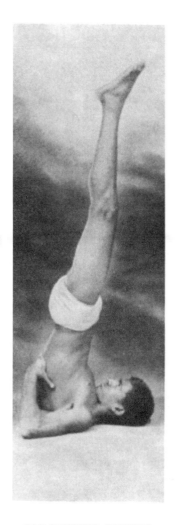 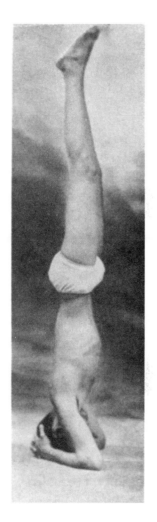

PAN-PHYSICAL POSTURE   TOPSY-TURVY POSTURE

THE RIGHT NOSTRIL CLOSED IN
YOGIC BREATHING

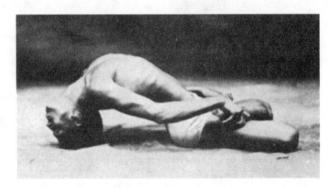

FISH POSTURE

teacher from time to time lays down the necessary instructions.

While yoga makes sufficient allowance for individual
differences, certain general rules are generally enforced.
The exercises described below are to be practised at
dawn and sunset on an empty stomach. Several hours
must elapse after a meal and before the exercise is begun.
Dietary regulations are to be strictly followed. The
yogin should not take sour, pungent, or spicy food.
Meat and intoxicating drinks are to be religiously avoided.
All yogic exercises are carried on in a place free from
disturbing factors. A firm but soft seat is chosen. Yogins
generally use some kind of tanned hide or carpets made
of grass to sit on.

Asanas, as these exercises are called, may be best translated as postures. It is interesting to note that, as against
Western exercises, a posture, once the position is assumed, is held for a long time—anywhere from three or
four minutes to half an hour. Rapid or violent movements are against the yogic tradition. Space does not
allow us to enumerate more than a few of the several
available postures which, it is hoped, will convince the
reader that an all-round development of the body is con-
templated in the yogic scheme of postures. There are one
or more exercises for every part of the body.

Apart from the general development that is claimed
to follow from these postures, some of them are said to
have specific therapeutic value. Traditional claims are
often exaggerations, if not entirely unfounded. It would
seem reasonable, however, to believe that there is a substratum of truth in these claims. One of the modern
yogins with a scientific turn of mind, Kuvalayananda,

who has utilized these postures in his work with patients, is convinced of their therapeutic advantages. We shall refer to some of his claims made for certain postures.

An immensely difficult posture and one of great discomfort to beginners is the lotus-posture.[1] Each leg is bent at the knee and the foot is kept resting at the opposite thigh-joint, with the soles turned up and the heels pressing against the lower side of the abdomen. The hands rest on the knees or on the toes, one on the other, with the palms turned upward. The beginner is repeatedly advised of the importance of maintaining an erect spine.

The lotus-posture, along with three others which all follow more or less the same principle, is utilized in the breathing and concentration exercises, and hence is known as the meditative posture. The technique of yogic deep breathing, described in the next chapter, demands certain movements of the head and hands. On the contrary, during meditation the head is held erect and the eyes closed.

The topsy-turvy-posture is an exercise in which the student stands straight on his head. After kneeling, the student makes a finger-lock by interlacing the fingers of both hands. With the forearms on the ground and with the elbows a foot apart, the head is placed in the curve formed by the fingers, which serves as a support to the back part of the head. As the toes are brought nearer the head, the trunk is raised to a vertical position. The legs

[1] Each posture has a Sanskrit name which often signifies the resemblance of the posture to an inanimate object or animal. I am following the very appropriate English translation by Kuvalayananda (Kuvalayananda-*Asanas*, Part 1, *Popular Yoga*, Vol. 1; Kaivalyadhama, Lonavla, India).

are then raised to form a straight line with the spine. Although this posture is rather uncomfortable in the beginning, practice enables one to maintain the position for twenty minutes or even more.[2]

The pan-physical-posture, as the name would indicate, is said to influence the whole body and its functions. As it is meant to direct a liberal supply of blood to the thyroid and parathyroid glands, it is possible that there is substance to this claim. It is also interesting to note that this exercise is very commonly practised in the West. After lying on the back, the legs are slowly raised, until they make a right angle to the ground. Next, with the elbows planted on the ground, the trunk is raised with the help of the forearms. The body is raised sufficiently high to allow the chest to keep pressing against the chin. The posture is sometimes maintained for half an hour or more.[3]

The fish-posture (so called because the posture enables one to float like a fish in water for a considerable time without exertion) is a complement of the pan-physical one. After assuming the lotus-posture, the student lies on his back and the trunk is raised with the help of the elbows, throwing the head backwards as far as it will go. The eyes keep looking across the forehead. The

[2] The main purpose of this exercise would seem to be to divert a large supply of blood to the brain. On the therapeutic side, it is maintained that dyspepsia and constipation, when caused by digestive disorders due to deficient blood supply, can be treated satisfactorily by means of this posture (*Asanas*, 67).

[3] Yogins hold this posture in high esteem and consider it to have great therapeutic value. Besides the general improvement in health through developing a healthy thyroid, according to Kuvalayananda, this posture has a beneficial influence on weak sex glands. A very ancient yogic tradition prescribes this posture with a milk diet for patients in the initial stages of leprosy (*Asanas*, 75).

posture is completed by taking hold of the toes with the fingers.

To assume the plough-posture (because it imitates the Indian plough), while lying on the back, first the legs are raised and then the lower part of the trunk. Slowly the legs are lowered beyond the head, the toes touching the ground as near the head as possible. The trunk is raised higher and higher, the toes are moved farther and farther away as far back as they will go. Now the hands are brought together to form a finger-lock around the head as in the topsy-turvy-posture. With this support for the head, the toes are pushed even farther back until the chest presses tightly against the chin.

To execute the cobra-posture, while lying on the back and with the palms on either side, first the head is raised and thrown back as far as possible. Very slowly, then, the thorax is raised, and then the lumbar section. As one advances in this practice, the pressure on the hands is reduced and the back muscles brought into action. Those who are well established in yogic deep breathing are expected to hold their breath while doing this exercise. As a complement to this, the locust-posture is practised. While lying on the chest and with the hands kept at the sides (with clenched fists), the legs are raised after deep inhalation by putting pressure on the chest and hands. When it is no longer possible to hold the breath, the legs are slowly lowered. The bow-posture combines the features of both cobra- and locust-postures. The ankles are held, and the head, chest, and the legs are raised.

In the posterior-stretching exercise, the student first sits with his legs stretched out. Hooks are made with the forefingers and the toes are grasped by bending the trunk a little forward. Next, the grasp is made firmer and the trunk is bent still farther forward until the face rests between the knees, and the elbows rest on the ground.

In most of the postures described so far, the spinal column is bent either backward or forward. But the semi-Matsyendra-posture (called after a famous yogin of ancient times) enables one to twist the spine sideways. The student sits on the floor with the legs stretched out. The right leg is bent, the heel is set against the perineum, and the sole against the left thigh. The left leg is bent and the foot made to rest on the right side of the right thigh. The right hand is passed around the left knee to grasp the left toe, so that the shoulder keeps pressing against the knee and allows the body to be twisted to the left. The maximum possible twist is effected by bringing the left hand behind the back to grasp the right thigh below the groin. The head is also turned to the left in line wth the left shoulder. To make the right twist, one may start with the left leg and introduce the corresponding changes.

The pelvic posture: while seated, either one of the legs is folded and, with the knees raised, the foot is made to rest in front of the corresponding buttock. If the student starts with the left leg, he leans a little to the right. The sole is turned up and the toes brought behind the corresponding buttock, where they remain pointing to the right. The right leg is then arranged likewise. With the spine held erect, the palms are brought to rest on the knees and the eyes are closed.[4] The supine pelvic-posture is a continuation of this, in which the student lies on his back with the forearms serving for cushions under the head.

[4.]This is a meditative posture, too.

In the peacock-posture the student balances the body horizontally on the two forearms—a very difficult posture to maintain and one which involves great expenditure of energy. While kneeling down and resting the body on the knees and toes, the palms are turned backwards and pressed against the floor. The elbows are brought together and held on the abdomen a little below the umbilicus. As pressure is put on the forearms, the toes are raised and thrown back in a line with the body. The head is held at a slight elevation to counterbalance the lower limbs.

We now come to the last posture, one which aims at the relaxation of all the muscles of the body. It is called the dead-posture because the subject lies on his back as motionless as a corpse. First the thoracic muscles are relaxed, then the abdominal, and so on. In attempting to relax, one concentrates on the part worked upon and imagines that the part thought about is relaxing. If necessary, the eyes are closed. Although one begins by working, one by one, on the different muscle groups, one's ultimate aim is to relax them all at once when so desired. With the muscles relaxed, one begins to regulate breathing. First, without attempting to control, one simply observes the inflow and outflow of breath. After a time the irregularities in breathing are rectified by voluntarily equalizing the time taken for both inhalation and exhalation. Finally, volume is increased, making respiration deeper. Each stage is attempted only after the successful completion of the previous one. If the student were to find that he had over-exercised himself, he would customarily practise the dead-posture to recover equilibrium.

If we are to get a complete picture of the purely

physical exercises of yoga, it is not enough to describe the postures. Several minor exercises, grouped under technical names, are utilized by the yogins. Some of them relate to the disposition of certain anatomical parts during the execution of the postures. Others are merely purificatory devices for cleansing the stomach, colon, etc. A few are practised independently of the postures. If we overlook the yogic way of grouping them (into *bandhas, mudras,* etc.) we may divide them into two broad groups, viz., those dealing with particular anatomical parts and those that are purificatory in nature. We shall first consider the former.

Two ways of steadily gazing at some point of the body are practised by yogins as a preliminary exercise in concentration, either as a part of the technique of the meditative postures or independently. In one of them, the nasal gaze, the student stares unflinchingly at the tip of the nose. Tradition considers this gaze a part of the lotus-posture. In the frontal gaze, the eyes are directed to the mid-point between the eyebrows. Since this gaze might sometimes injure the eyes, yogins always take care to warn the enthusiastic beginner against overdoing. It is claimed, however, that when cautiously done these gazes help immensely to conquer the wandering propensities of the mind.

Yogins place a great deal of emphasis on abdominal exercises. One of these is designed to raise the diaphragm. The student stands with the feet a few inches apart and the knees and the trunk bent a little forward. The hands rest a little above the knees. As the knees are pressed, he exhales completely. A vigorous mock inhalation is then attempted by raising the ribs and producing a pronounced depression of the abdomen. When it is no longer possible to refrain from inhaling, the abdomen is brought back to its normal position.[5] This exercise may be practised in several positions, sitting cross-legged, squatting, etc.

In the chin-lock, the head is bent down so that the chin presses the jugular notch. Throughout the period of retention in yogic breathing, the head is held in this position. It is claimed that this exerts an upward pull on the spine.

Yogins attempt from very early in their practice to gain control over the anal sphincters. The first effort in this direction consists of repeated contraction and relaxation of the sphincters for several minutes in succession. The same procedure is repeated during the diaphragm-raising exercise. With every inhalation the sphincters are relaxed and in exhalation they are contracted. One of the developments of the topsy-turvy-posture consists of practising the diaphragm-raising exercise while maintaining this posture with slight modifications. While inhaling and exhaling in this position, the sphincters are also manipulated. A few days' practice in various positions enables the student to accomplish his objective—that of gaining complete voluntary control over the sphincters.[6] Once the control is established, while the abdomen is withdrawn for the diaphragm-raising exercise, the sphincters are opened to force out the gases from the lower part of the colon. When the abdominal muscles are re-

[5] This is claimed to have great therapeutic value against many abdominal troubles (*Asanas*, 51).

[6] This is not merely idle claim. In one of the purificatory exercises, to be described shortly, we shall see how this voluntary control over the sphincters is utilized.

laxed, the same process is repeated, this time to take fresh air in from the outside.[7]

An exercise called the symbol of yoga is executed by forming a foot-lock as in the lotus-posture. The hands are brought behind the back, the right hand grasping the left wrist. With the body bent over the heels, the forehead is made to touch the ground.[8]

There are a few exercises that are generally practised only by advanced yogins. One such is the tongue-rolling exercise in which the tongue is rolled backward and upward to cover up the nasal cavities posteriorly leading into the pharynx at the base of the skull. Ordinarily, since the tongue is tied to the region below by the frenulum, its movements are checked and hence cannot reach the posterior openings. To overcome this difficulty the frenulum is cut. According to the prescribed procedure this cutting is done, little by little, once every week until the fibrous band is removed. Every day the student enhances the flexibility of the tongue by rolling it to both sides. He lengthens it by pulling it out slowly until it is long enough to reach the posterior openings of the nasal cavities and to cover them up. This is practised as an adjunct to the breathing exercises by those who are able to hold their breath for a considerable time. While it may

[7] "The nerve supply of the rectum and the anus is mainly from the sympathetic; and the nerve endings in the skin at the anal orifice are exceedingly numerous. The work of Asvini-Mudra [the anal exercise to control the sphincters] principally lies with this part and through it the sympathetic is probably stimulated." (*Yoga-Mimansa*, Vol. I, 133, ed. by Kuvalayananda; Kaivalyadhama, Lonavla, India.)

[8] On the therapeutic side it is claimed that the pressure exerted by the heels against the pelvic loop and the cecum induces movements in these portions of the colon, and hence this pressure is a good remedy for constipation (*Asanas*, 118).

be difficult for the layman to see what could possibly be accomplished by this the yogins are unanimous in attributing great value to it. It is claimed by some that this practice induces secretions of great physiological value. All of them maintain, however, that it helps the practitioner to advance towards *samadhi*—the highest stage of yoga practice, the ideal and the supreme objective of all yogins.

We may now take up the purificatory exercises which are utilized to cleanse the different parts of the body. It is not necessary for every yogin to practise any or all of them as a regular part of the daily yogic routine; only those with certain irregularities or those suffering from defective functioning of any particular region need undertake them. Everyone, however, is expected to know the technique of doing these so that, when the occasion arises, he may easily utilize them.

The most important of the purificatory exercises is the one in which the two muscles, recti abdomini, are isolated; first together and then each independently. In a sense this is a continuation of the diaphragm-raising exercise described above. When the diaphragm has been raised, with the practitioner in a standing position, a downward and forward push is given to the abdominal portion above the pubic bone. After considerable practice, sometimes running over several months, one is able to isolate the two muscles. This forms the first stage. Next, the attempt is directed to isolating either one, keeping the other one relaxed. If the isolation of the left rectus is desired, the body is bent a little to that side and a corresponding change is introduced for isolating the right muscle.

When the student has succeeded in isolating the two recti, together and then independently, he is ready to pass on to the final stage, which consists of rolling manipulations. This is achieved by the rapid contraction and relaxation of the two muscles in quick succession and is also practised both ways, from left to right and vice versa.[9]

Yogins have developed a very interesting method for washing the colon. While the recti abdomini muscles are isolated a partial vacuum is created in the colon which enables the student to take water up through the rectum, provided the sphincters can be voluntarily opened.[10] We have already described the practices by which one can gain control over the sphincters. In traditional practice, for those who could not voluntarily open their sphincters, it is customary to insert a bamboo tube into the rectum. After the water is in, the student practises the diaphragm-raising exercise and the isolation and the rolling manipulation of the recti abdomini before the water is let out.

Another interesting consequence of the isolation of the two muscles is the development of a partial vacuum in the bladder as well. Just as in the case of the colon, this is utilized by the yogins to wash this organ. In traditional practice a silver or lead tube is used to force open the urethral sphincter which gives ready access to the bladder. The student inserts the first one as far as the bladder.

[9] Kuvalayananda, after some X-ray studies as well as some therapeutic application of this exercise, concludes that it is one of the finest exercises for several abdominal and intestinal complaints (*Yoga-Mimansa*, Vol. I, Nos. 2 and 3).

[10] On experimental evidence, Kuvalayananda claims that a partial vacuum of 30 to 47 mm.Hg. was in evidence every time the two muscles were isolated (*Yoga-Mimansa*, Vol. I, 28).

The outer end of the tube is left in a bowl of water and the recti abdomini are isolated. Immediately the water rushes up through the tube. Before the muscles are relaxed, the tube is pulled out and the water is retained in the bladder for a few minutes, after which it is let out. Sometimes in modern yogic practice rubber catheters are used.[11]

There are several exercises to improve the stomach. One of them is aimed to develop control over the stomach to the extent that one could voluntarily vomit the contents. The student drinks four or five glasses of water on an empty stomach. The student bends the trunk slightly forward, spreads the legs and rests the hands on the knees, and then inhales deeply. With the hands pressed firmly against the knees, the abdominal muscles are thrown backward and upward and then relaxed again. This is repeated at the rate of approximately seven or eight times a minute. After a few months of practice, most students gain full control over the stomach and can vomit the contents at will.

In an unusually striking practice to cleanse the stomach and massage its walls, the yogins swallow a long piece of cloth. A strong but thin piece of cloth about twenty-two feet long and three inches wide is used for the purpose. One end of the cloth, which is moistened and held in one hand, is inserted into the mouth and the student begins to swallow it bit by bit. Very often it

[11] The writer has seen both these practices, viz., taking water into the colon and the bladder by isolating the recti abdomini. In the former no tube was used, since the practitioner was able to open the rectal sphincters voluntarily, while the traditional silver tube was availed of in the case of the bladder. About half a glass of water was drawn into the bladder.

takes considerable practice to swallow the whole piece, leaving out only a few inches. With the cloth in, the student practises the diaphragm-raising exercise for a few minutes and follows this by the isolation and the rolling manipulations of the recti abdomini. The cloth is pulled out after twenty minutes or so by the alternate use of the two hands.[12]

The breathing exercises, described in the next chapter, constitute, according to the yogic classification, the fourth among the eight stages. Yet there is a type of rhythmic, shallow breathing known as *kapalabhati* which is considered a purificatory exercise. The pause between inhalation and exhalation, the main feature of all yogic varieties of breathing which are claimed to have spiritual value, is conspicuous by its absence in kapalabhati.

It may be practised in any one of the four meditative postures, preferably the lotus-posture.[13] Since this is a diaphragmatic variety of breathing, the abdominal muscles play the major rôle. The student starts with an exhalation brought about by an inward stroke of the abdomen. Inhalation follows immediately after exhalation, there being no interval between the two. Muscular con-

---

[12] Two specific advantages are claimed for this practice—absorption by the cloth of the fluids collected in the stomach and the massage given to its walls (*Yoga-Mimansa*, Vol. II, 174).

[13] Any one of these postures is good enough as long as kapalabhati is practised for a short time, say, four or five minutes. When practised for a longer period, however, the lotus-posture is the only one available. The reason is that when the breathing is carried on over long periods certain vibrations are started all over the body and this, coupled with a feeling of exhilaration, results in a lessening of the motor control over the limbs. But in the lotus-posture the legs are formed into such a firm lock that it is impossible to undo them without the help of the hands, and hence not likely to be disturbed by the lessening motor control.

traction beyond that involved in one moderate inward stroke is avoided. In actual practice, inhalation is so passive and automatic that the student pays no attention to this phase. Two exhalations per second is about the usual rate, and one minute the duration of one round (one hundred and twenty respirations). After the maximum number in one round is reached, the student rests for a short period ranging from a few seconds to one minute. Then the second round begins. Three such rounds are generally practised in one sitting. Students who have had long practice, however, sometimes prolong the session to thirty minutes and increase the speed to four exhalations per second.[14]

We may now conclude this chapter with the observation that, from the yogic point of view, a correct and harmonious physiological functioning of the various organs of the body is more important than either mere physical strength or muscular power. The exercises described above seem to have been developed primarily for that purpose. It is a well-rounded system in that no part of the body has been left without an appropriate exercise or exercises for its development. These, coupled with the breathing exercises, help the yogins to maintain their bodies at a high level of physical efficiency.

[14] "As an exercise of great oxygen value, kapalabhati has no parallel. Its nerve culture value is also very great. Its effect upon the circulatory and digestive systems are of considerable physiological importance. The massage of the abdominal viscera which the exercise effects is obvious." (Kuvalayananda—*Pranayama*, Part I, 97; Kaivalyadhama, Lonavla, India.)

CHAPTER XI

VARIETIES OF BREATHING

IN THE minds of many people, both in India and in the West, yoga is very often associated with *pranayama*, i.e., with certain types of breathing, sometimes to the exclusion of all other practices. In point of fact pranayama occupies the fourth stage in the yogic curriculum, which in turn is followed by the mental exercises.

There is a substantial reason why yoga has come to be associated with pranayama in the popular mind; it is the connecting link between the physical and the mental aspects of yoga. We can make this point clear by considering the general nature of the postures and the effect they are supposed to bring about in the organism. They are physical exercises intended to develop a physiological balance and as such have very little to do with the induction of any extraordinary mental experiences. But with sufficient practice in pranayama the yogin finds that changes occur in his mental states; in a marked way his awareness of the external world diminishes.

Pranayama comprises different types of breathing. "Prana" means "breath" and "ayama", "pause"; hence the compound "pranayama" literally means a cessation or pause in the movement of breath. While in the earlier writings, especially in Patanjali's *Yoga Sutras*, the word is free from all mystical and symbolic interpretations, in the hands of later writers it became equivalent to some psychic force or cosmic element. We shall ignore this unnecessary mystification of the word and use it in its original and correct sense, referring to the normal function of respiration.

Each act of breathing, according to yogic teachers, consists of three parts: inhalation (*puraka*), holding (*kumbhaka*), and exhalation (*rechaka*). Holding may refer to the stage when the air is held in the body or outside of it. The time relation between these three parts of respiration is one of great importance to yogins. The most authentic tradition demands that if inhalation should take one time-unit, then holding and exhalation should take four and two respectively. This means that in the successive order of inhalation, holding, and exhalation the ratio is 1:4:2. There are two other traditions, one of which prescribes the proportion as 1:2:2 and the other has a uniform measure for all the three acts.

Beginners generally follow the second ratio, i.e., 1:2:2, although one may practise according to the first proportion after a time when it is deemed desirable. For that matter the beginner is even advised to omit retention altogether in the first few days of pranayamic practice. It may be taken up after the student has made satisfactory progress in inhalation and exhalation in the proportion 1:2. All yogic pranayamas are practised slowly, and one should not continue under a sense of discomfort or feeling of suffocation. The adjustments that may demand conscious attention in the beginning follow as a matter of course with practice.

Advanced yogins practise pranayama four times in the

course of twenty-four hours, i.e., morning (at dawn), midday, evening (at sunset), and midnight; for beginners, however, morning and evening is sufficient. Just as a light stomach is necessary in the case of the postures, so also it is imperative in pranayama. If the postures and pranayama are both practised in one session, the latter should invariably come second. Concentration exercises, if practised with either postures or pranayama or both, should always come last.

According to one of the generally accepted traditions there are eight varieties of pranayama: *ujjayi, bhastrika, suryabhedana, sitkari, sitali, bhramari, murchchha,* and *plavini.* We shall now turn our attention to a description of these.

Ujjayi

After assuming one of the meditative postures in which the spine and the head are held erect, the student is ready to start the first part of the respiratory act, inhalation. After a slow, but complete, exhalation the chest is expanded and the air allowed to flow in. Inhalation is done slowly and deliberately. The disposition of the glottis deserves particular notice. In normal breathing it is customary to keep the glottis wide open. But in ujjayi the glottis is partially closed. When the student inhales, consequently, a sound similar to that produced in sobbing is heard even at a little distance. The frictional sound sometimes produced when the nasal passages are not clear is religiously avoided. It is important to bear in mind that the force exerted during inhalation must be uniform until the last cubic centimeter of air is in, and further, that no jerky movements of the muscles of inspiration should take place.

Since ujjayi is a thoracic variety of breathing, the abdominal muscles play only a passive rôle. It is customary, for most people, to draw out the abdomen in any kind of deep breathing. This, however, is not countenanced in yogic pranayamas. On the contrary, the abdominal muscles are held in a state of slight contraction throughout inhalation.

Inhalation is followed by holding, and a few changes are introduced in the disposition of some parts of the body. First, the glottis, which remained partially closed during inhalation, is now tightly closed. Next, the chinlock is formed, i.e., the head is bent down in front so that the chin presses firmly against the jugular notch. This position is maintained throughout the period of retention.

The student then closes his nostrils, using the right hand for this purpose. With the index and the middle fingers bent so as to touch the palmar side, the thumb and the other fingers are held straight. While arranged in this fashion the fingers are kept on the bridge of the nose. If the practitioner desires to close the right nostril, the thumb is moved down and pressed against the septum and the hard bone above. Similarly, to close the left nostril, the extended fingers are brought down. If both nostrils are to be closed the fingers as well as the thumb are brought down and pressed against the septum.[1] In ujjayi both nostrils are closed during retention.

---

[1] In some varieties of breathing, as we shall see later, it is necessary to open and close the right and left nostrils alternately; hence this arrangement of the fingers is a convenient device.

Before exhalation begins, pressure is relieved from the left nostril, and the right one still remains closed. The head is then raised and brought back to its original position; and the glottis is partially opened. The student then exhales through the left nostril, maintaining a uniform speed to the end. In order to make the exhalation complete, the abdominal muscles are contracted more and more as the air supply is exhausted. This completes one round of ujjayi.

One may begin with a few rounds and increase the number every day. With some practice one is enabled to increase the duration of each round and develop the right ratio. It is desirable to practise eighty rounds in one sitting. In doing this, care should be taken to avoid the inhalation of extra air between the rounds.

So far we have described ujjayi as it is taught according to tradition. But Swami Kuvalayananda suggests a slight change which is based on his experiences as well as those of his several disciples. According to him, instead of exhaling through the left nostril, beginners would do well to make use of both nostrils for this purpose. He is also convinced that this minor change in technique does not greatly affect the results. Beginners generally find the frequent manipulation of fingers for opening and closing the nostrils very irksome. The advantage of the suggestion is that this part of the technique, i.e., closing both nostrils after inhalation and later opening the left one before exhalation, may be conveniently avoided.

We have already mentioned that all yogic pranayamas are practised in one or another of the meditative postures. Even according to traditional teaching there is one exception to this. This is ujjayi. One may practise this also while walking. The chin-lock, etc., which generally go with the different kinds of pranayamas, are avoided in this case. This then becomes nothing more than deep breathing. When so practised, yogins maintain that one cannot expect from ujjayi those spiritual results that are claimed to follow from pranayamas.

Utmost concentration is invariably demanded in all yogic pranayamas. The student is asked to concentrate on that point in the nasal passage where the first touch of inhaled air is felt. It is claimed by yogins that such concentration has, in the long run, a steadying effect on the mind.

Bhastrika

Bhastrika is a pranayama which is held in high esteem by yogins. This type of breathing is claimed to be best among all the yogic pranayamas for arousing the spiritual forces and for preparing the practitioner for concentration (*dharana*) and meditation (*dhyana*). There are four varieties of bhastrika, the one common characteristic of them all is the short-rhythm-breathing, i.e., quick and sudden exhalations followed by equally sudden inhalations. The short-rhythm-breathing part of bhastrika is exactly the same as in *kapalabhati*, described under the purificatory exercises in the previous chapter. This is, however, only the first part of bhastrika which is followed in all the four varieties by the same sort of deep breathing that is found in ujjayi. The sound produced by the incessant expulsions in the first part of bhastrika is similar to that of the bellows of a village smith; hence the name, "bhastrika", meaning "bellows".

In the first type of bhastrika one starts with kapalabhati, the number of rounds being determined by the needs of the individual. Twenty rounds is considered a good average for beginners. After this is completed, one round of ujjayi is practised with a slight change, viz., the glottis remains wide open throughout inhalation and exhalation. Because of the kapalabhatic type of breathing preceding ujjayi, the duration of the latter in bhastrika is longer than it would be otherwise, because the student takes advantage of the apnœa resulting from the short-rhythm-breathing. The end of deep exhalation completes one round of bhastrika. Several such rounds, depending on individual needs, are practised.

In the second variety of bhastrika the kapalabhatic part is slightly different from that of the first. Instead of keeping the glottis completely open, as is generally done in kapalabhati proper, it is slightly contracted. The student takes particular care to see that the closure effected is so slight as not to cause any friction consequent on the rapid movement of the breath in and out. After the prescribed rounds of kapalabhati are over, the student begins ujjayi. Here he inhales through the right nostril, effecting the necessary closure of the left nostril with the fingers of the right hand. This is followed by retention, the formation of the chin-lock, etc. In exhalation, air is let out through the left nostril in the same manner generally used in ujjayi. This completes one round of the second variety of bhastrika. As soon as the ujjayic part of bhastrika is over, the right hand is brought down and held against the right knee. The hand is again raised to make the adjustments during the ujjayic part in every round.

The most conspicuous feature of the third variety is the alternation between the right and left nostrils for the expulsion of air during the first part of every round. If the right nostril, for example, is used for expelling air in the first round, the left is used in the second, and so on for every odd and even number. Inhalation in the ujjayic part is done through the same nostril as in the preceding kapalabhatic part and exhalation through the other. Since the right hand is frequently used for closing one or the other of the nostrils in the kapalabhatic and ujjayic parts of this bhastrika, the student finds it helpful to keep the hand on the bridge of the nose throughout this exercise.

In the fourth variety there is a change in technique only in the first part of the exercise. The student inhales through the right nostril and exhales through the left. The order is reversed in the second round. Thereafter all odd rounds follow the first and even rounds the second. The second part of this exercise is similar to the corresponding part of the second variety of breathing: the student inhales through the right nostril and exhales through the other nostril.

Suryabhedana

The name "suryabhedana" is related to the yogic claim about the effect of this particular pranayama on the organism. It is generally held by yogins that inhalation through the right nostril increases the temperature of the body, while inhalation through the left lowers it. Since inhalation is done through the right nostril in this pranayama, it is called "suryabhedana" and the word "surya" (meaning "sun") is expressive of the result expected.

After making the adjustments with the right hand to close the left nostril, the student inhales with partially-closed glottis through the right nostril. This is followed by retention as in ujjayi. Exhalation is done through the right nostril. The distinguishing feature of suryabhedana, in short, is the use of the right nostril for both inhalation and exhalation.

Sitkari

This pranayama involves inhaling through the mouth, although the disposition of the various parts is as in ujjayi. The tip of the tongue is kept between the two lips with sufficient space between the upper lip and the tongue to allow the air to flow in. With this arrangement the student inhales through the mouth, producing a wheezing sound. A kind of breezy and pleasant sensation is felt on the forepart of the tongue. As soon as inhalation is over, the lips are brought together and the mouth closed. The chin-lock is formed at the beginning of retention. Exhalation is done through both nostrils.

Sitali

This pranayama is very much like sitkari, in that inhalation is done through the mouth and exhalation through the nostrils. The arrangement of the tongue and the lips is, however, slightly different. Both lips are contracted and between the two the tongue is folded like the beak of a bird. The tongue is found to protrude a little beyond the lips. After inhalation the mouth is closed and retention begins. This is followed by exhalation through both nostrils, thus completing one round.

Bhramari

This is usually practised at some time past midnight when external sounds are at a minimum. The ears are closed with the thumbs and inhalation and exhalation produce a sound like the humming of bees ("bhramari" means "a bee"). It is claimed by yogins that in this pranayama the palate is set vibrating.

Murchchha

As far as inhalation and exhalation are concerned there is nothing unique about this pranayama. It is, however, the only pranayama in which exhalation is done with the chin-lock and thus is an exception to the general rule. It is claimed that this type of breathing is particularly capable of calming the mind.

Plavini

The unique feature of this pranayama is that it is practised while floating on water. The legs are crossed in a fashion similar to that of the fish-posture which is described in the previous chapter. The disposition of the head is just the opposite to what is done in the chin-lock, i.e., it is thrown back and the hands are crossed behind to give it support. This arrangement of the body helps one to float in water with considerable ease.

We have so far described the eight varieties of pranayamas that are available to the yogins. It is not always necessary to practise all of the eight kinds to obtain the desired results, and very often yogins confine themselves to the most important varieties like bhastrika and ujjayi. In the texts all of them are said to possess spiritual significance, inasmuch as they are all conducive to the awakening of spiritual forces. Some of them are claimed to have specific virtues. Ujjayi and suryabhedana, for example, increase the heat in the body, while sitkari and sitali have the opposite effect. Bhastrika is supposed to preserve even temperature. Murchchha is particularly effective in producing a state of mental passivity that is highly desired by yogins. As far as physical health is concerned, all the pranayamas are said to have a beneficial effect on the system. In actual practice *gurus* attach utmost importance to ujjayi and bhastrika.

In one form or another the different kinds of yogic pranayamas are, from a physiological point of view, variations of deep breathing with a few changes in technique, e.g., the meditative postures in which the flexor muscles remain contracted, the partial closure of the glottis, the chin-lock, etc. It is perhaps possible that the unusual disposition of the different anatomical parts of the body may have something to do with the mental changes claimed by yogins to follow upon these practices. Equally important are the results that are likely to be produced in the retention period. When we realize that the yogins attach a great deal of importance to, and try their utmost to prolong, the holding period, we are justified in concluding that this stage in pranayama probably has important bearing on the physico-chemical changes leading to the mental states alleged to supervene and hence deserving of our experimental attention. The subjective experiences that arise in the course of pranayama are so varied that it would be very unscientific to advance any hypothesis which does not take all the phenomena into consideration. Very many avenues will have to be experimentally explored before we shall be in a position to state exactly the changes that take place in the organism as a result of the yogic pranayamas.

Chapter XII

EXERCISES IN CONCENTRATION

It is our task in this chapter to explain the last stage of yoga, a stage which involves mental exercises or exercises in concentration. They are meant to influence directly the mind as against the gymnastic and breathing practices designed to control the body. The four stages comprise: sense-withdrawal (*pratyahara*), concentration (*dharana*), contemplation (*dhyana*), and trance (*samadhi*). Anyone who seeks precise theoretical distinctions between these four stages will be disappointed, for there is considerable overlapping and gradual but distinguishable development from one stage to another. For practical purposes, however, it is possible to differentiate each stage from the others.

It would be useful at this point to clarify the technical meaning of the word "concentration" in yogic terminology. In popular language the process implied by the word is one of intense application to a particular subject, to the exclusion of extraneous thoughts that have no relevance to the subject on hand. But within the circumscribed "area", attention is allowed to range over innumerable ideas before a decision or solution is arrived at. One might characterize this as the intensification of the process of discursive reasoning within a narrow field. The mind, by an effort of the will, is made to limit its range, but within the chosen "circle" the stream of consciousness knows no cessation, passing from idea to idea and thought to thought. Reason and intellect function at their highest level of efficiency. If the attention is directed to an external happening, then the appropriate sense would also participate in the process.

How different is all this from the yogic idea of concentration may be easily grasped by the following consideration. The objective that the yogin lays before himself in practising the exercises is the complete elimination of thoughts, or, rather that of getting behind thoughts, i.e., transcending the activities and fluctuations of the *citta* or mind-stuff. The ideal is not reached until all thoughts are suppressed. To the mind as such, yoga attaches no importance, regarding it as an obstacle or veil, so to say, that hides the true self. When the yogin succeeds in suppressing the activities of the mind by means of his mental exercises, then he is said to have realized himself. This is the "pure consciousness", untarnished by the modifications of the mind-stuff which usually result in sense-perception, reasoning, intellectual activities, etc.

To reach such a goal, the mind has to take a different turn and concentration has to be of an entirely different order. The yogin is advised, therefore, not to place a premium on discursive faculties, to ignore the primary as well as the secondary qualities of the object of concentration, and to retain just the bare idea of the object in the mind. Attention is to be narrowed down to a vague, "qualityless" point—a kind of monoideism claimed to be essential for autohypnosis. The reader may gain some idea of this kind of concentration by gazing steadily at a minute object or by thinking continuously of the meaning of a word. This would result first in a cloudiness leading sometimes to a mental vacuum. The distinction in the use of the word "concentration" should convince us that as practised by yogins the process is one of regression, i.e., he begins with the fluctuating mind-stuff with its propensity to "fly" from thought to thought; he then steadies the mind-stuff by practice and effort of the will, until at last by intense concentration even the steady mind and its single thought are surpassed.

After this digression we may turn now to the practical, if not the theoretical, differentiation of the four stages in the development of yogic mental practice. The exercises in concentration usually come after a few rounds of deep breathing (pranayama) and it is needless to reiterate that the practitioner continues to sit in one of the meditative postures described in a previous chapter. In *pratyahara* or the sense-withdrawal stage, a deliberate effort is made to diminish the impulses streaming in through the sense organs. The student attempts to establish a control over the senses which restrains the communication of external impressions to the mind. This is only the negative aspect. On the positive side, the physical exhilaration and mental passivity induced by the heavy breathing facilitate the sense-withdrawal.

The state of the mind in this condition may be thought of as one of detachment from the external world, but in no way does it approach a rigid immobility. The yogin, for example, is alive, and advised to be so, to certain sensations in the body that are produced by the pranayamic breathing. It is claimed that certain vibrations are generated in the lower part of the spine.[1] The impulses

[1] Yoga has devoted considerable attention to the anatomical and physiological description of the human body. Here is an illustrative description: "In the body of man there are 350,000 *nadis* [nerves?]; of them, the principal are fourteen . . . All these principal *nadis* . . . are like thin threads of lotus. The other *nadis* rising from *muladhara* [a region in the pelvic area, sacro-coccygeal plexus?] go to the various parts of the body, e.g., the tongue, organ of generation, eyes, feet, toes, ears, abdomen, armpit, fingers of the hands, scrotum and the anus. Having risen from their proper places they stop at their respective destinations, as above described. From all these fourteen *nadis*, there arise gradually other branches and sub-branches, so that at last they become three hundred thousand and a half in number, and supply their respective places. These *nadis* are spread through the body crosswise and lengthwise; they are vehicles of sensation and keep watch over the movements of the air . . . These *nadis* are the seeds of mystery, or the sources of all principles which constitute a man and show the road to Brahma." (*Siva-Samhita*, II.13,17,29,30,31 and V.121; ed. by Major B. D. Basu, The Panini Office, Allahabad.)

Brahmadanda or the *merudanda* [spinal column?] is said to be like a column or stick that extends from the lowest part of the trunk to the occiput. Within this column is the thin cord *sushumna* [spinal cord?] which, because of its supreme importance, is called *Brahmanadi* (nerve of Brahma) by the wise. The rest of the *nadis* are subordinate to it. To the left side of the long column is *Ida* and to the right *Pingala*, each ending in the opposite nostril [the two ganglionic chains?]. Both of these have their connection with the *sushumna* [spinal cord?] somewhere in the *navichakra* (pelvic area).

It should be borne in mind, however, that what the yogins have said on this subject is clothed in such mystical and allegorical phraseology that it is difficult, if not impossible, to gauge the precise significance of the terms used. Any attempt to interpret this terminology in modern scientific language is very likely to end in confusion, since the yogic conceptions of the functional significance of the different parts of the body are far removed from those of the present day.

Even the higher experiences of the yogins are said to be generated by the arousal of a psychic energy known as *kundalini*. The importance attached to this force, *kundalini*, is unsurpassed by anything in the whole realm of yogic theory and practice. Under ordinary circumstances *kundalini* is claimed to be sleeping like a coiled serpent. Although psychical in nature, it has a physical counterpart and is located in the region somewhere at the end of the spinal column (*Brahmadanda*). The paramount aim of yoga practice is to arouse this normally static energy into action. Once aroused, its influence extends thus initiated are in some indirect way responsible for inducing those higher experiences that are yet to come. As one advances in his practices, these sensations are not confined to the lower part of the spine alone, but slowly ascend along the spine, step by step, until they reach the head. No doubt individual difference plays a part. It is claimed, for example, that in some people these vibrations may originate anywhere along the spine. Instead of vibrations, one may experience a sensation of throbbing.

To summarize: in *pratyahara* or the stage of sense-withdrawal one is responsive only to those stimuli that have a spiritual value. When the yogin finds that his mind is able to "detach" itself from those stimuli that are unnecessary and useless for his spiritual progress, he is ready for the next stage, *dharana*.

The word *dharana* means restricting the mind to one point. In practice, however, this stage is more comprehensive and connotes more than the literal meaning of the word would indicate. What is known as introversion of the mind, for example, plays a conspicuous rôle in *dharana*. While introversion and one-pointed concentration are both included in this stage, the former is only a step or aid in achieving the latter condition.

The practitioner is asked to let the continuous procession of thoughts, a kind of reverie which inevitably becomes real when relaxation follows upon pranayamic

through the *sushumna* [spinal cord?] to the *sahasrara* or the thousand-petalled center [upper cerebrum?]. *Kundalini*, then, is the divine power in man which when liberated becomes the causal factor in all higher experiences of the yogin. Quite naturally yogic descriptions are interspersed with references to this force. Some yogins have pointed out that, in the case of those who lay claim to casual mystical experiences, *kundalini* might be accidentally released.

breathing, take its own course. The mind may observe the thoughts in this stream as they come and go without attempting to restrict or control them. The mind is turned on itself, becoming a disinterested spectator of its own processes. The precept has been well described thus:

Seat yourself for a while and allow your thoughts to take their own course freely. It behaves like a frisky monkey. Let the monkey jump about; wait and take note. Your thoughts will entertain ugly ideas, so ugly that you will be surprised. But day by day, these errings will become less numerous and less extensive. During the first months you will have a thousand thoughts; then you will have no more than seven hundred; and the number will progressively diminish.[2]

The next development in introspective observation is one of singling out the thoughts. Up to this point the thoughts have been observed as a continuous stream, but now they are separated as distinct from one another. This is found, of course, to introduce a certain amount of artificial interference with the free flow of thoughts. In trying to observe each thought, one should make sure that the vague beginning, the rise, the highest peak, the fall, and the vague disappearance of each thought are well observed. Similarly, the next thought is taken as a separate entity and the student likewise follows its course. This procedure, according to yoga, reveals the fact that, although our thoughts appear to be continuous, in reality they are discrete.

Next, attention is to be directed to the interval between succeeding thoughts. One can understand the

[2] Baudouin, C.—*Suggestion and Autosuggestion*, 178; Dodd, Mead and Company, 1922.

yogic contention that the most important part of this stage begins with the observation of the vacuous gap between successive thoughts, when one realizes that their immediate aim is to make the *citta* (mind) calm and still. Since thoughts are the fluctuations or modifications of the mind-stuff, it is impossible to reach this goal until they are eliminated. The interval, however, is free from fluctuations and consequently it is to the yogins a good handle, as it were, for the prolongation of the vacuous state and the suppression of the rising thought. He who succeeds in this endeavor may be said to be well on his way to succeed in yoga. The idea that the pure self lies hidden behind the thoughts is conveyed by a metaphor in which the mind is compared to a necklace of beads where every bead is a thought. The thread runs through all the beads, but its existence, because it is covered by the beads, is not obvious. By separating two beads the hidden thread is bared. Likewise, when the gap between two thoughts is prolonged, one gets a "taste" of what the pure self is like. All the studied introspective efforts of yoga, therefore, are only attempts to bring the mind to a thoughtless state which is then prolonged.

Another road open to the yogin to achieve his special goal is that of concentration, where attention is focussed on a point. If a flower is chosen as the object of concentration, there is no consideration of its size, weight, or any other qualities whatsoever; it is mentally reduced to a point and kept before the mind as a mere idea. Any thought about the qualities or relations of objects only leads to a perpetual succession of ideas and this is precisely what the yogin wants to avoid. However barren this kind of focussing of the attention may seem, yogins claim that one-pointed concentration is dynamic enough to reach deeper levels of consciousness.

The object chosen for concentration may be mental or physical, the latter being either external to the body or within it. It is a usual practice of yogins to concentrate on certain spots in the body—the tip of the nose, the point between the eyebrows, the navel, etc. Imaginary objects also are sometimes employed.

Another method of creating a mental vacuum is by repeating innumerable times some sacred word like "ŌM". The two letters in the word are separated and uttered distinctly at a pitch that is kept more or less uniform throughout the period of repetition.[3]

Whatever the means, the goal is the same: to have before the mental eye nothing more than a bare idea. Attention remains spontaneously immobilized. An important point, the rôle of the will, should receive careful attention here. Does the yogin, in this state, have any sense of effort? In the initial stage of practice, before one gets used to holding the object for any considerable time, it may be necessary to exercise the will. But the

[3] It is a well-known fact that certain words have the power to arouse mild and sometimes intense states of ecstasy. Words like "Mesopotamia", "Philadelphia", "woods", "forests", etc., can sometimes transport people into realms of ecstatic feeling. Certain fragrant odors and musical sounds can open undreamt-of vistas. In a lesser degree words and phrases of lyric poetry have a similar effect on a great many minds. Repetition of one's own name can bring about a transformation in the mind. "A kind of waking trance I have frequently had," wrote Tennyson to a friend, "quite up from boyhood when I have been alone. This has generally come upon me through repeating my own name two or three times to myself silently, till all at once, as it were out of the intensity of the consciousness of individuality, the individuality itself seemed to dissolve and fade away into boundless being, and this is not a confused state, but the clearest of the clearest, the surest of the surest. . . ."

yogins claim that until one is able to induce this as a matter of habit and without any feeling of effort, one cannot be considered to have advanced very far. Whatever the will may be in philosophic language, it is, to the psychologist, nothing more than a muscular adjustment, with the accompanying feeling of effort.

One of the tangible results of relaxation is the diminution of effort and progressive disappearance of the will. The greatest contribution of the Nancy school of Coué is the demonstration that autosuggestion, to be effective, must be practised in that somnolent state just before sleep and after waking. To relax is passively to withdraw into ourselves—a condition contrary to the activities of the waking hours where the will is more or less an important determinant.

It would seem, therefore, that in the mental exercises of yoga a progressive relaxation is also accompanied by the diminution of the will until at last in the highest stage, that of *samadhi*, a complete paralysis of the will is reached. The will may intervene in the early stages to give a general twist to the mind in the direction of introversion and also to bring the wandering one-pointed object or idea again and again before the mental eye. But once the habit is developed, effort is replaced by spontaneity and, instead of having the attention hold the object, the object holds the attention.

The next stage, *dhyana* (meditation), in spite of its many points of likeness to the previous one, is technically considered a step beyond concentration (*dharana*). In actual fact both are merely stages of concentration. Even those who are not given to yogic practices may sometimes legitimately claim that they, too, can concen-

trate though only for a short period; hence the question
arises whether this can be classed as *dharana* or *dhyana*.
To make a practical distinction, yogins have introduced
the time factor. In pranayamic breathing, a holding period of a 12-second duration is usually considered the
lower limit. The upper limit is 108 seconds. A *dharana*
would then be twelve times pranayama, i.e., lower limit
144 seconds and the upper limit 1296 seconds, and a
dhyana twelve times *dharana*.

There is, in addition to the quantitative factor, a qualitative difference between *dharana* and *dhyana*. The nature of the object of concentration in the *dharana* stage
is invariably gross; during *dhyana*, on the contrary, the
gross matter "disappears" and leaves in its place the
subtle infra-atomic constituents which make up the ultimate elements of matter. The gross objects begin to give
way to their subtle form. The ability to perceive these
subtle things depends on the "purity" of the concentrat-
ing mind. Some minds do not advance beyond the gross
matter, but those that do are able to penetrate deeper
levels. By passing through varying degrees of subtlety
the yogin finally reaches the last state, trance-contemplation (*samadhi*).

Since *samadhi* is the last of the eight stages and the
goal towards which all efforts are directed, it is important to understand the nature of the yogin's experiences
in this condition. Even here several grades are said to
exist and the one quality which characterizes them all
is the relative or total loss of subject-object awareness.
That state in which the mind is one with the object
(*artha*), together with the concept (*jnana*) and the
name (*sabda*), called *savitarka*, is the lowest kind of

samadhi. The object remains gross because it is identified with concept and name. In short, the associations formed in our waking life still persist.

The next stage of samadhi, *nirvitarka*, is a grade higher than the above, in that the associations of name and concept are dropped off. The object is just the object without predicate relations. In the *savicara prajna*, the grossness of the object is no longer felt; its place is taken by the subtle constituents of matter (*tanmatras*). Perception, if one may call it such, is determinate because the tanmatras are subject to time, space, and causality. In the fourth kind of samadhi, *nirvicara*, the *tanmatras* are finally dispossessed of the conceptual notions of time, etc.

These four stages are also called *conscious-samadhi* (*samprajnata-samadhi*), because there is, though only vaguely, a union between the subject and the object; the object is, so to say, still there. The *buddhi* continues to function as long as the object remains and the feeling of personality, accompanied by deliberation (*vitarka*), reflection (*vicara*), and joy (*ananda*), persists.

But the yogin's aim is to surpass the *citta* stage entirely. This condition is reached in the *superconscious-samadhi* (*asamprajnata-samadhi*). Prakriti (nature), through *citta*, does not bind the purusha any more, the sense of personality and the resultant joy are no longer experienced. The ultimate truth dawns on the yogin and the purusha abides in itself. Inasmuch as it is not possible to remain in this condition indefinitely, complete deliverance is attained only after death.

Yoga claims, as we have mentioned before, that our ordinary knowledge is vitiated by concepts dealing with the general characteristics of things. This artificial cloak

—a veritable symbolic structure—keeps us from knowing things as they are. Consequently, the superconscious "perception" is the door that leads to a new insight, an insight which is considered superior to the knowledge derived through perception, inference, and valid testimony. If our language is not an effective vehicle for conveying this experience, it is because it deals with a different order of reality. Frequently, however, the yogin warns us that his negative description should not mislead us into thinking that it is a state of nescience. Consciousness in its purest form, with the potentiality for ideation, remains. It is not a negative state of absolute silence and darkness, but one of pure consciousness free from thoughts—a mill that does not grind.

Chapter XIII

YOGA: AN APPRAISAL

Our exposition of yoga in the previous chapters had one essential purpose: to reveal the basic metaphysical and metapsychological theories on which the system is based and the goal toward which the practitioner is striving. Judged from this angle, it is both an intellectual system and a practical way of life which give purpose and direction to its adherents.

Every culture has its own distinctive characteristics or patterns, its own particular *Weltanschauung*. In this respect yoga, like every other product of Hindu civilization, has shared the features of religion. While, to be sure, the philosophical aspects and intricacies of the practices of yoga were known only to a few, and were kept alive by oral transmission from one generation to the next, the masses inchoately felt it to be the natural consummation of the general trend of the culture.

Philosophical systems are an attempt of the human mind to present the problems of existence, life, meaning, and values in a comprehensive and consistent framework. It is probably fair to say that in all such systems, whether Eastern or Western, no problem has evoked a keener interest than that of the mind, particularly in its relation to the body. But the speculative theories advanced to explain the mind-body problem are invariably based on assumptions that are inaccessible to scientific methods. Religious and philosophical approaches, like the yoga, aim to explain the *ultimate nature of the mind*. The limbo of the unknown is admirably passive to all questions concerning ultimates; we may ask any question and receive the answer that pleases us most. Perhaps this is nature's kind way of making our otherwise precarious existence moderately reasonable and acceptable.

An intelligent evaluation of yoga, therefore, should make a distinction between its metapsychological theories, which are speculative, and the elements of practice that are amenable to experimental treatment. Our acceptance or rejection of the former as articles of belief would be influenced by our philosophical bias. But the experiences and developments claimed to follow upon yogic practices can and should be objectively verified.

In contrast with the religio-philosophical approach, modern psychology makes a modest, yet far-reaching, analysis of the mind-body problem. We say modest because, unlike the religio-philosophical approach, it does not and can not claim to reveal the ultimate nature of the mind or the body; yet far-reaching, because scientific method traces the delicate operations of the mind and their relationships in terms of cause and effect.

Traditional modes of thinking have in general perpetuated the notion that the mind and the body are two different substantial entities. As long as this notion persisted, it was difficult to make a scientific appraisal of psychological problems. Today, closely following the findings of the various biological sciences, we are forced to think of the mind as a function of the integrated organism. Mental operations no doubt constitute the highest function of the delicately balanced organism. Any deep-going structural change is inevitably accompanied by a corresponding change in the function. We all know that physical illness is accompanied by low spirits, mental cloudiness and lack of "pep". Would any religio-philosophical theory of the mind advance our knowledge of the causes determining this change? Obviously not. This would demand an experimental study of the bodily processes.

For all practical purposes it is simple enough to distinguish mental and muscular work. No one would ever doubt that the conclusions embodied in Einstein's formulae involved work of a kind different from that of ditch-digging. In both cases, however, there is transformation of energy from one form to another which may be measured in various ways. Work, muscular or mental, is invariably accompanied by a general increase in metabolism and the factors that contribute to this change are present, though in different degrees, in both kinds of work. Although we do not consider Johnny's effort at multiplication physical work, for purposes of description and analysis we are forced to take into consideration all the physical and chemical changes that take place in the organism, realizing full well that much concerning the underlying processes is still unknown to us. Instead of classifying certain types of work as mental and others as physical, the psychologists are more and more beginning to study all work as activities of an integrated organism. As long as we bear in mind that the underlying cause of all changes in the organism is physico-chemical, it is equally possible, and sometimes necessary, to approach certain problems from the mental side.

The above remarks lead to one conclusion. No matter whether we approach from the side of the higher mental processes or from that of the physical aspects, the organism emerges as an integrated whole—an inseparable but distinguishable unity of physical and mental factors. The treatment of the mind-body problem as two aspects of an integrated organism, distinguishable for purposes of experimentation and understanding but wholly unreal when separated, has proved more fertile and seems to offer a very satisfactory explanation of the problems of psychology. The trend in this direction has always existed, but today more than ever before would no experimentalist present or discuss psychological problems in any other framework.

We may now turn our attention to the results of a few experiments in which the writer was the only subject. It is only proper, however, to warn the reader against an over-enthusiastic evaluation of our results. The limitations are too manifold for that. All of the studies were made with one subject—a very unsatisfactory condition for any precise experimental conclusion. The preliminary preparation, conformation to all regulations concerning diet and daily routine, etc., was by no means what it would be in the case of one who determinedly undergoes yogic discipline as a way of life and a means to salvation. In short, what is presented here should be regarded chiefly as exploratory work with no claims to conclusiveness. The lesson that some of these problems can be isolated from the totality of the system and brought into the laboratory is, however, significant. With further advance in the technique of psychological experimentation, we should undoubtedly be able to deepen our knowledge of the mental modifications and experiences of the higher stages of yoga.

The writer learned the technique of the yogic practices from Swami Kuvalayananda, of Lonavla, with whom he spent a year in India from April, 1932 to March, 1933. In order to conform as much as possible to the yogic demands of a life of "detachment", the subject has tried his best, with partial success, to lead a relatively quiet life. When the experiments were commenced in the spring of 1935 he had nearly three years of experience in some varieties of yogic breathing. His daily practice generally consisted of 30 minutes of *ujjayi* (one of the important types of pranayama) followed by 20-30 minutes of concentration.

The well-known method of mental testing was utilized to derive a quantitative measure of the mental changes. Five tests were employed. In setting up the experiments we were particularly anxious to answer two important questions: What is the effect on the mind, as revealed by the results of the tests, of (1) 30 minutes of ujjayi (one variety of breathing) and (2) 30 minutes of ujjayi followed by 20 minutes of concentration? To answer both of these questions, it was necessary to take the tests under two experimental conditions. On 36 days the tests were administered both before and after breathing only, and on another 36 days before and after breathing followed by concentration. These two situations were alternated, i.e., if on a certain day the subject did only the yogic breathing, the day after would be devoted to

TABLE SHOWING THE RESULTS OF THE FIVE TESTS

NAME OF THE TEST	BREATHING					BREATHING AND CONCENTRATION					
	(1) Normal Time in Seconds	(2) Experimental Time in Seconds	(3) Amount of Increase in Experimental Time in Seconds	(4) Percent Change in Efficiency	(5) Chances in 100 that the Difference is Genuine (Nearly)	(6) Normal Time in Seconds	(7) Experimental Time in Seconds	(8) Amount of Increase in Experimental Time in Seconds	(9) Percent Change in Efficiency	(10) Chances in 100 that the Difference is Genuine (Nearly)	(11) Percent Change in Efficiency when Concentration was introduced
ADDING TEST	274.6	300.7	26.1	—9.5	100	274.2	305.2	31.0	—11.3	100	—1.8
CODE TEST	222.0	231.0	9.0	—4.0	100	217.6	231.9	14.3	—6.6	100	—2.6
COLOR NAMING TEST	51.0	57.7	6.7	—13.1	100	50.3	57.2	6.9	—13.7	100	—0.6
COÖRDINATION TEST	24.6	25.6	1.0	—4.1	99	25.2	26.6	1.4	—5.6	100	—1.5
CHINESE PUZZLE TEST	188.6	195.3	6.7	—3.6	93.5	188.2	201.4	13.2	—7.0	100	—3.4

breathing and concentration, and so on. In the preceding Table we have summarized the results of the five tests.

We can readily gather from column 11 that the introduction of the 20-minute period of concentration has increased the test time over the first experimental condition, i.e., when the yogic practice consisted of breathing only. Both of these increases are not any too appreciable. In trying to answer the question concerning the effect of mental concentration as revealed by the tests, let us remind ourselves of the following query: What would probably be the result if the subject had practised yogic breathing for 50 minutes instead of introducing the 20-minute period of concentration after 30 minutes of breathing? The figures in column 4 show the percent change in efficiency after 30 minutes of breathing. On the basis of these figures we may naturally expect a greater increase of time (this is the same as decrease in efficiency) if breathing were continued for a further period of 20 minutes (a total of 50 minutes). This is not to say that concentration did not influence the results. We may rightly conclude, therefore, that breathing and concentration tend to decrease the mental functions. As to whether concentration is better adapted for this purpose than breathing, as is sometimes popularly thought, we must give a negative answer.

While the mental state as borne out by the tests indicates a retardation of mental functions in both pranayama (breathing) and concentration, it does not necessarily follow that the subjective experiences of the practitioner under both conditions are similar; on the contrary, yogins maintain that they are different. Breathing alone, no matter for how long, would not induce the higher experiences so ardently longed for by them. Concentration practices constitute an essential preliminary condition for these.[1]

Here we may touch upon another popular misconception concerning yoga in relation to mental training. Those who are inclined to believe that yoga is a beneficial training for mental development may be a little surprised by our conclusion that there is a retardation of mental functions after yogic practices. But we have not even raised, let alone answered, the question as to what effect these practices have on the mind over a long period of time. While the retardation effect is apparent immediately after the practices, we do not know how long the effect would be operative, or whether our normal intellectual faculties are improved after the immediate effect has waned.[2] There is no experimental evidence, therefore, either to support or disprove the popular notion that these practices can improve one's intellectual faculties (in the broad sense including memory, logical acumen, etc.).

The yogic contention that by these practices the mind is turned inward and "detached" from the external world of normal waking life is to some extent confirmed by our results. This, however, does not give us an insight into the nature of the bodily changes occurring in this condition. We would like to know, for example, whether the state of the organism during the yogic practices is comparable, at any rate in certain respects, to that in-

[1] The writer is convinced from his own practices that concentration introduces a new stage in the subjective experiences of the practitioner.

[2] My conclusion (subjective, of course) is that yogic practices do not influence intellectual life either way, favorably or unfavorably.

duced by voluntary relaxation. From our own experience we can distinguish the difference in the feelings of tension accompanying a state of mental activity and one of mental passivity. The same task sometimes requires greater effort on one's part under a different stimulational setting. When we are disturbed by noises pouring in from all sides, nothing but greater effort can accomplish the same task which might have been performed easily under more favorable circumstances. But what are the physiological accompaniments of such concepts as "effort", "attention", etc., which we are so accustomed to use in everyday life? Or, what makes reactions relatively slower in a state of relaxation?

The results of an elaborate study by Dr. Edmund Jacobson on the effects of voluntary relaxation upon mental functions are contained in his book, *Progressive Relaxation.*[3] He found that many patients and normal subjects could develop, after considerable training with one muscle-group after another, the skill and ability to relax the whole body at once. Under extreme relaxation the subject would lie entirely motionless except for the movement of the respiratory muscles. His subjects agreed that visual imagery failed to appear with relaxation of the ocular region. Furthermore, when the muscles of the lips, tongue, and throat were relaxed, the so-called "silent speech" also disappeared.

In another important study, Dr. A. G. Bills[4] of Chicago created tension in his subjects by making them

[3] Jacobson, E.—*Progressive Relaxation;* The University of Chicago Press, 1929.

[4] Bills, A. G.—"The Influence of Muscular Tension on the Efficiency of Mental Work", *American Journal of Psychology*, Vol. 38, 1927..

grasp a dynamometer during the performance of a variety of mental tests like memorization of syllables, adding columns of digits, etc. In general it was found that efficiency increased with tension, that is to say, heightened muscular tone increased mental effectiveness.

The general conclusion to be drawn from experiments of this nature is that neuromuscular tension is closely related to mental functions. When the tension is less, such functions become proportionately less efficient. The physiological correlate of mental activity is, therefore, the contraction of the musculature which in turn is controlled by the nervous system. In technical language the tense state of the muscle is referred to as one of tonicity. It is true that in our experiments we have no objective record of the measure of tension or muscle tone during deep breathing and concentration. Yet, as judged by the results of our tests, it is difficult to refrain from the conclusion that there is a similarity between the neuromuscular condition under yogic breathing and concentration, on the one hand, and the state of relaxation and reduced tension indicated by the above experiments, on the other.

It seems very probable, then, that the pranayamic breathing of yoga induces a state of relaxation, thereby influencing the mind to take an "inward" course.[5] In the period of concentration following upon breathing this relaxation is further advanced by the reduction in the movement of the body which in turn lessens propriocep-

[5] In the writer's opinion the subjective evidence for the relaxation during yogic breathing and concentration is incontrovertible. One becomes aware of progressive relaxation as the breathing proceeds. During concentration relaxation is so complete as to make one "forget the presence of the body".

tive stimulation, i.e., the stimuli that have their origin in the body.

But one might ask why the yogic way of inducing relaxation does not lead to sleep, while Jacobson's subjects pointed out that progressive relaxation culminated in a complete loss of consciousness. As a matter of fact, yogic teachers invariably advise the practitioner to guard against a natural inclination to sleep in the course of concentration and meditation—an indirect proof of the underlying similarity between the two states. The yogins, however, counteract this inclination with their effort to concentrate. This, we should think, is enough to explain the differential result. Since relaxation leads to a condition of general passivity, any attempt at concentration—and that too according to the difficult technique of yoga—would be like trying to swim against the current. Yogins are the only persons who, as a group, have made such practices a part of their mental training. We may presume, therefore, that such practices may lead, as the yogins claim, to interesting mental modifications as yet unknown to present-day experimental psychology.

Inasmuch as yoga has sometimes been equated with partial or complete hypnosis, we may make a few relevant observations in passing. Recent researches [6] have conclusively shown that sleep and hypnosis are different phenomena when viewed from the angle of underlying physiological changes. While automatic reactions (reflexes) are abolished in sleep, they are not influenced by hypnosis. These reactions are reduced, however, under

[6] Hull, C. L.—*Hypnosis and Suggestibility;* D. Appleton-Century Company, 1933.

progressive relaxation. If, as we have already indicated, the earlier stages of yoga are anything like the state induced by progressive relaxation, we may venture the opinion that hypnotic phenomena are far removed from the mental modifications of yoga. Intellectual functions, furthermore, are not abolished or even reduced in hypnotic trances. Our experiments have shown, however, that yogic practices, as in progressive relaxation, retard the mental functions.

An hypnotized person has no memory of what had transpired during the trance (except when it is suggested that he remember). But the yogins are relatively conscious of their experience during and after the trance. Their statements of indescribable joy and blissfulness certainly are indicative of a *real* remembered experience which, because of its sheer ineffability, is found difficult to convey through the medium of language. The experience itself may be transitory, but it does leave a vivid impression on the practitioner—so vivid and blissful as to make him long for further trance experiences. This is an important point of difference between the two.

There is one feature which is strikingly common to both hypnosis and yoga. It is well known that hypnosis can be induced by staring steadily at an object or by thinking exclusively of one idea. This monoideism has its parallel in yoga during the meditative period when the yogin aims to eliminate from the mind everything but the thought of the minute object of concentration.

Hypnosis comprises various stages ranging from mild drowsiness to deep trance. Yoga, likewise, has its gradations of experience. We might expect, therefore, that it would be possible to indicate, as we have done, elements that are similar and others that are different. Experimentally, however, we know only very little about hypnotic phenomena and practically nothing about the *samadhic* (trance) stage of yoga. It would be mere speculation of doubtful value either to affirm or deny that the two are essentially similar. Without further research no fruitful purpose would be served by such speculations.

It is well known that oxygen is the prime sustainer of life. Apparently the breathing exercises of yoga must be, on the physiological side, a direct aid to increasing oxygen consumption. In a series of experiments we measured the rate of oxygen consumption in *ujjayi*, *bhastrika*, and *kapalabhati*.[7]

Taking normal breathing as a basis of comparison it was found that oxygen consumption increased 24.5 percent in ujjayi, 18.5 percent in bhastrika, and 12 percent in kapalabhati. The three types have, therefore, distinctively great oxygen value—the greatest increase was noted in ujjayi. Since each cycle of bhastrika and kapalabhati is preceded by several rapid, shallow respirations, the duration of each cycle for these two types would naturally be longer than the corresponding cycles in ujjayi. From the average rate of 28 cycles in 22 minutes in ujjayi, it was seen that the subject could conveniently manage with 76 respirations per hour. It may be pointed out that the wearing of the mask and other inconveniences of laboratory experimentation must have tended to reduce the duration of each cycle.

It is popularly thought that the yogic period of concentration is characterized by a lower level of breathing

[7] The technique of these breathing practices is described in Chapter XI.

than is found during normal. In our experiments, when concentration came after ujjayi, oxygen consumption increased 5 percent over normal. In bhastrika and kapalabhati, however, there was a decrease of 5 and 2 percent, respectively. The decrease of 5 percent in concentration when it came after bhastrika was striking enough to deserve further experimental attention. But the results showed no appreciable reduction in the level of breathing. In short, the popular notion concerning the lower level of breathing during yogic concentration practices is not borne out by our results. If there be any significant difference, it is not translatable in terms of oxygen consumption.

Yogic breathing routines on the physical side constitute a bodily exercise. Can we say that this is any different from other kinds of gymnastic exercises? Is there anything that may be considered unique about this? Increased oxygen consumption, which is characteristic of yogic breathing, in itself does not mark it off as different from other kinds of exercises, because any kind of exertion involves an increase in metabolic rate which is manifested by the greater intake of oxygen. A few details, like the tipping of the head during the holding period and inspiration and expiration with half-closed glottis, may appear to be unique features. Until we have positive evidence concerning the physiological changes introduced by these details, however, it does not seem reasonable to believe that they are a very important part of the system.

One thing seems rather unique. In yogic breathing, while the respiratory muscles are exercised in the execution of deep cycles, the other groups of muscles remain

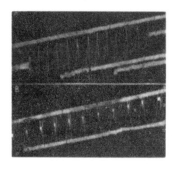

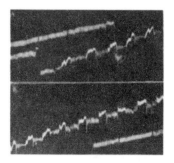

RECORDS OF TWO VARIETIES
OF YOGIC BREATHING

A. Ujjayi
B. Bhastrika

A RECORD OF THE KAPALA-
BHATIC VARIETY OF YOGIC
BREATHING

A. First Part
B. Second Part

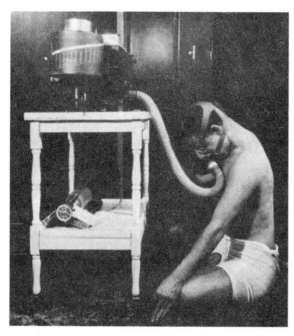

SUBJECT AND THE APPARATUS IN OXYGEN CONSUMP-
TION EXPERIMENTS

relatively inactive. Thus it differs markedly from the deep breathing incident to riding a bicycle. Here, although the trunk and arms are rather inactive, they can hardly be relaxed and the lower limbs are called upon to do vigorous exercise.

The different stages of the respiratory act are executed with calculated deliberation. The contraction and relaxation of the respiratory muscles are accomplished slowly, while jerky movements are avoided. It would seem reasonable, therefore, to believe that the chief purpose of the yogic breathing exercises is to increase the consumption of oxygen with the minimum of physical exertion, under conditions probably favorable to the storage of oxygen.

At best, the above experimental results have answered certain specific questions. We should like, however, to make a qualitative appraisal of yoga as well. Does it help the practitioner to arouse deeper levels of energy? Is it conducive to a feeling of equanimity? In short, we may ask whether the sum total of these practices leads to an alteration of personality, attitudes, and the manner in which we react to the ups and downs of everyday life.

One of the great problems of individual psychology is to map out the upper and lower limits of human efficiency and powers. Just as it is possible to stretch a rubber band to a certain limit without breaking it, so the human mind, in like fashion, has always shown an unusual capacity to muster untapped reserves of energy when confronted with obstacles. Biographies are full of episodes in which, by infinite patience and perseverance, human beings have demonstrated their ability to rise higher than they had ever dreamed possible. Of course,

like everything else, this phenomenon has its limits; but
it should make us wonder if we are fully aware of the
limits of our powers. One who has been too weak to
carry a load across the street may be seen carrying his
wife and children out of a house which is on fire. Everyone must be familiar with such examples of heroism of
which the human organism is capable under excitement.

The key that unlocks these deeper reservoirs may
differ with individuals. A passing display of the American flag is enough in some to open the flood-gates of
moral enthusiasm and great deeds. Religious, economic,
and political conversions are equally crystallized emotional transitions that call forth higher degrees of moral
ardor. Who could deny that there has been an alteration
in the personality of a new recruit to Christian Science?
All these are realities of daily life which we are as yet
unable to represent in terms of charts and weights.

The systematized practices of yoga seem somehow to
be able to arouse, little by little as the practice progresses, this indomitable power of the human mind. The
late William James devoted a great deal of his time to
gathering the personal testimony of those who had undergone mental regeneration, including Western practitioners of yoga. Basing his evaluations on a letter from a
European friend of his who had practised yoga, James
has the following to say:

But the most venerable ascetic system, and the one whose
results have the most voluminous experimental [?] corrobo-
ration is undoubtedly the Yoga system in Hindustan. . . .
The result claimed, and certainly in many cases accorded by
impartial judges, is strength of character, personal power,
unshakability of soul . . . a very gifted European friend of

mine who, by persistently carrying out for several months its methods of fasting from food and sleep, its exercises in breathing and thought-concentration, and its fantastic posture gymnastics, seems to have succeeded in waking up deeper and deeper levels of will and moral and intellectual power in himself, and to have escaped from a decidedly menacing brain-condition of the "circular" type, from which he had suffered for years. . . . A profound modification has unquestionably occurred in the running of his mental machinery. The gearing has changed, and his will is available otherwise than it was.[8]

My own experience with yoga and yogins agrees so well with the opinion of James that the above quotation, though lengthy, is an apt introduction to what I have to say.

I have had no complaints whatsoever which may be considered as due to organic defects either before starting yogic practices or since engaging in them. In the few years before taking up these practices, however, I was in a generally run-down condition, a victim of frequent headaches and a general condition which may be colloquially described as one of lack of "pep". Needless to say, I did not commence yogic practices for any amelioration of these ills; on the contrary, the mere belief that an objective study would be facilitated by practising the exercises myself led me to undertake them.

A few months after beginning the practices in April, 1932, a distinct change was noticeable in my health. No work, physical or mental, could tire me so rapidly as it did before. This phase may be summarized as an increase in my resistance capacity or power of endurance. My

[8] James, W.—*On Vital Reserves*, 26-28; Henry Holt and Company, 1911.

susceptibility to frequent headaches also was diminished considerably.

Sitting in one of the meditative postures to practise yogic breathing was, in the beginning, a matter of considerable difficulty, causing severe pain. The knees tended to form an angle to the floor. Since the difficulty centered mainly around the inflexibility of the hips, I began by folding one leg and by keeping it in that position for several minutes. With practice, the hips became very flexible. It would be interesting to point out that this posture, which gave me considerable difficulty in the beginning, now, after four years, is executed with perfect ease and gives an unmistakable feeling of relaxation and passivity.

Maintaining an erect spine while sitting in the meditative posture did not involve any discomfort. There are two gazes, described in Chapter X, which form part of the technique of the meditative postures. In one of them the gaze is directed to the tip of the nose, and in the other, to the midpoint between the eyebrows. These are claimed to be helpful in concentration. I am convinced that the nasal gaze—this alone of the two was utilized by me—is an aid to checking the wandering propensities of the mind, but when practised too long in one sitting it resulted sometimes in a feeling of strain. I have no doubt that, if carelessly done, this practice might lead to unfavorable complications.

The most difficult part in mastering the technique of the breathing exercises was that of regulating the speed of each cycle and the time ratio between inspiration, retention, and exhalation—a matter claimed by yogins to be of considerable importance. I overcame this difficulty by mental counting. Here, also, a few months of practice enabled me to achieve a satisfactory uniformity. I no longer find it necessary to count; the act has attained the precision of a well-established habit.[9] Tipping the head to bring the chin to touch the jugular notch forms a characteristic feature of yogic breathing, and great results are said to follow from it. My feeling, however, is that it merely makes retention easier.

The breathing part of my practices may be divided into two phases. In the first few minutes (approximately 15 to 20) I feel a "physical excitement", if I may use this uncommon expression. I feel as if my system were very active and alive; an activeness which sometimes leads to the erection of hairs in the follicles on the trunk and hands, and this phenomenon is followed by a tingling sensation. Sometimes muffled sounds are heard within the ears and the phenomenon generally known as the "flight of colors"—different colors seen in rapid succession—is not an uncommon occurrence.[10]

In the second stage all this excitement dies down and is followed by an extremely pleasant feeling of quietude and relaxation. Every kind of noise now becomes very disturbing. Kinesthetic sensations are at a minimum. Slowly, but unmistakably, one begins to feel that the mind takes a turn, becoming more and more "centripetal". When I find that I have practised breathing for a time sufficiently long—generally about 30 minutes—to

[9] That this remarkable consistency of time proportion between each cycle holds throughout the practice period has been borne out by the laboratory experiments.

[10] The highly metaphorical and allegorical language of the yogic literature may easily be explained as superb exaggeration of these well-known physiological phenomena.

induce this pleasant feeling of quietude and isolation, I begin ordinarily the period of concentration.[11]

It has been very difficult for me to keep the object of concentration before the mental eye. Before I know it, I am thinking of something else, and considerable effort is required to keep up concentration successfully. Practice has shown progressive improvement, and what was accomplished with great effort in the early days has become relatively easy. Very often it happens that, when and if concentration is successful, the object becomes vague and ill-defined, a condition which leads to a kind of mental vacuity. In this condition any sense of effort is lacking, though dimly I am aware of what is happening. On the affective side, this condition is one of extreme pleasantness, and I would like to prolong it indefinitely if it were in my power to do so. Before I know it, however, I am out of this state and there is no more vagueness about the object of concentration. An interesting observation that I have made just as I come out of this hazy period is the consciousness of a change in the level of respiration, i.e., I am struck with the fact that in that condition my respirations have been very few and shallow. Our experiments, however, do not point to an actual decrease in the rate or depth of respiration; hence I am inclined to believe that this is a purely subjective feeling. All through the period of concentration one becomes less and less aware of the body, and as concentration wanes the process of respiration forces itself on one's consciousness. Probably this may lead one to believe, as in my case, that respiration may have been at a reduced

[11] Yogic breathing and concentration are practised with the eyes closed.

level during concentration and more particularly in the state of relative mental vacuity.

In spite of the inevitable subjectivity of the above remarks, I cannot refrain from putting on record a change in my own emotional life which seems somehow to be an outgrowth of these practices. They have led to an emotional stability and balance which I do not remember having possessed prior to taking up these exercises. Of what does this mental-emotional integration consist? In the final analysis, I think, it is that quality of inner feeling which is the subjective counterpart of our reactions to the events of the world, particularly those that immediately affect our own personality. This inner quality, immeasurable though it may be, has changed in me as yogic discipline has progressed. My mental-emotional life is no longer a blind catch-as-catch-can and, unlike the two snakes that intertwined their bodies so inextricably as to make each feel the other a part of itself, I seem relatively able to prevent self-victimization by emotional extremes. Here I may add that this discipline has in no way influenced my intellectual outlook.

James' appraisal is in my opinion essentially correct. I have had the privilege of watching at close range the daily lives of more than a half-dozen yogins for over a period of one year. I can testify without any reservation that they were the happiest personalities that I have known. Their serenity was contagious and in their presence I felt always that I was dealing with people who held great "power" in reserve. If the saying "radiant personality" means anything, it should be applied to them.

The physiological basis of the emotions is becoming

more and more one of the important fields of research. In his book, *The Wisdom of the Human Body*, Professor Cannon [12] has discussed at length how organisms composed of materials characterized by the utmost inconstancy and unsteadiness have somehow learned the methods of maintaining constancy and steadiness in the face of profoundly disturbing physical conditions. The physical basis, according to him, is to be sought in the "homeostasis of blood sugar", etc. Yogic practices perhaps lead to what may be called the homeostasis of emotion. It seems to awaken deeper levels of energy. Recent studies have shown the supreme importance of the changes in the secretions of certain endocrine glands for personality development. The changes in the mental-emotional life and consequently in the personality of the practitioner may, in all probability, be mediated through transformations in the glandular system.

The graduated series of exercises, which offers a practical way of achieving emotional stability, distinguishes yoga from other systems of discipline whether religious or moral. Almost all systems expect of their adherents some kind of change in attitudes and the quality of inner response, but they fail to offer a practical way of achieving this change. Whatever may be one's opinion of the yogic theory of the mind and its evolution, its success in developing a healthy emotional equilibrium is empirically verifiable. Nor does one need to reach the higher stages of its practices to attain this desirable adjustment. Whether or not the yogic way of life is desirable in its entirety is beside the point. It offers a practical program

[12] Cannon, W. B.—*The Wisdom of the Human Body;* W. W. Norton and Company, 1932.

for the attainment of what any judicious person would admit is an enviable frame of mind—one that is not easily perturbed by emotional conflicts.

In defending their metaphysical system the yogins, along with other mystics, may claim that their certainty is based on supernormal experiences. Their experiences are claimed to be face-to-face presentations rather than logical deductions and, to them, the reality experienced is not of doubtful validity but of a certainty that is equal to, if not greater than, the knowledge presented through sense data. While there is unanimity of agreement among all mystics with regard to the affective nature of their experiences, irrespective of the extreme diversity of the philosophical presuppositions, we search in vain for any kind of clear, objective interpretation of the content of experience. The vedantist [13] in his mystical state finds that Brahman is the sole reality in which the individual soul (Atman) is merged, while the yogin "sees" his own soul (purusha) existing as a separate entity. On the other hand, the Christian mystics in general conclude that personality is never lost. Again, from the point of view of the intellectual content, naturalistic mystics fall into a different group. To each, then, the absolutely certain experience of the mystical state provides a valid justification for his own particular intellectual outlook.

In the face of such extreme diversity of intellectual interpretations, the objectivity of mystical perception becomes a matter of questionable validity. To be sure, the experience itself is sufficiently real and valid to the yogin

[13] Indian school of monistic idealism which believes that the physical universe is only an appearance—illusion (maya)—and that Brahman is the sole reality.

to be the starting point of a new set of values. The "measuring rod" of value which we employ in our judgments is peculiarly our own, and in this respect the mystics differ from the vast majority of mankind whose "rod" is based on the reality of knowledge and experience arrived at through the senses.

But is an intensely real experience, no matter how certain it might seem to the experiencer, by itself a proof of the objectivity of what is experienced? [14] On the contrary, the diversity of intellectual interpretations should incline us to believe that the supernormal experiences are, to say the least, predominantly subjective. They constitute no valid source of knowledge. For those who are incorrigibly wedded to the belief that philosophical superstructure can reveal absolute truth we can do no better than quote the words of a contemporary philosopher, George Santayana:

What is the function of philosophy? To disclose absolute truth? But is it credible that the absolute truth should descend into the thoughts of a mortal creature, equipped with a few special senses and a biassed intellect, a man lost amidst millions of his fellows and a prey to the epidemic delusions of the race? [15]

As far as the metaphysical tenets of yoga are concerned, they are an audacious and poetic leap in the dark

[14] "To distinguish between what is subjective and what is objective about our experience is frequently difficult, even in physical observation; but especially in the experience of the mystic, the objects are difficult to grasp, while the inner event is comparatively tangible. It would be strange if there were not a general tendency to mistake one for the other." (Hocking, W. E.—*The Meaning of God in Human Experience*, 352; Yale University Press, 1912.)

[15] Santayana, G.—*The Realm of Essence*, Preface XIII; Constable and Company, London, 1928.

—worthy enough to occupy a spacious hall in the "Mansions of Philosophy" that the human mind has spun in its irresistible desire to explain the warp and woof of the unknown.

> *"With his night-cap and his night-shirt tatters*
> *He botches up the loop-holes in the structure of the*
> *world."*

APPENDIX

Kaivalyadhama was founded by Swami Kuvalayananda in 1924 with a view towards furthering the objectives of yoga and of developing the social usefulness of its practices. This institution is located in Lonavla, a hill station in the Bombay Presidency.

The activities of Kaivalyadhama have received encouragement and support from several Indian States and two Provincial Governments of British India. A system of *yogic physical culture* has been worked out by the founder-director, Swami Kuvalayananda. *Yogic therapy* is rendering valuable service to many patients from all parts of India. A new Health Center under the auspices of Kaivalyadhama has been opened in Bombay.

The results of laboratory researches conducted at Kaivalyadhama are published in the quarterly journal, *Yoga-Mimansa*. This journal gives accurate descriptions of various yogic postures and other exercises.

In spite of the various cultural and humanitarian activities in which it is engaged, Kaivalyadhama has not lost sight of the ultimate goal of yoga. An exclusively spiritual center is available for those who seek salvation through complete adherence to the yogic discipline.

GLOSSARY

AHAM BRAHMA ASMI, I am Brahman; I am one with the universal soul.

AHAMKĀRA, the "I" sense.

AHIMSĀ, the doctrine of non-violence.

ĀKĀŚA, ether; space; sky.

ĀNANDA, bliss.

ANTAḤ-KARAṆA, the inner-organ; a collective name for *buddhi* (*intellect*), *ahaṃkāra* (the "I" sense), and *manas* (the organ of synthesis and coördination).

AP, water.

ARTHA, the object in its meaning.

ĀRYAN, noble; a member of the ethnic group of the Indo-Europeans who invaded India probably in the first half of the second millennium B.C.

ASAMPRAJÑĀTA-SAMĀDHI, the stage of trance-contemplation in which the subject is not conscious of the object of concentration.

ĀSANA, posture; the third stage in the yogic curriculum.

AŚVINĪ-MUDRĀ, an exercise of the anal sphincters.

ĀTMAN, self; soul.

AVIDYĀ, cosmic ignorance; non-discrimination.

AVIŚESHA, unspecialized form.

ĀYĀMA, pause.

BANDHA, lock; one of a group of yogic exercises involving certain anatomical parts.

BHAGAVAD GĪTĀ, The Song of the Lord; the most sacred book of the Hindu Scriptures.

BHASTRIKĀ, one of the eight varieties of the yogic breathing exercises.

BHRĀMARĪ, one of the eight varieties of the yogic breathing exercises.

BHŪTĀDI, rudimentary matter devoid of physical characters.

BRAHMADANDA, the rod of Brahman; the spinal column.

BRAHMAN, the ultimate reality; a member of the priestly caste.

BRĀHMAŅA, a theological commentary on the vedic sacrifices.

BRAHMANĀDĪ, the nerve of Brahman; the spinal cord.

BRAHMIN, a member of the priestly caste.

BUDDHI, the individual basis of intellection.

CIT (pronounced *chit*), the pure, relating element of consciousness.

CITTA (pronounced *chitta*), the mind-stuff.

DHĀRAŅĀ, concentration; the sixth stage in the yogic curriculum.

DHYĀNA, meditation; the seventh stage in the yogic curriculum.

GUŅA, strand; quality; constituent.

GURU, teacher.

IŅĀ, the left ganglionic chain; the left nostril.

ĪŚVARA, personal god.

JÑĀNA, conceptual experience; mental modification.

KAPĀLABHĀTI, a purificatory exercise for the body consisting of short-rhythm, shallow breathing.

KĀRAŅACITTA (pronounced *kāraṇachitta*), the mind-stuff in its causal aspect; collective mind-stuff.

KARMA, the doctrine of causality in the mental-moral world.

KĀRYACITTA (pronounced *kāryachitta*), the mind-stuff in its resultant aspect; individual mind-stuff.

KSHAŅA, moment.

KSHITI, earth.

KUMBHAKA, retention (of air in or out of the body).

KUŅŅALINĪ, the spiritual or psychical energy said to be located somewhere in the lower abdominal region.

LIŅGA ŚARĪRA, subtle or psychical body.

MAHAT, the first evolute of *prakriti*; *buddhis* in the collective aspect.

MANAS, mind; the organ of coördination and assimilation.

MĀYĀ, appearance; illusion; mystical nature.

MERUDĀNDA, a vertical rod; the spinal column.

MUDRĀ, a symbol; one of a group of yogic exercises involving certain anatomical parts.

MŪLĀDHĀRA, the principal source; sacro-coccygeal plexus(?).

MŪRCHCHHĀ, one of the eight varieties of the yogic breathing exercises.

NĀDĪ, nerve.

NĀVICHAKRA, the pelvic area.

NIRVĀNA, the Buddhist conception of the highest good; the spiritual equilibrium in which the passions have ceased to rage.

NIRVIKALPA, indeterminate.

NIRVITARKA, the stage of concentration in which the object appears without the name-concept associations.

NIYAMA, moral law in its positive aspect; the second stage in the yogic curriculum.

ŌM, a sacred syllable symbolic of vedic knowledge.

PARAMĀNU, a gross atom.

PIÑGALĀ, the right ganglionic chain; the right nostril.

PLĀVINĪ, one of the eight varieties of the yogic breathing exercises.

PRAKRITI, primordial, undifferentiated matter.

PRALAYA, the quiescent state of cessation from evolution.

PRĀNA, breath.

PRĀNĀYĀMA, breath control; a yogic breathing exercise; the fourth stage in the yogic curriculum.

PRATYĀHĀRA, sense-withdrawal; the fifth stage in the yogic curriculum.

PŪRAKA, inhalation.

PURUSHA, soul.

RAJAS, energy-stuff.

RECHAKA, exhalation.

RIG-VEDA, the oldest of the four vedas.

ŚABDA, sound.

ŚABDA TANMĀTRA, sound-potential.

SAHASRĀRA, thousand-petalled [nerve center]; cerebrum.

SAMĀDHI, trance-contemplation; the last stage (eighth) in the yogic curriculum.

SĀMKHYA, one of the six systems of Indian philosophy; the philosophy of number (25 categories).

SĀMKHYA KĀRIKĀ, the basic text of the sāmkhya philosophy; sāmkhya aphorism.

SAMPRAJÑĀTA-SAMĀDHI, the stage of trance-contemplation in which the subject is conscious of the object of concentration.

SAMSKĀRA, the root-impression of past deeds.

SĀMYĀVASTHĀ, undifferentiated condition; state of equilibrium.

SATTVA, intelligence-stuff.

SAVICĀRA PRĀJÑĀ (pronounced *savichara*), the stage of concentration in which the object has lost its grossness.

SAVIKALPA, determinate.

SAVITARKA, the stage of concentration in which the mind is aware of the name and qualities of the object.

SĪTALĪ, one of the eight varieties of the yogic breathing exercises.

SĪTKĀRĪ, one of the eight varieties of the yogic breathing exercises.

SMRITI, memory; law books.

SOMA, an intoxicating juice.

SPHOTA, notion; concept.

SROTRAYA, a professional vedic student.

SŪRYA, the sun.

SŪRYABHEDANA, one of the eight varieties of the yogic breathing exercises.

SUSHUMNĀ, the spinal cord.

TAMAS, inertia-stuff.

TANMĀTRA, mere thatness; potentiality devoid of qualities.

TAT TVAM ASI, that thou art.

TATTWA, category; reality; product.

TEJAS, light; brilliance; refulgence.

UJJĀYĪ, one of the eight varieties of the yogic breathing exercises.

UPANISHAD, secret teaching; a philosophical treatise.

VAIRĀGYA, passionlessness.

VAISHAMYA, differentiatedness.

VĀSANĀ, the tendency determined by past lives.

VĀYU, air.

VEDA, one of the four earliest compositions of the Āryans.

VEDĀNTA, the end of the veda; the most idealistic system of Indian philosophy.

VICĀRA (pronounced *vichara*), reflection.

VIŚESHA, specialized form.

VITARKA, deliberation.

VRITTI, perception.

YAMA, moral law in the negative aspect; the first stage in the yogic curriculum.

YOGA SŪTRA, the basic text of the yoga system; yoga aphorism.

INDEX

A

Abdominal exercise, 196

Ahamkara (self-sense), 80-83; father of self-love, 81; its practical function, 81; both cause and effect, 86

Ahimsa (abstention from injuring others), 119

Akasa (ether), 37; relation of finite objects in space to, 89

Alexander, S., his definition of philosophy, 42

Alexander the Great, 1

Ambivalence, 158

American Journal of Psychology, 233fn.

Amnesia, 138

Ampère, French electrician, 174

Ananda (bliss), quality of Atman (q.v.), 45; persistence of, 223

Anatomy, yoga, 216fn., 217fn.

Anaximander, Greek philosopher, claimed fish-origin for man, 68

Anthropomorphism, 65

Anthroposophy, 165

"Archetypes," 155, 156

Aristotle, 12, 13, 144; theory of form and matter, 50, 51; his conception of God compared with that of samkhya, 55, 56; concept of evolution, 68

Artha (object), 222

Aryan invasion of India, 1

Aryans, prehistoric, 6-8

Asamprajnata-Samadhi (super-conscious Samadhi), 223. *See also* Samadhi

Asanas (yogic postures), 111, 187, 188; therapeutic value of, 187, 188. *See also* Discipline, Postures

Asia, Central, 6

Asvini-Mudra (anal exercise), 195fn.

Atman (individual soul), 12, 43, 49; explanation of term, 13; the imperishable self, 14, 17; mystical intuition, 17; difference from Brahman equation, 20; plurality of souls doctrine, 44

Atoms, 70

Austerities, extremes prohibited in yoga, 120

Avidya (ignorance), 104, 112, 128; practical definition of, 113; its uprooting supreme ethical task, 113; cause of all misery, results analyzed, 114 ff.; as root-cause in citta modification, 118

Avisesha (indeterminate unspecialized product), 76, 89

B

Bahva, teacher, 19

Baudouin, C., au. *Suggestion and Autosuggestion,* quoted, 218

Becquerel, French physicist, 71

Bergson, Henri, French philosopher, 110; his *élan vital* cosmic theory, 53

A CATALOG OF SELECTED
DOVER BOOKS
IN ALL FIELDS OF INTEREST

A CATALOG OF SELECTED DOVER
BOOKS IN ALL FIELDS OF INTEREST

CONCERNING THE SPIRITUAL IN ART, Wassily Kandinsky. Pioneering work by father of abstract art. Thoughts on color theory, nature of art. Analysis of earlier masters. 12 illustrations. 80pp. of text. 5⅜ x 8½. 23411-8

ANIMALS: 1,419 Copyright-Free Illustrations of Mammals, Birds, Fish, Insects, etc., Jim Harter (ed.). Clear wood engravings present, in extremely lifelike poses, over 1,000 species of animals. One of the most extensive pictorial sourcebooks of its kind. Captions. Index. 284pp. 9 x 12. 23766-4

CELTIC ART: The Methods of Construction, George Bain. Simple geometric techniques for making Celtic interlacements, spirals, Kells-type initials, animals, humans, etc. Over 500 illustrations. 160pp. 9 x 12. (Available in U.S. only.) 22923-8

AN ATLAS OF ANATOMY FOR ARTISTS, Fritz Schider. Most thorough reference work on art anatomy in the world. Hundreds of illustrations, including selections from works by Vesalius, Leonardo, Goya, Ingres, Michelangelo, others. 593 illustrations. 192pp. 7⅛ x 10¼. 20241-0

CELTIC HAND STROKE-BY-STROKE (Irish Half-Uncial from "The Book of Kells"): An Arthur Baker Calligraphy Manual, Arthur Baker. Complete guide to creating each letter of the alphabet in distinctive Celtic manner. Covers hand position, strokes, pens, inks, paper, more. Illustrated. 48pp. 8¼ x 11. 24336-2

EASY ORIGAMI, John Montroll. Charming collection of 32 projects (hat, cup, pelican, piano, swan, many more) specially designed for the novice origami hobbyist. Clearly illustrated easy-to-follow instructions insure that even beginning papercrafters will achieve successful results. 48pp. 8¼ x 11. 27298-2

THE COMPLETE BOOK OF BIRDHOUSE CONSTRUCTION FOR WOODWORKERS, Scott D. Campbell. Detailed instructions, illustrations, tables. Also data on bird habitat and instinct patterns. Bibliography. 3 tables. 63 illustrations in 15 figures. 48pp. 5¼ x 8½. 24407-5

BLOOMINGDALE'S ILLUSTRATED 1886 CATALOG: Fashions, Dry Goods and Housewares, Bloomingdale Brothers. Famed merchants' extremely rare catalog depicting about 1,700 products: clothing, housewares, firearms, dry goods, jewelry, more. Invaluable for dating, identifying vintage items. Also, copyright-free graphics for artists, designers. Co-published with Henry Ford Museum & Greenfield Village. 160pp. 8¼ x 11. 25780-0

HISTORIC COSTUME IN PICTURES, Braun & Schneider. Over 1,450 costumed figures in clearly detailed engravings–from dawn of civilization to end of 19th century. Captions. Many folk costumes. 256pp. 8⅜ x 11¾. 23150-X

STICKLEY CRAFTSMAN FURNITURE CATALOGS, Gustav Stickley and L. & J. G. Stickley. Beautiful, functional furniture in two authentic catalogs from 1910. 594 illustrations, including 277 photos, show settles, rockers, armchairs, reclining chairs, bookcases, desks, tables. 183pp. 6½ x 9¼. 23838-5

AMERICAN LOCOMOTIVES IN HISTORIC PHOTOGRAPHS: 1858 to 1949, Ron Ziel (ed.). A rare collection of 126 meticulously detailed official photographs, called "builder portraits," of American locomotives that majestically chronicle the rise of steam locomotive power in America. Introduction. Detailed captions. xi+ 129pp. 9 x 12. 27393-8

AMERICA'S LIGHTHOUSES: An Illustrated History, Francis Ross Holland, Jr. Delightfully written, profusely illustrated fact-filled survey of over 200 American lighthouses since 1716. History, anecdotes, technological advances, more. 240pp. 8 x 10¾.
25576-X

TOWARDS A NEW ARCHITECTURE, Le Corbusier. Pioneering manifesto by founder of "International School." Technical and aesthetic theories, views of industry, economics, relation of form to function, "mass-production split" and much more. Profusely illustrated. 320pp. 6⅛ x 9¼. (Available in U.S. only.) 25023-7

HOW THE OTHER HALF LIVES, Jacob Riis. Famous journalistic record, exposing poverty and degradation of New York slums around 1900, by major social reformer. 100 striking and influential photographs. 233pp. 10 x 7⅞. 22012-5

FRUIT KEY AND TWIG KEY TO TREES AND SHRUBS, William M. Harlow. One of the handiest and most widely used identification aids. Fruit key covers 120 deciduous and evergreen species; twig key 160 deciduous species. Easily used. Over 300 photographs. 126pp. 5⅜ x 8½. 20511-8

COMMON BIRD SONGS, Dr. Donald J. Borror. Songs of 60 most common U.S. birds: robins, sparrows, cardinals, bluejays, finches, more—arranged in order of increasing complexity. Up to 9 variations of songs of each species.
Cassette and manual 99911-4

ORCHIDS AS HOUSE PLANTS, Rebecca Tyson Northen. Grow cattleyas and many other kinds of orchids—in a window, in a case, or under artificial light. 63 illustrations. 148pp. 5⅜ x 8½. 23261-1

MONSTER MAZES, Dave Phillips. Masterful mazes at four levels of difficulty. Avoid deadly perils and evil creatures to find magical treasures. Solutions for all 32 exciting illustrated puzzles. 48pp. 8¼ x 11. 26005-4

MOZART'S DON GIOVANNI (DOVER OPERA LIBRETTO SERIES), Wolfgang Amadeus Mozart. Introduced and translated by Ellen H. Bleiler. Standard Italian libretto, with complete English translation. Convenient and thoroughly portable—an ideal companion for reading along with a recording or the performance itself. Introduction. List of characters. Plot summary. 121pp. 5¼ x 8½. 24944-1

TECHNICAL MANUAL AND DICTIONARY OF CLASSICAL BALLET, Gail Grant. Defines, explains, comments on steps, movements, poses and concepts. 15-page pictorial section. Basic book for student, viewer. 127pp. 5⅜ x 8½. 21843-0

THE CLARINET AND CLARINET PLAYING, David Pino. Lively, comprehensive work features suggestions about technique, musicianship, and musical interpretation, as well as guidelines for teaching, making your own reeds, and preparing for public performance. Includes an intriguing look at clarinet history. "A godsend," *The Clarinet,* Journal of the International Clarinet Society. Appendixes. 7 illus. 320pp. 5⅜ x 8½. 40270-3

HOLLYWOOD GLAMOR PORTRAITS, John Kobal (ed.). 145 photos from 1926-49. Harlow, Gable, Bogart, Bacall; 94 stars in all. Full background on photographers, technical aspects. 160pp. 8⅜ x 11¼. 23352-9

THE ANNOTATED CASEY AT THE BAT: A Collection of Ballads about the Mighty Casey/Third, Revised Edition, Martin Gardner (ed.). Amusing sequels and parodies of one of America's best-loved poems: Casey's Revenge, Why Casey Whiffed, Casey's Sister at the Bat, others. 256pp. 5⅜ x 8½. 28598-7

THE RAVEN AND OTHER FAVORITE POEMS, Edgar Allan Poe. Over 40 of the author's most memorable poems: "The Bells," "Ulalume," "Israfel," "To Helen," "The Conqueror Worm," "Eldorado," "Annabel Lee," many more. Alphabetic lists of titles and first lines. 64pp. 5 3/16 x 8¼. 26685-0

PERSONAL MEMOIRS OF U. S. GRANT, Ulysses Simpson Grant. Intelligent, deeply moving firsthand account of Civil War campaigns, considered by many the finest military memoirs ever written. Includes letters, historic photographs, maps and more. 528pp. 6⅛ x 9¼. 28587-1

ANCIENT EGYPTIAN MATERIALS AND INDUSTRIES, A. Lucas and J. Harris. Fascinating, comprehensive, thoroughly documented text describes this ancient civilization's vast resources and the processes that incorporated them in daily life, including the use of animal products, building materials, cosmetics, perfumes and incense, fibers, glazed ware, glass and its manufacture, materials used in the mummification process, and much more. 544pp. 6⅛ x 9¼. (Available in U.S. only.) 40446-3

RUSSIAN STORIES/RUSSKIE RASSKAZY: A Dual-Language Book, edited by Gleb Struve. Twelve tales by such masters as Chekhov, Tolstoy, Dostoevsky, Pushkin, others. Excellent word-for-word English translations on facing pages, plus teaching and study aids, Russian/English vocabulary, biographical/critical introductions, more. 416pp. 5⅜ x 8½. 26244-8

PHILADELPHIA THEN AND NOW: 60 Sites Photographed in the Past and Present, Kenneth Finkel and Susan Oyama. Rare photographs of City Hall, Logan Square, Independence Hall, Betsy Ross House, other landmarks juxtaposed with contemporary views. Captures changing face of historic city. Introduction. Captions. 128pp. 8¼ x 11. 25790-8

AIA ARCHITECTURAL GUIDE TO NASSAU AND SUFFOLK COUNTIES, LONG ISLAND, The American Institute of Architects, Long Island Chapter, and the Society for the Preservation of Long Island Antiquities. Comprehensive, well-researched and generously illustrated volume brings to life over three centuries of Long Island's great architectural heritage. More than 240 photographs with authoritative, extensively detailed captions. 176pp. 8¼ x 11. 26946-9

NORTH AMERICAN INDIAN LIFE: Customs and Traditions of 23 Tribes, Elsie Clews Parsons (ed.). 27 fictionalized essays by noted anthropologists examine religion, customs, government, additional facets of life among the Winnebago, Crow, Zuni, Eskimo, other tribes. 480pp. 6⅛ x 9¼. 27377-6

FRANK LLOYD WRIGHT'S DANA HOUSE, Donald Hoffmann. Pictorial essay of residential masterpiece with over 160 interior and exterior photos, plans, elevations, sketches and studies. 128pp. 9¹/₄ x 10¾. 29120-0

THE MALE AND FEMALE FIGURE IN MOTION: 60 Classic Photographic Sequences, Eadweard Muybridge. 60 true-action photographs of men and women walking, running, climbing, bending, turning, etc., reproduced from rare 19th-century masterpiece. vi + 121pp. 9 x 12. 24745-7

1001 QUESTIONS ANSWERED ABOUT THE SEASHORE, N. J. Berrill and Jacquelyn Berrill. Queries answered about dolphins, sea snails, sponges, starfish, fishes, shore birds, many others. Covers appearance, breeding, growth, feeding, much more. 305pp. 5¼ x 8¼. 23366-9

ATTRACTING BIRDS TO YOUR YARD, William J. Weber. Easy-to-follow guide offers advice on how to attract the greatest diversity of birds: birdhouses, feeders, water and waterers, much more. 96pp. 5³/₁₆ x 8¼. 28927-3

MEDICINAL AND OTHER USES OF NORTH AMERICAN PLANTS: A Historical Survey with Special Reference to the Eastern Indian Tribes, Charlotte Erichsen-Brown. Chronological historical citations document 500 years of usage of plants, trees, shrubs native to eastern Canada, northeastern U.S. Also complete identifying information. 343 illustrations. 544pp. 6½ x 9¼. 25951-X

STORYBOOK MAZES, Dave Phillips. 23 stories and mazes on two-page spreads: Wizard of Oz, Treasure Island, Robin Hood, etc. Solutions. 64pp. 8¼ x 11. 23628-5

AMERICAN NEGRO SONGS: 230 Folk Songs and Spirituals, Religious and Secular, John W. Work. This authoritative study traces the African influences of songs sung and played by black Americans at work, in church, and as entertainment. The author discusses the lyric significance of such songs as "Swing Low, Sweet Chariot," "John Henry," and others and offers the words and music for 230 songs. Bibliography. Index of Song Titles. 272pp. 6½ x 9¼. 40271-1

MOVIE-STAR PORTRAITS OF THE FORTIES, John Kobal (ed.). 163 glamor, studio photos of 106 stars of the 1940s: Rita Hayworth, Ava Gardner, Marlon Brando, Clark Gable, many more. 176pp. 8⅜ x 11¼. 23546-7

BENCHLEY LOST AND FOUND, Robert Benchley. Finest humor from early 30s, about pet peeves, child psychologists, post office and others. Mostly unavailable elsewhere. 73 illustrations by Peter Arno and others. 183pp. 5⅜ x 8½. 22410-4

YEKL and THE IMPORTED BRIDEGROOM AND OTHER STORIES OF YIDDISH NEW YORK, Abraham Cahan. Film Hester Street based on *Yekl* (1896). Novel, other stories among first about Jewish immigrants on N.Y.'s East Side. 240pp. 5⅜ x 8½. 22427-9

SELECTED POEMS, Walt Whitman. Generous sampling from *Leaves of Grass*. Twenty-four poems include "I Hear America Singing," "Song of the Open Road," "I Sing the Body Electric," "When Lilacs Last in the Dooryard Bloom'd," "O Captain! My Captain!"–all reprinted from an authoritative edition. Lists of titles and first lines. 128pp. 5³/₁₆ x 8¼. 26878-0

THE BEST TALES OF HOFFMANN, E. T. A. Hoffmann. 10 of Hoffmann's most important stories: "Nutcracker and the King of Mice," "The Golden Flowerpot," etc. 458pp. 5⅜ x 8½. 21793-0

FROM FETISH TO GOD IN ANCIENT EGYPT, E. A. Wallis Budge. Rich detailed survey of Egyptian conception of "God" and gods, magic, cult of animals, Osiris, more. Also, superb English translations of hymns and legends. 240 illustrations. 545pp. 5⅜ x 8½. 25803-3

FRENCH STORIES/CONTES FRANÇAIS: A Dual-Language Book, Wallace Fowlie. Ten stories by French masters, Voltaire to Camus: "Micromegas" by Voltaire; "The Atheist's Mass" by Balzac; "Minuet" by de Maupassant; "The Guest" by Camus, six more. Excellent English translations on facing pages. Also French-English vocabulary list, exercises, more. 352pp. 5⅜ x 8½. 26443-2

CHICAGO AT THE TURN OF THE CENTURY IN PHOTOGRAPHS: 122 Historic Views from the Collections of the Chicago Historical Society, Larry A. Viskochil. Rare large-format prints offer detailed views of City Hall, State Street, the Loop, Hull House, Union Station, many other landmarks, circa 1904-1913. Introduction. Captions. Maps. 144pp. 9⅜ x 12¼. 24656-6

OLD BROOKLYN IN EARLY PHOTOGRAPHS, 1865-1929, William Lee Younger. Luna Park, Gravesend race track, construction of Grand Army Plaza, moving of Hotel Brighton, etc. 157 previously unpublished photographs. 165pp. 8⅞ x 11¾. 23587-4

THE MYTHS OF THE NORTH AMERICAN INDIANS, Lewis Spence. Rich anthology of the myths and legends of the Algonquins, Iroquois, Pawnees and Sioux, prefaced by an extensive historical and ethnological commentary. 36 illustrations. 480pp. 5⅜ x 8½. 25967-6

AN ENCYCLOPEDIA OF BATTLES: Accounts of Over 1,560 Battles from 1479 B.C. to the Present, David Eggenberger. Essential details of every major battle in recorded history from the first battle of Megiddo in 1479 B.C. to Grenada in 1984. List of Battle Maps. New Appendix covering the years 1967-1984. Index. 99 illustrations. 544pp. 6½ x 9¼. 24913-1

SAILING ALONE AROUND THE WORLD, Captain Joshua Slocum. First man to sail around the world, alone, in small boat. One of great feats of seamanship told in delightful manner. 67 illustrations. 294pp. 5⅜ x 8½. 20326-3

ANARCHISM AND OTHER ESSAYS, Emma Goldman. Powerful, penetrating, prophetic essays on direct action, role of minorities, prison reform, puritan hypocrisy, violence, etc. 271pp. 5⅜ x 8½. 22484-8

MYTHS OF THE HINDUS AND BUDDHISTS, Ananda K. Coomaraswamy and Sister Nivedita. Great stories of the epics; deeds of Krishna, Shiva, taken from puranas, Vedas, folk tales; etc. 32 illustrations. 400pp. 5⅜ x 8½. 21759-0

THE TRAUMA OF BIRTH, Otto Rank. Rank's controversial thesis that anxiety neurosis is caused by profound psychological trauma which occurs at birth. 256pp. 5⅜ x 8½. 27974-X

A THEOLOGICO-POLITICAL TREATISE, Benedict Spinoza. Also contains unfinished Political Treatise. Great classic on religious liberty, theory of government on common consent. R. Elwes translation. Total of 421pp. 5⅜ x 8½. 20249-6

MY BONDAGE AND MY FREEDOM, Frederick Douglass. Born a slave, Douglass became outspoken force in antislavery movement. The best of Douglass' autobiographies. Graphic description of slave life. 464pp. 5⅜ x 8½.　　22457-0

FOLLOWING THE EQUATOR: A Journey Around the World, Mark Twain. Fascinating humorous account of 1897 voyage to Hawaii, Australia, India, New Zealand, etc. Ironic, bemused reports on peoples, customs, climate, flora and fauna, politics, much more. 197 illustrations. 720pp. 5⅜ x 8½.　　26113-1

THE PEOPLE CALLED SHAKERS, Edward D. Andrews. Definitive study of Shakers: origins, beliefs, practices, dances, social organization, furniture and crafts, etc. 33 illustrations. 351pp. 5⅜ x 8½.　　21081-2

THE MYTHS OF GREECE AND ROME, H. A. Guerber. A classic of mythology, generously illustrated, long prized for its simple, graphic, accurate retelling of the principal myths of Greece and Rome, and for its commentary on their origins and significance. With 64 illustrations by Michelangelo, Raphael, Titian, Rubens, Canova, Bernini and others. 480pp. 5⅜ x 8½.　　27584-1

PSYCHOLOGY OF MUSIC, Carl E. Seashore. Classic work discusses music as a medium from psychological viewpoint. Clear treatment of physical acoustics, auditory apparatus, sound perception, development of musical skills, nature of musical feeling, host of other topics. 88 figures. 408pp. 5⅜ x 8½.　　21851-1

THE PHILOSOPHY OF HISTORY, Georg W. Hegel. Great classic of Western thought develops concept that history is not chance but rational process, the evolution of freedom. 457pp. 5⅜ x 8½.　　20112-0

THE BOOK OF TEA, Kakuzo Okakura. Minor classic of the Orient: entertaining, charming explanation, interpretation of traditional Japanese culture in terms of tea ceremony. 94pp. 5⅜ x 8½.　　20070-1

LIFE IN ANCIENT EGYPT, Adolf Erman. Fullest, most thorough, detailed older account with much not in more recent books, domestic life, religion, magic, medicine, commerce, much more. Many illustrations reproduce tomb paintings, carvings, hieroglyphs, etc. 597pp. 5⅜ x 8½.　　22632-8

SUNDIALS, Their Theory and Construction, Albert Waugh. Far and away the best, most thorough coverage of ideas, mathematics concerned, types, construction, adjusting anywhere. Simple, nontechnical treatment allows even children to build several of these dials. Over 100 illustrations. 230pp. 5⅜ x 8½.　　22947-5

THEORETICAL HYDRODYNAMICS, L. M. Milne-Thomson. Classic exposition of the mathematical theory of fluid motion, applicable to both hydrodynamics and aerodynamics. Over 600 exercises. 768pp. 6⅛ x 9¼.　　68970-0

SONGS OF EXPERIENCE: Facsimile Reproduction with 26 Plates in Full Color, William Blake. 26 full-color plates from a rare 1826 edition. Includes "The Tyger," "London," "Holy Thursday," and other poems. Printed text of poems. 48pp. 5¼ x 7.
24636-1

OLD-TIME VIGNETTES IN FULL COLOR, Carol Belanger Grafton (ed.). Over 390 charming, often sentimental illustrations, selected from archives of Victorian graphics—pretty women posing, children playing, food, flowers, kittens and puppies, smiling cherubs, birds and butterflies, much more. All copyright-free. 48pp. 9¼ x 12¼.
27269-9

PERSPECTIVE FOR ARTISTS, Rex Vicat Cole. Depth, perspective of sky and sea, shadows, much more, not usually covered. 391 diagrams, 81 reproductions of drawings and paintings. 279pp. 5⅜ x 8½. 22487-2

DRAWING THE LIVING FIGURE, Joseph Sheppard. Innovative approach to artistic anatomy focuses on specifics of surface anatomy, rather than muscles and bones. Over 170 drawings of live models in front, back and side views, and in widely varying poses. Accompanying diagrams. 177 illustrations. Introduction. Index. 144pp. 8⅜ x11¼. 26723-7

GOTHIC AND OLD ENGLISH ALPHABETS: 100 Complete Fonts, Dan X. Solo. Add power, elegance to posters, signs, other graphics with 100 stunning copyright-free alphabets: Blackstone, Dolbey, Germania, 97 more—including many lower-case, numerals, punctuation marks. 104pp. 8⅛ x 11. 24695-7

HOW TO DO BEADWORK, Mary White. Fundamental book on craft from simple projects to five-bead chains and woven works. 106 illustrations. 142pp. 5⅜ x 8.
20697-1

THE BOOK OF WOOD CARVING, Charles Marshall Sayers. Finest book for beginners discusses fundamentals and offers 34 designs. "Absolutely first rate . . . well thought out and well executed."–E. J. Tangerman. 118pp. 7¾ x 10⅝. 23654-4

ILLUSTRATED CATALOG OF CIVIL WAR MILITARY GOODS: Union Army Weapons, Insignia, Uniform Accessories, and Other Equipment, Schuyler, Hartley, and Graham. Rare, profusely illustrated 1846 catalog includes Union Army uniform and dress regulations, arms and ammunition, coats, insignia, flags, swords, rifles, etc. 226 illustrations. 160pp. 9 x 12. 24939-5

WOMEN'S FASHIONS OF THE EARLY 1900s: An Unabridged Republication of "New York Fashions, 1909," National Cloak & Suit Co. Rare catalog of mail-order fashions documents women's and children's clothing styles shortly after the turn of the century. Captions offer full descriptions, prices. Invaluable resource for fashion, costume historians. Approximately 725 illustrations. 128pp. 8⅜ x 11¼. 27276-1

THE 1912 AND 1915 GUSTAV STICKLEY FURNITURE CATALOGS, Gustav Stickley. With over 200 detailed illustrations and descriptions, these two catalogs are essential reading and reference materials and identification guides for Stickley furniture. Captions cite materials, dimensions and prices. 112pp. 6½ x 9¼. 26676-1

EARLY AMERICAN LOCOMOTIVES, John H. White, Jr. Finest locomotive engravings from early 19th century: historical (1804–74), main-line (after 1870), special, foreign, etc. 147 plates. 142pp. 11⅜ x 8¼. 22772-3

THE TALL SHIPS OF TODAY IN PHOTOGRAPHS, Frank O. Braynard. Lavishly illustrated tribute to nearly 100 majestic contemporary sailing vessels: Amerigo Vespucci, Clearwater, Constitution, Eagle, Mayflower, Sea Cloud, Victory, many more. Authoritative captions provide statistics, background on each ship. 190 black-and-white photographs and illustrations. Introduction. 128pp. 8⅞ x 11¾.
27163-3

LITTLE BOOK OF EARLY AMERICAN CRAFTS AND TRADES, Peter Stockham (ed.). 1807 children's book explains crafts and trades: baker, hatter, cooper, potter, and many others. 23 copperplate illustrations. 140pp. 4⅝ x 6.   23336-7

VICTORIAN FASHIONS AND COSTUMES FROM HARPER'S BAZAR, 1867–1898, Stella Blum (ed.). Day costumes, evening wear, sports clothes, shoes, hats, other accessories in over 1,000 detailed engravings. 320pp. 9⅜ x 12¼. 22990-4

GUSTAV STICKLEY, THE CRAFTSMAN, Mary Ann Smith. Superb study surveys broad scope of Stickley's achievement, especially in architecture. Design philosophy, rise and fall of the Craftsman empire, descriptions and floor plans for many Craftsman houses, more. 86 black-and-white halftones. 31 line illustrations. Introduction 208pp. 6½ x 9¼.   27210-9

THE LONG ISLAND RAIL ROAD IN EARLY PHOTOGRAPHS, Ron Ziel. Over 220 rare photos, informative text document origin (1844) and development of rail service on Long Island. Vintage views of early trains, locomotives, stations, passengers, crews, much more. Captions. 8⅞ x 11¾.   26301-0

VOYAGE OF THE LIBERDADE, Joshua Slocum. Great 19th-century mariner's thrilling, first-hand account of the wreck of his ship off South America, the 35-foot boat he built from the wreckage, and its remarkable voyage home. 128pp. 5⅜ x 8½.
40022-0

TEN BOOKS ON ARCHITECTURE, Vitruvius. The most important book ever written on architecture. Early Roman aesthetics, technology, classical orders, site selection, all other aspects. Morgan translation. 331pp. 5⅜ x 8½.   20645-9

THE HUMAN FIGURE IN MOTION, Eadweard Muybridge. More than 4,500 stopped-action photos, in action series, showing undraped men, women, children jumping, lying down, throwing, sitting, wrestling, carrying, etc. 390pp. 7⅞ x 10⅝.
20204-6 Clothbd.

TREES OF THE EASTERN AND CENTRAL UNITED STATES AND CANADA, William M. Harlow. Best one-volume guide to 140 trees. Full descriptions, woodlore, range, etc. Over 600 illustrations. Handy size. 288pp. 4½ x 6⅜.   20395-6

SONGS OF WESTERN BIRDS, Dr. Donald J. Borror. Complete song and call repertoire of 60 western species, including flycatchers, juncoes, cactus wrens, many more–includes fully illustrated booklet.   Cassette and manual 99913-0

GROWING AND USING HERBS AND SPICES, Milo Miloradovich. Versatile handbook provides all the information needed for cultivation and use of all the herbs and spices available in North America. 4 illustrations. Index. Glossary. 236pp. 5⅜ x 8½.
25058-X

BIG BOOK OF MAZES AND LABYRINTHS, Walter Shepherd. 50 mazes and labyrinths in all–classical, solid, ripple, and more–in one great volume. Perfect inexpensive puzzler for clever youngsters. Full solutions. 112pp. 8⅛ x 11.   22951-3

PIANO TUNING, J. Cree Fischer. Clearest, best book for beginner, amateur. Simple repairs, raising dropped notes, tuning by easy method of flattened fifths. No previous skills needed. 4 illustrations. 201pp. 5⅜ x 8½. 23267-0

HINTS TO SINGERS, Lillian Nordica. Selecting the right teacher, developing confidence, overcoming stage fright, and many other important skills receive thoughtful discussion in this indispensible guide, written by a world-famous diva of four decades' experience. 96pp. 5⅜ x 8½. 40094-8

THE COMPLETE NONSENSE OF EDWARD LEAR, Edward Lear. All nonsense limericks, zany alphabets, Owl and Pussycat, songs, nonsense botany, etc., illustrated by Lear. Total of 320pp. 5⅜ x 8½. (Available in U.S. only.) 20167-8

VICTORIAN PARLOUR POETRY: An Annotated Anthology, Michael R. Turner. 117 gems by Longfellow, Tennyson, Browning, many lesser-known poets. "The Village Blacksmith," "Curfew Must Not Ring Tonight," "Only a Baby Small," dozens more, often difficult to find elsewhere. Index of poets, titles, first lines. xxiii + 325pp. 5⅝ x 8¼. 27044-0

DUBLINERS, James Joyce. Fifteen stories offer vivid, tightly focused observations of the lives of Dublin's poorer classes. At least one, "The Dead," is considered a masterpiece. Reprinted complete and unabridged from standard edition. 160pp. 5³⁄₁₆ x 8¼. 26870-5

GREAT WEIRD TALES: 14 Stories by Lovecraft, Blackwood, Machen and Others, S. T. Joshi (ed.). 14 spellbinding tales, including "The Sin Eater," by Fiona McLeod, "The Eye Above the Mantel," by Frank Belknap Long, as well as renowned works by R. H. Barlow, Lord Dunsany, Arthur Machen, W. C. Morrow and eight other masters of the genre. 256pp. 5⅜ x 8½. (Available in U.S. only.) 40436-6

THE BOOK OF THE SACRED MAGIC OF ABRAMELIN THE MAGE, translated by S. MacGregor Mathers. Medieval manuscript of ceremonial magic. Basic document in Aleister Crowley, Golden Dawn groups. 268pp. 5⅜ x 8½. 23211-5

NEW RUSSIAN-ENGLISH AND ENGLISH-RUSSIAN DICTIONARY, M. A. O'Brien. This is a remarkably handy Russian dictionary, containing a surprising amount of information, including over 70,000 entries. 366pp. 4½ x 6⅛. 20208-9

HISTORIC HOMES OF THE AMERICAN PRESIDENTS, Second, Revised Edition, Irvin Haas. A traveler's guide to American Presidential homes, most open to the public, depicting and describing homes occupied by every American President from George Washington to George Bush. With visiting hours, admission charges, travel routes. 175 photographs. Index. 160pp. 8¼ x 11. 26751-2

NEW YORK IN THE FORTIES, Andreas Feininger. 162 brilliant photographs by the well-known photographer, formerly with *Life* magazine. Commuters, shoppers, Times Square at night, much else from city at its peak. Captions by John von Hartz. 181pp. 9¼ x 10¾. 23585-8

INDIAN SIGN LANGUAGE, William Tomkins. Over 525 signs developed by Sioux and other tribes. Written instructions and diagrams. Also 290 pictographs. 111pp. 6⅛ x 9¼. 22029-X

ANATOMY: A Complete Guide for Artists, Joseph Sheppard. A master of figure drawing shows artists how to render human anatomy convincingly. Over 460 illustrations. 224pp. 8⅜ x 11¼. 27279-6

MEDIEVAL CALLIGRAPHY: Its History and Technique, Marc Drogin. Spirited history, comprehensive instruction manual covers 13 styles (ca. 4th century through 15th). Excellent photographs; directions for duplicating medieval techniques with modern tools. 224pp. 8⅜ x 11¼. 26142-5

DRIED FLOWERS: How to Prepare Them, Sarah Whitlock and Martha Rankin. Complete instructions on how to use silica gel, meal and borax, perlite aggregate, sand and borax, glycerine and water to create attractive permanent flower arrangements. 12 illustrations. 32pp. 5⅜ x 8½. 21802-3

EASY-TO-MAKE BIRD FEEDERS FOR WOODWORKERS, Scott D. Campbell. Detailed, simple-to-use guide for designing, constructing, caring for and using feeders. Text, illustrations for 12 classic and contemporary designs. 96pp. 5⅜ x 8½. 25847-5

SCOTTISH WONDER TALES FROM MYTH AND LEGEND, Donald A. Mackenzie. 16 lively tales tell of giants rumbling down mountainsides, of a magic wand that turns stone pillars into warriors, of gods and goddesses, evil hags, powerful forces and more. 240pp. 5⅜ x 8½. 29677-6

THE HISTORY OF UNDERCLOTHES, C. Willett Cunnington and Phyllis Cunnington. Fascinating, well-documented survey covering six centuries of English undergarments, enhanced with over 100 illustrations: 12th-century laced-up bodice, footed long drawers (1795), 19th-century bustles, 19th-century corsets for men, Victorian "bust improvers," much more. 272pp. 5⅝ x 8¼. 27124-2

ARTS AND CRAFTS FURNITURE: The Complete Brooks Catalog of 1912, Brooks Manufacturing Co. Photos and detailed descriptions of more than 150 now very collectible furniture designs from the Arts and Crafts movement depict davenports, settees, buffets, desks, tables, chairs, bedsteads, dressers and more, all built of solid, quarter-sawed oak. Invaluable for students and enthusiasts of antiques, Americana and the decorative arts. 80pp. 6½ x 9¼. 27471-3

WILBUR AND ORVILLE: A Biography of the Wright Brothers, Fred Howard. Definitive, crisply written study tells the full story of the brothers' lives and work. A vividly written biography, unparalleled in scope and color, that also captures the spirit of an extraordinary era. 560pp. 6⅛ x 9¼. 40297-5

THE ARTS OF THE SAILOR: Knotting, Splicing and Ropework, Hervey Garrett Smith. Indispensable shipboard reference covers tools, basic knots and useful hitches; handsewing and canvas work, more. Over 100 illustrations. Delightful reading for sea lovers. 256pp. 5⅜ x 8½. 26440-8

FRANK LLOYD WRIGHT'S FALLINGWATER: The House and Its History, Second, Revised Edition, Donald Hoffmann. A total revision–both in text and illustrations–of the standard document on Fallingwater, the boldest, most personal architectural statement of Wright's mature years, updated with valuable new material from the recently opened Frank Lloyd Wright Archives. "Fascinating"–*The New York Times*. 116 illustrations. 128pp. 9¼ x 10¾. 27430-6

PHOTOGRAPHIC SKETCHBOOK OF THE CIVIL WAR, Alexander Gardner. 100 photos taken on field during the Civil War. Famous shots of Manassas Harper's Ferry, Lincoln, Richmond, slave pens, etc. 244pp. 10⅝ x 8¼.   22731-6

FIVE ACRES AND INDEPENDENCE, Maurice G. Kains. Great back-to-the-land classic explains basics of self-sufficient farming. The one book to get. 95 illustrations. 397pp. 5⅜ x 8½.   20974-1

SONGS OF EASTERN BIRDS, Dr. Donald J. Borror. Songs and calls of 60 species most common to eastern U.S.: warblers, woodpeckers, flycatchers, thrushes, larks, many more in high-quality recording.   Cassette and manual 99912-2

A MODERN HERBAL, Margaret Grieve. Much the fullest, most exact, most useful compilation of herbal material. Gigantic alphabetical encyclopedia, from aconite to zedoary, gives botanical information, medical properties, folklore, economic uses, much else. Indispensable to serious reader. 161 illustrations. 888pp. 6½ x 9¼. 2-vol. set. (Available in U.S. only.)   Vol. I: 22798-7
Vol. II: 22799-5

HIDDEN TREASURE MAZE BOOK, Dave Phillips. Solve 34 challenging mazes accompanied by heroic tales of adventure. Evil dragons, people-eating plants, blood-thirsty giants, many more dangerous adversaries lurk at every twist and turn. 34 mazes, stories, solutions. 48pp. 8¼ x 11.   24566-7

LETTERS OF W. A. MOZART, Wolfgang A. Mozart. Remarkable letters show bawdy wit, humor, imagination, musical insights, contemporary musical world; includes some letters from Leopold Mozart. 276pp. 5⅜ x 8½.   22859-2

BASIC PRINCIPLES OF CLASSICAL BALLET, Agrippina Vaganova. Great Russian theoretician, teacher explains methods for teaching classical ballet. 118 illustrations. 175pp. 5⅜ x 8½.   22036-2

THE JUMPING FROG, Mark Twain. Revenge edition. The original story of The Celebrated Jumping Frog of Calaveras County, a hapless French translation, and Twain's hilarious "retranslation" from the French. 12 illustrations. 66pp. 5⅜ x 8½.
22686-7

BEST REMEMBERED POEMS, Martin Gardner (ed.). The 126 poems in this superb collection of 19th- and 20th-century British and American verse range from Shelley's "To a Skylark" to the impassioned "Renascence" of Edna St. Vincent Millay and to Edward Lear's whimsical "The Owl and the Pussycat." 224pp. 5⅜ x 8½.
27165-X

COMPLETE SONNETS, William Shakespeare. Over 150 exquisite poems deal with love, friendship, the tyranny of time, beauty's evanescence, death and other themes in language of remarkable power, precision and beauty. Glossary of archaic terms. 80pp. 5³⁄₁₆ x 8¼.   26686-9

THE BATTLES THAT CHANGED HISTORY, Fletcher Pratt. Eminent historian profiles 16 crucial conflicts, ancient to modern, that changed the course of civilization. 352pp. 5⅜ x 8½.   41129-X

THE WIT AND HUMOR OF OSCAR WILDE, Alvin Redman (ed.). More than 1,000 ripostes, paradoxes, wisecracks: Work is the curse of the drinking classes; I can resist everything except temptation; etc. 258pp. 5⅜ x 8½. 20602-5

SHAKESPEARE LEXICON AND QUOTATION DICTIONARY, Alexander Schmidt. Full definitions, locations, shades of meaning in every word in plays and poems. More than 50,000 exact quotations. 1,485pp. 6½ x 9¼. 2-vol. set.
Vol. 1: 22726-X
Vol. 2: 22727-8

SELECTED POEMS, Emily Dickinson. Over 100 best-known, best-loved poems by one of America's foremost poets, reprinted from authoritative early editions. No comparable edition at this price. Index of first lines. 64pp. 5$\frac{3}{16}$ x 8¼. 26466-1

THE INSIDIOUS DR. FU-MANCHU, Sax Rohmer. The first of the popular mystery series introduces a pair of English detectives to their archnemesis, the diabolical Dr. Fu-Manchu. Flavorful atmosphere, fast-paced action, and colorful characters enliven this classic of the genre. 208pp. 5$\frac{3}{16}$ x 8¼. 29898-1

THE MALLEUS MALEFICARUM OF KRAMER AND SPRENGER, translated by Montague Summers. Full text of most important witchhunter's "bible," used by both Catholics and Protestants. 278pp. 6⅝ x 10. 22802-9

SPANISH STORIES/CUENTOS ESPAÑOLES: A Dual-Language Book, Angel Flores (ed.). Unique format offers 13 great stories in Spanish by Cervantes, Borges, others. Faithful English translations on facing pages. 352pp. 5⅜ x 8½. 25399-6

GARDEN CITY, LONG ISLAND, IN EARLY PHOTOGRAPHS, 1869–1919, Mildred H. Smith. Handsome treasury of 118 vintage pictures, accompanied by carefully researched captions, document the Garden City Hotel fire (1899), the Vanderbilt Cup Race (1908), the first airmail flight departing from the Nassau Boulevard Aerodrome (1911), and much more. 96pp. 8⅞ x 11¾. 40669-5

OLD QUEENS, N.Y., IN EARLY PHOTOGRAPHS, Vincent F. Seyfried and William Asadorian. Over 160 rare photographs of Maspeth, Jamaica, Jackson Heights, and other areas. Vintage views of DeWitt Clinton mansion, 1939 World's Fair and more. Captions. 192pp. 8⅞ x 11. 26358-4

CAPTURED BY THE INDIANS: 15 Firsthand Accounts, 1750-1870, Frederick Drimmer. Astounding true historical accounts of grisly torture, bloody conflicts, relentless pursuits, miraculous escapes and more, by people who lived to tell the tale. 384pp. 5⅜ x 8½. 24901-8

THE WORLD'S GREAT SPEECHES (Fourth Enlarged Edition), Lewis Copeland, Lawrence W. Lamm, and Stephen J. McKenna. Nearly 300 speeches provide public speakers with a wealth of updated quotes and inspiration–from Pericles' funeral oration and William Jennings Bryan's "Cross of Gold Speech" to Malcolm X's powerful words on the Black Revolution and Earl of Spenser's tribute to his sister, Diana, Princess of Wales. 944pp. 5⅜ x 8⅜. 40903-1

THE BOOK OF THE SWORD, Sir Richard F. Burton. Great Victorian scholar/adventurer's eloquent, erudite history of the "queen of weapons"–from prehistory to early Roman Empire. Evolution and development of early swords, variations (sabre, broadsword, cutlass, scimitar, etc.), much more. 336pp. 6⅛ x 9¼.
25434-8

AUTOBIOGRAPHY: The Story of My Experiments with Truth, Mohandas K. Gandhi. Boyhood, legal studies, purification, the growth of the Satyagraha (nonviolent protest) movement. Critical, inspiring work of the man responsible for the freedom of India. 480pp. 5⅜ x 8½. (Available in U.S. only.) 24593-4

CELTIC MYTHS AND LEGENDS, T. W. Rolleston. Masterful retelling of Irish and Welsh stories and tales. Cuchulain, King Arthur, Deirdre, the Grail, many more. First paperback edition. 58 full-page illustrations. 512pp. 5⅜ x 8½. 26507-2

THE PRINCIPLES OF PSYCHOLOGY, William James. Famous long course complete, unabridged. Stream of thought, time perception, memory, experimental methods; great work decades ahead of its time. 94 figures. 1,391pp. 5⅜ x 8½. 2-vol. set.
Vol. I: 20381-6 Vol. II: 20382-4

THE WORLD AS WILL AND REPRESENTATION, Arthur Schopenhauer. Definitive English translation of Schopenhauer's life work, correcting more than 1,000 errors, omissions in earlier translations. Translated by E. F. J. Payne. Total of 1,269pp. 5⅜ x 8½. 2-vol. set. Vol. 1: 21761-2 Vol. 2: 21762-0

MAGIC AND MYSTERY IN TIBET, Madame Alexandra David-Neel. Experiences among lamas, magicians, sages, sorcerers, Bonpa wizards. A true psychic discovery. 32 illustrations. 321pp. 5⅜ x 8½. (Available in U.S. only.) 22682-4

THE EGYPTIAN BOOK OF THE DEAD, E. A. Wallis Budge. Complete reproduction of Ani's papyrus, finest ever found. Full hieroglyphic text, interlinear transliteration, word-for-word translation, smooth translation. 533pp. 6½ x 9¼. 21866-X

MATHEMATICS FOR THE NONMATHEMATICIAN, Morris Kline. Detailed, college-level treatment of mathematics in cultural and historical context, with numerous exercises. Recommended Reading Lists. Tables. Numerous figures. 641pp. 5⅜ x 8½. 24823-2

PROBABILISTIC METHODS IN THE THEORY OF STRUCTURES, Isaac Elishakoff. Well-written introduction covers the elements of the theory of probability from two or more random variables, the reliability of such multivariable structures, the theory of random function, Monte Carlo methods of treating problems incapable of exact solution, and more. Examples. 502pp. 5⅜ x 8½. 40691-1

THE RIME OF THE ANCIENT MARINER, Gustave Doré, S. T. Coleridge. Doré's finest work; 34 plates capture moods, subtleties of poem. Flawless full-size reproductions printed on facing pages with authoritative text of poem. "Beautiful. Simply beautiful."—*Publisher's Weekly.* 77pp. 9¼ x 12. 22305-1

NORTH AMERICAN INDIAN DESIGNS FOR ARTISTS AND CRAFTSPEOPLE, Eva Wilson. Over 360 authentic copyright-free designs adapted from Navajo blankets, Hopi pottery, Sioux buffalo hides, more. Geometrics, symbolic figures, plant and animal motifs, etc. 128pp. 8⅜ x 11. (Not for sale in the United Kingdom.) 25341-4

SCULPTURE: Principles and Practice, Louis Slobodkin. Step-by-step approach to clay, plaster, metals, stone; classical and modern. 253 drawings, photos. 255pp. 8⅜ x 11. 22960-2

THE INFLUENCE OF SEA POWER UPON HISTORY, 1660–1783, A. T. Mahan. Influential classic of naval history and tactics still used as text in war colleges. First paperback edition. 4 maps. 24 battle plans. 640pp. 5⅜ x 8½. 25509-3

CATALOG OF DOVER BOOKS

THE STORY OF THE TITANIC AS TOLD BY ITS SURVIVORS, Jack Winocour (ed.). What it was really like. Panic, despair, shocking inefficiency, and a little heroism. More thrilling than any fictional account. 26 illustrations. 320pp. 5⅜ x 8½.
20610-6

FAIRY AND FOLK TALES OF THE IRISH PEASANTRY, William Butler Yeats (ed.). Treasury of 64 tales from the twilight world of Celtic myth and legend: "The Soul Cages," "The Kildare Pooka," "King O'Toole and his Goose," many more. Introduction and Notes by W. B. Yeats. 352pp. 5⅜ x 8½.
26941-8

BUDDHIST MAHAYANA TEXTS, E. B. Cowell and others (eds.). Superb, accurate translations of basic documents in Mahayana Buddhism, highly important in history of religions. The Buddha-karita of Asvaghosha, Larger Sukhavativyuha, more. 448pp. 5⅜ x 8½.
25552-2

ONE TWO THREE . . . INFINITY: Facts and Speculations of Science, George Gamow. Great physicist's fascinating, readable overview of contemporary science: number theory, relativity, fourth dimension, entropy, genes, atomic structure, much more. 128 illustrations. Index. 352pp. 5⅜ x 8½.
25664-2

EXPERIMENTATION AND MEASUREMENT, W. J. Youden. Introductory manual explains laws of measurement in simple terms and offers tips for achieving accuracy and minimizing errors. Mathematics of measurement, use of instruments, experimenting with machines. 1994 edition. Foreword. Preface. Introduction. Epilogue. Selected Readings. Glossary. Index. Tables and figures. 128pp. 5⅜ x 8½.
40451-X

DALÍ ON MODERN ART: The Cuckolds of Antiquated Modern Art, Salvador Dalí. Influential painter skewers modern art and its practitioners. Outrageous evaluations of Picasso, Cézanne, Turner, more. 15 renderings of paintings discussed. 44 calligraphic decorations by Dalí. 96pp. 5⅜ x 8½. (Available in U.S. only.)
29220-7

ANTIQUE PLAYING CARDS: A Pictorial History, Henry René D'Allemagne. Over 900 elaborate, decorative images from rare playing cards (14th–20th centuries): Bacchus, death, dancing dogs, hunting scenes, royal coats of arms, players cheating, much more. 96pp. 9¼ x 12¼.
29265-7

MAKING FURNITURE MASTERPIECES: 30 Projects with Measured Drawings, Franklin H. Gottshall. Step-by-step instructions, illustrations for constructing handsome, useful pieces, among them a Sheraton desk, Chippendale chair, Spanish desk, Queen Anne table and a William and Mary dressing mirror. 224pp. 8⅛ x 11¼.
29338-6

THE FOSSIL BOOK: A Record of Prehistoric Life, Patricia V. Rich et al. Profusely illustrated definitive guide covers everything from single-celled organisms and dinosaurs to birds and mammals and the interplay between climate and man. Over 1,500 illustrations. 760pp. 7½ x 10⅛.
29371-8

Paperbound unless otherwise indicated. Available at your book dealer, online at **www.doverpublications.com**, or by writing to Dept. GI, Dover Publications, Inc., 31 East 2nd Street, Mineola, NY 11501. For current price information or for free catalogues (please indicate field of interest), write to Dover Publications or log on to **www.doverpublications.com** and see every Dover book in print. Dover publishes more than 500 books each year on science, elementary and advanced mathematics, biology, music, art, literary history, social sciences, and other areas.